Spenser's Image of Nature:
Wild Man and Shepherd
in "The Faerie Queene"

Yale Studies in English
Benjamin Christie Nangle, Editor
Volume 161

New Haven and London, Yale University Press, 1966

Spenser's Image of Nature:
Wild Man and Shepherd
in "The Faerie Queene"

by Donald Cheney

Copyright © 1966 by Yale University.
Designed by Arthur G. Beckenstein,
set in Times Roman type,
and printed in the United States of America by
the Carl Purington Rollins Printing-Office of
the Yale University Press, New Haven, Connecticut.
Distributed in Canada by McGill University Press.
All rights reserved. This book may not be
reproduced, in whole or in part, in any form
(except by reviewers for the public press),
without written permission from the publishers.
Library of Congress catalog card number: 66–12490

for my parents

Preface

In its original form, this study was a dissertation submitted in candidacy for the degree of Doctor of Philosophy at Yale University, under the title: "Wild Man and Shepherd in the Spenserian Ethic: Studies in The Faerie Queene *and Renaissance Pastoral Motifs." I am indebted to John C. Pope for his direction of the thesis, which grew out of work done in his graduate course on Spenser, and for his kind help in revision; to Maynard Mack, Louis L. Martz, and Charles T. Prouty, readers of the thesis, for their suggestions; to Geoffrey Hartman, Eugene Vance, and Sally Wiseley, for informal discussions of relevant matters; and to Wayland W. Schmitt for his editorial assistance. Harold Bloom has lived with the manuscript in its various untidy states, and has offered advice and encouragement at every stage. Since I have not had the opportunity before this to thank them publicly, I should like to express my sense of gratitude to Beatrice P. Westerfield and Norman Holmes Pearson, for their earlier acts of encouragement. And I owe a special debt to my wife, who has given unstintingly of her time and learning.*

D.S.C.

Rome
June 1965

Contents

Introduction
The Uses of Pastoral
in Spenser's Allegory

Two questions may be raised concerning my choice
of title for this study of *The Faerie Queene*. In the first place,
it may seem odd that I have claimed to be dealing with a single
image of Nature in the poem, since I have not tried to arrange
in any single perspective the vast array of good, bad, and in-
different savages and natural settings that appears there. I have
sought to avoid a mere catalogue of pastoral motifs, or even
more a simplification of Spenser's cosmology, and have tried
instead to consider how these varied motifs shed light on a much
more general, if perhaps rather blurred, concept of Nature as
the world external to the poet and the poet's art, as the sense
of reality which the poem is trying to illuminate. Yet this very
desire to give a unified or at least comprehensive account of an
elusive concept exposes me to another challenge: whether in
fact my subject is, properly speaking, Spenser's pastoral imagery at all, or whether my study could not more honestly have
been entitled "The Nature of Imagery in *The Faerie Queene*."

This latter question is less easily turned aside; perhaps the only answer to it lies in an account of the book's origin.

I began with a desire to explore the implications of a part of the poem to which many readers have responded with enthusiasm: the pastoral episodes at the end of Book VI. That these episodes happen to conclude the completed portion of the poem has seemed eminently fitting to those readers who take a lively pleasure in paradox.[1] The point at which the patron of Courtesy forsakes the court seems a wholly appropriate ending to an action which began in Book I with the repudiation of pastoral for the loftier strains of epic; that Calidore should encounter here the rejected pastoral mask of Spenser, Colin Clout, only underscores the irony of this return. To an older generation of readers, who were less concerned with paradox or with formal symmetry, the pastoral episodes were equally pleasing in terms of plot and character: they offered an oasis of "natural" or spontaneous emotion at a point when many readers had been bored and repulsed by the sterile justice of Artegall in Book V, and inadequately recompensed by the inconsecutive and largely heroless episodes of the first two thirds of Book VI. Explicitly or implicitly, then, appreciation of these pastoral scenes has tended to be at the expense of what precedes them. It has seemed that the poet found, after much barrenness, a furrow where the soil is "both fayre and frutefull," and better suited to the techniques of cultivation which he had been developing ever since his first experiments in the *Shepheardes Calender*. Spenser's finest effects are often derived from his ability to join the worlds of public ceremony and private emotion in a richly patterned equilibrium of tone: this was true of the striking sense of a unique literary personality conveyed by the "new Poete" with his pastorals in 1579 and is outstandingly true of his marriage poems, where the traditional invocations are given a

1. The case for the poem's completeness is argued most directly by Northrop Frye, "The Structure of Imagery in *The Faerie Queene*," *Toronto Quarterly, 30* (1961), 109–27.

new pertinence and an almost elegiac poignancy through the introduction of the image of the poet.[2] These same terms might be used to describe the presentation of Calidore's glimpse of Colin's celebration of the Graces. And at the end of Book VI, when Spenser speaks directly of his own harassment by the Blatant Beast, he is still employing this characteristic mode of personal reference.

It seemed useful to inquire, therefore, in what senses these pastoral and personal strains were characteristic of the poem as a whole. In the strictest sense of the term the pastoralism of Book VI is unique; and Spenser's repeated emphases on the contrasting "styles" of Calidore and the shepherds—in dress, song, conversation, and attitude—call attention to the foreignness of the pastoral setting. But literary criticism, in the twentieth century at least, employs the term "pastoral" in a variety of senses, ranging (sometimes rather glibly) from the strictly formal considerations of a genre which demands the literal presence of shepherds, sheep, and a suitably Arcadian setting (and will provide a subdivision for such nonconformists as Sannazaro's fishermen only when they come fully equipped with the machinery of established pastoral conventions) to the opposite extreme of more loosely thematic definitions which take the fundamental pastoral situation as a figure or prototype or archetype of a number of literary presentations involving the contrast between Art and Nature or the technique of "putting the complex into the simple."[3] The process of generalization which leads from the former to the latter senses contains no guide to restraint; each critic must determine for himself the

2. T. M. Greene, "Spenser and the Epithalamic Convention," *Comparative Literature, 9* (1957), 215 ff.
3. William Empson, *Some Versions of Pastoral* (Norfolk, Conn., New Directions, n.d.), p. 23. Empson's recognition of this problem seems to account for his discussing the different aspects of pastoral in a historical context; but there is nothing in his theory to keep him from considering these versions as existing simultaneously.

point at which the term best combines breadth of relevance with depth of focus.

In the present instance this problem of limiting one's terms is particularly difficult, since the pastoral mode is so explicitly related to the figure of the poet. The broadest sense of "pastoral" would include all literary imitation, since art is necessarily selective in its presentation of data. And in the case of *The Faerie Queene,* the very concept of Fairyland is a "pastoral" projection of human motives into a simplified world where they can be challenged and anatomized while escaping temporarily some of the confusion and murkiness of our own fallen natures. By repeatedly insisting on the differences between Faery and Briton—their modes of perception, their roles in time and history, their relation to Providence—Spenser maintains a double awareness of human desire and limit. The poem's point of view, therefore, consistently involves a narrator who sometimes speaks directly to the reader but is more generally felt in the transforming power of a highly artificial stanzaic form and in the rich patterning of bewilderingly complex echoes of imagery and plot detail. The emergence of the narrator in the form of Colin Clout at the end of Book VI, and the concurrent emergence of explicit, literal pastoral, may be felt to bring into focus a perspective which has been more dimly felt throughout the poem.

This perspective, which I am trying to approach through the concept of pastoral, depends on a sense of abstraction from the immediate plot context which is frequently treated under the heading of "allegory," a convenient but treacherous term. Not even Spenser himself was able to speak of his poem (in the Letter to Ralegh) without calling it an allegory; and, like most of his critics, he must have done so with some recognition of the term's elusiveness, for he no sooner introduced it than he sought to modify it by describing *The Faerie Queene* as "a continued Allegory, or darke conceit." Although in one sense this study is an attempt to define the nature of Spenser's allegory, it is not couched in terms of any general theory of allegory;

and for this reason it may be helpful to explain at once what I consider to be the meaning of the term.[4]

At heart the notion of allegory seems inextricably a part of genetic theory. It is thus that the term is typically defined—for example, "An allegory undertakes to make a doctrine or thesis interesting and persuasive by converting it into a narrative in which the agents, and sometimes the setting as well, represent general concepts, moral qualities, or other abstractions."[5] The emphasis on intention, on the priority of the thesis to the form in which it is expressed, offers a clue to our assumptions in using the term. If we set aside such evidence as the poet's own, authoritative but personal comment on his work and consider the evidence on which a reader can base his recognition of a work as allegory, it appears that this evidence generally consists of a certain distracting cleavage between image and "meaning." The work seems to be concerned with something other (*allos*) than its ostensible subject. Frequently there is some defective naturalism involved: a mixed metaphor which suggests that the author is too busy thinking of that something else (his thesis) to pay attention to the fiction in which he has clothed it; or perhaps a rigorously narrow definition of characters through names which give them only a capital letter to distinguish them from the qualities they are supposed to embody.

In any case, the concept of allegory implies a division of interests abhorrent to a view of literature which sees the poet's main business as the direct imitation of reality. From such a viewpoint it is tempting to dismiss the allegorist as a man concerned with extra-literary, doctrinal goals, and to consider his mixed metaphors as evidence of carelessness, of the absent-minded pursuit of a theme. The apologist for allegory, on the other hand, must account for these evidences of double vision

4. Angus Fletcher, *Allegory: The Theory of a Symbolic Mode* (Ithaca, Cornell University Press, 1964) appeared too late for me to make use of its valuable contributions to allegorical theory.

5. Dan S. Norton and Peters Rushton, *A Glossary of Literary Terms*, rev. ed. M. H. Abrams (New York, Holt, Rinehart, and Winston, 1961), p. 2.

as best he can; they are too disconcertingly evident, too much in fact a part of the definition of allegory, to be shrugged aside as unimportant. Perhaps the most useful approach to this problem has been elaborated by Harry Berger under the rubric of "conspicuous irrelevance":[6] the image (be it simile or plot incident) is seen as an ironic projection of a will to order which is simultaneously deflated by an awareness of contrary forces. So considered, allegory may even be precariously close to the mock-heroic in its use of epic conventions.

With regard to the decorum of allegory, Spenser's treatment of character might be considered in terms of the two meanings of "patron" found in Elizabethan English (and still current in French). The more abstract sense of "pattern" or paradigm had begun to break off into a distinct pronunciation and spelling; according to the *OED* (*s.v.* "pattern"), the shift was complete by 1700, leaving "patron" to refer solely to a protector or supporter, in the sense of Latin *patronus*. Spenser's heroes generate a dramatic irony through being both abstract and personal in these senses. In the case of some lesser figures this irony is obvious and relatively superficial: Morpheus, Sloth, or Despair embody the forces of their respective appetites in working on their victims and at the same time show themselves to be the victims of their own vices. A similar interplay of active and passive references attaches to the patrons of the various virtues. They may appear to be embodiments of the virtues in their dealings with others—showing the operation of Holiness or Justice on those who supplicate or challenge them—and at the same time they are human figures struggling to realize their own identities in terms of these virtues. The conflict between these two concepts of character, as abstractly formulated datum and as dramatic quest, may diminish our sense of consistency, since the poem's emphasis is translated from a single dramatic decorum to the level of a witty play on imagery.

6. Harry Berger, Jr., *The Allegorical Temper: Vision and Reality in Book II of Spenser's "Faerie Queene,"* Yale Studies in English, 137 (New Haven, Yale University Press, 1957).

To read Spenser in this fashion is in effect to bring his long and diffuse poem under the intensive scrutiny which has been applied in recent decades to metaphysical lyrics and—most notably among longer works—to *Paradise Lost,* where clear plot lines and a coherent exegetical tradition have served as useful guidelines to the literary analyst. It is to extend Robert Penn Warren's concept of "impure poetry"—poetry which tests its vision by exposing it to ironic, discordant impulses.[7] It is not merely to stress the "richness" of *The Faerie Queene*— readers are agreed that it is rich in one sense or another—but to suggest that this richness is not primarily a factor of its encyclopedic range: that an ideal Elizabethan reader, thoroughly conversant with Spenser's references, would still find the poem difficult, since its meaning lies in the juxtaposition of references, not in the references themselves.

In speaking of Spenser's "allegory," therefore, I would point to a multiplicity of meaning, not to any supposed otherness of reference. I would suggest that allegory is far from being a lazy or intermittent exercise of the poetic faculty, but is instead a highly energetic collocation of awarenesses which demands an equally high degree of attentive response from the reader. It may be objected that a long poem cannot make demands of this sort without offering some rewards to the less than ideal reader who expends at times a less than ideal energy. Without such rewards for ordinary diligence and good will the poem is merely a puzzle: wholly meaningless until wholly solved. In the case of *The Faerie Queene* intimations of order may be drawn from various sources. One is what Ruskin meant by "the allegory" in his famous summary of Book I: the extended analogy with the Christian scheme of personal salvation. To a lesser degree other extended comparisons, historical or mythological or more loosely ethical in nature, offer similar opportunities for orientation. The rhythms of meter and canto structure offer a different sense of order; allied to them are the patterned repeti-

7. Robert Penn Warren, "Pure and Impure Poetry," *Kenyon Review,* 5 (1943), 228–54.

tions of motif, the musical logic of the poem. And even less demonstrable is the authority which the poem obtains by appealing to the logic of dreams: implicitly basing itself on medieval dream allegory, its discontinuous narrative has a consistency and credibility of its own.

All of these structuring forces can be treated as avenues of approach to the poem; most of them, especially the former approaches through analogy, have been explored in detail as means of illuminating Spenser's meaning. In offering a study of Spenser's treatment of pastoral motifs I am trying to suggest still another controlling force in the poem: a force which might be called a generic allegory in analogy to the moral, theological, and historical allegories. This force makes itself felt in repeated assertions of conflict between epic and pastoral, public and personal, idealist and realist. Though Spenser is not the first to introduce such controlling forces in his epic (Homeric simile and Virgilian melancholy have much the same role), he does develop them with unprecedented complexity and self-consciousness, in proportion as his poem is more directly concerned with a study of the imaginative process.

Spenser's contrasts between Faery and Briton afford an example of how "nature" is seen as a controlling force, opposing man's formless ambitions and yet capable of giving them meaningful shape. The Faery is untouched by the burden of Time in the Christian sense of the word: his relationship to the world of seasonal change (seen in his easy access to the Gardens of Adonis, for example) is more direct than the Briton's. Yet this lack of complication, though enviable at first appearance, is a gauge of his radical limitations. If he is unfallen, he is also unredeemed; although he is free of direct, ancestral guilt, his creator Prometheus is subject to a higher punishment for the prideful act of creation. The history of Fairyland, as recounted in Book II, is a uniformly glorious expansion of human achievement, carried out by successive generations barely distinguishable from one another. Like the flowers in the Gardens of Adonis, the race flourishes, dies, and is replenished in a continual springtime and harvest of earthly glory. It is possible to see this antique image of Fairyland as being at once a celebration and a critique of the humanist vision. The Faeries are creations of the human will for symmetry: their chief characteristic seems to be their relative ability to remain true to a narrow definition of self. In Spenser's vision, and in contrast to the view of the Britons as fallen man, the Faeries resemble Darwinian man, raised from the earth and from beastly nature by the animating gift of stolen fire. They are a product, so to speak, of a naïvely allegorical fusion "of many partes from beasts deriued" (II.x.70). Their creator languishes in visceral torment, reft of his heartstrings as an apt punishment for his act. Prometheus is only one of the makers of images who are shown in fetters in the first books of the poem; but as the creator of Fairyland he is clearly the closest to the figure of the poet himself. The world he has created offers a flattering but selective picture of Elizabeth's heritage; it needs the corrective of the more brutally realistic history perused by Arthur.[8]

The relationship between Faery and Briton is thus rather like that between Houyhnhnm and Yahoo: the very attractiveness of the former is suggestive of a fault in one's standards of value, in one's sense of what distinguishes man from the beasts. But the difference cannot be simply stated in terms of a rather smug preference for a more painful, less self-sufficient relationship to nature as the price of eternal bliss hereafter. So narrowly Christian a reading of the poem weakens it and ignores the larger question of the proper uses of nature as a guide.

It must be noted that Spenser's distinctions between Faery and Briton are infrequent and generally refer to specific contexts within the poem. In Book I the reader is encouraged to take Gloriana simply as a glorified image of Elizabeth, without stopping to consider what that "glorification" entails; and it is surprising to hear the hermit Contemplation speaking of "base Elfin brood" (I.x.65), and to learn that Redcross cannot com-

---

8. Berger, *The Allegorical Temper*, pp. 89–114; Isabel E. Rathborne, *The Meaning of Spenser's Fairyland* (New York, Columbia University Press, 1937).

plete his quest until he is revealed to be a Briton subject to the Christian dispensation. In general, Spenser tends to distinguish between his two orders of creation most clearly in Books I and II, where he is concerned with virtues—Holiness and Temperance—which relate to the isolated individual; for it is with respect to these, the most "private" of the virtues,[9] that the question of personal identity is most crucial. As the poem proceeds to consider the relationships between one individual and another (informed by Chastity and Friendship), and those among the many and varied individuals constituting a society (informed by Justice and Courtesy), this problem becomes secondary, for increasing prominence is attached to the necessity of reconciling differences and of recognizing the extent to which in any case man's life in this world involves a working compromise between his higher and lower natures. With this shift in emphasis comes a greater reliance on pastoral motifs to suggest the precise extent to which nature (and the Natural Law) can instruct both Faery and Briton in the operation of these more social virtues.

Although it is true that the chief characteristic of Fairyland is its emphasis on earthly glory, as the hermit points out to Redcross, the larger implications of this glory, as it is contrasted both with man's more limited achievement and with his more spacious goals, cannot be simply stated. Part of the difficulty of defining the poem's milieu derives from the fact that Spenser's presentation involves a number of distinct contrasts, not all of which are necessarily operative at every point in the poem and not all of which can be wholly assimilated in any single coherent formula. Just as Spenser is prepared to derive authority for his poem's action by reference to a wide range of allusions, similarly he will shift from one area of contrast to another. If any thematic image may be said to persist through-

---

9. Not, apparently, in the sense which Spenser himself gives to the term in his Letter to Ralegh, where "private" and "public" virtues relate to distinctions between ethics and politics. But Spenser's meaning here can be variously interpreted, in accordance with one's theory of the poem's evolution.

out these changes it is that of the intermediate state of man, caught between God and beast, forced to resolve an opposition of impulses within himself which is not ultimately an opposition between good and evil so much as a rivalry of various virtues, each representing motivations good in themselves but tending toward such different conditions as freedom or responsibility, submission or control.

One distinction which has long been observed with respect to the pastoral genre is that between "hard" and "soft" views of nature. As Lovejoy and Boas indicate in their survey of these concepts in antiquity,[10] it is seldom possible to find the one in clear isolation from the other. It seems that whenever civilized man contemplates the state of nature (seeing it as remote from him in time, like the Golden Age or the pre-lapsarian Garden, or in space, like the Arcadia or Sicily of the classical eclogue), he invariably tends to regard it with a mixture of attitudes, to see it as somehow embodying both a welcome absence of civilized tensions and a Spartan simplicity which contrasts with his own depraved ease. The dominant tendency of a particular epoch may tend to weight the relative emphasis on these two attitudes—medieval asceticism may tend toward the realistic or "hard" view, or Renaissance nostalgia for past splendor may favor the "softer" view[11]—but an absolute exclusion of either is rare; more frequently, the notions of virtue and comfort are joined in the pastoral impulse. Such a mixture is of course in keeping with both biblical and classical views of history: man's paradise has been lost through his own sinfulness; a universal flood divides this hardier and more brutish race of mankind from the memory of an earlier, easier life. If a spontaneous and unconstrained pursuit of virtue is characteristic of mankind

10. A. O. Lovejoy and G. Boas, *Primitivism and Related Ideas in Antiquity,* A Documentary History of Primitivism and Related Ideas, *1* (Baltimore, The Johns Hopkins Press, 1935).

11. Cf. Erwin Panofsky, *"Et in Arcadia Ego:* Poussin and the Elegiac Tradition," in *Meaning in the Visual Arts* (Garden City, N.Y., Doubleday, 1955), p. 302.

during the Golden Age, it follows that both man and nature have been changed as a consequence of the Fall.

Spenser employs this contrast between "hard" and "soft" views of nature in various ways. In a seasonal presentation such as that of the *Shepheardes Calender,* the two aspects are presented in a manner that suggests that a cyclical change from one to the other and back again is the means by which Nature achieves her goals; a similar emphasis on permanence in the midst of change is found in the *Mutabilitie Cantos.* Ease leads to generation; disease leads to death; and the alternation of the two halves of the cycle maintains the unchanging balance of creation. Again, these two aspects of nature may be separated for the purpose of examining the lessons which each can offer to man. Belphoebe is trained to an unassailable virginity in the harsh rigors of Diana's forests; her virtue makes her invulnerable and an adept in the social aspects of a courtly ethic (as evidenced by her control not only over Timias but over every person and circumstance she encounters). On the other hand, Amoret's education amid an idyllic and orderly nature in Venus' Gardens of Adonis prepares her for a more meaningful participation in the natural cycle than Belphoebe can achieve; but at the same time it renders her vulnerable to the assaults of Busyrane, whose castle with its masques of a cruelly destructive Cupid opposes a courtly love to the simple, generative love cherished in the Gardens. Thus the conditions of civilized life demand an assimilation of both lessons; and in some respects Britomart may be said to link the chastity and fortitude demonstrated by Belphoebe (the lesson of Diana and of "hard" primitivism: a defense against the chaos which surrounds the human world) with the prospect of marriage and hence an involvement in the order of nature as seen by Amoret (the lesson of Venus and of "soft" primitivism: a glimpse of positive value in the outer world, in the form of the physical immortality of kind provided by the cycle of generation and death).

Yet the mention of Britomart and her dynastic role as predicted by Merlin (III.iii.26ff.) raises the question of man's relationship to nature as it is seen from the viewpoint of Christian revelation. Here the dimension of time is introduced, and the distinction between "hard" and "soft" aspects of nature is related to the environment of man before and after the Fall. In this context pastoral motifs may evoke the contrast of man's present, degraded state with the condition enjoyed in the Garden. Even without a specifically biblical frame of reference, the mention of the Golden Age at the beginning of Book V can function in this manner; and the emphasis on man's descent from a blissful, spontaneously virtuous world into one in which men behave like beasts, oppressing one another and submitting to right only when it is accompanied with a superior force, is appropriate for the role to which the exiled Astraea has prepared Artegall. In connection with these presentations of nature, it may be relevant to recall the contrast between Nature and Grace, in the sense in which A. S. P. Woodhouse invoked it in his interpretation of the different roles assigned to Redcross and Guyon,[12] particularly if this contrast is translated into the tripartite distinction with which theologians mark the three periods of human history: *ante legem, sub lege,* and *sub gratia.* With respect to man's relationship to nature, these three periods can be seen dialectically, the garden world before the Fall being opposed by the image of the wilderness (in which man is subject to Mosaic or classical Law, the harsh justice of an Artegall), and the synthesis being that of an "Eden rais'd in the waste Wilderness." It is this view of man's capacity, through Grace, to regain his Paradise through an act of understanding impossible before the Fall, that provides a constant frame of reference for the presentation of pastoral motifs in Western literature. Most frequently this biblical version of pastoral is so inexplicit that it is not really distinguished from the classical irony seen in Horace, for example (*Epodes* II), whereby the city dweller realizes at the end of his pastoral reverie that, however genuine his longing for the simplicity of the country life, he will never

12. A. S. P. Woodhouse, "Nature and Grace in the *Faerie Queene*," *ELH*, *16* (1949), 194–228.

literally and permanently abandon his present life. Here, and in the still more common mixture of "hard" and "soft" elements mentioned above, where a nostalgic view of nature is tempered by an awareness of its disadvantages or limitations (its seasonal discomforts, its lack of civilized companionship or of the virtues which civilization alone can foster), there is no need to look for a specifically religious context. But in the case of a poem whose larger themes establish such a context, these conventional pastoral elements may be readily adapted to its support. In this sense it is pertinent to speak of the Christian context of Spenser's treatment of nature, and to examine the ways in which readily accessible motifs are assimilated into the structure of *The Faerie Queene.*

In describing Spenser's treatment of nature under these various aspects, I have tried to follow the sequence of presentation established by the poem as a control over any tendency to betray its own poetic logic by rearranging its elements to fit a conceptual framework foreign to it. I realize that this conscientiousness occasionally places a heavy burden on the reader's attention and may seem unjustified by a book which can make no pretense of providing a comprehensive reading of the poem. Both to minimize the difficulty of keeping in mind the complexities of Spenser's plot and to make more immediately clear my own choice of passages for discussion in greater or lesser detail, I have appended an Index of Episodes which can serve usefully as a summary of the poem's action, while enabling the specialized or preoccupied reader of Spenser to see whether I have addressed myself to his problems.

In my frequent attempts to discuss the structure of *The Faerie Queene,* I should hope to have illuminated some general questions of interpretation which its allegory raises. In stressing its sequential logic, I am urging a technique of "explication" which is at variance with any theory of exegesis which would reduce the poem's meaning to a systematic thesis. I suggest that the poem's motion is itself one of explication, and that the critic's task is to reveal the lines of force which carry out this motion.

When Hamlet expresses scorn for the groundlings "who for the most part are capable of nothing but inexplicable dumb-shows and noise," he is clearly using "inexplicable" in a different sense from that in which a modern reader might apply it to the heraldic obscurities of Elizabethan literature. What evokes his disdain is the obviousness of a slapstick which contains no complexity to be unfolded: statements with a single referent or subverbal gestures are for him no more than noise. In this sense of the term, Spenser's poem is supremely explicable. Its stanzaic form is an instrument of its creator's desire to elaborate to the full the narrative particles of his epic. The enfolding rhymes, capped by the summary Alexandrine, arrest the forward motion of the poem, and subject each detail to a sedately intricate perusal.[13] Hamlet, whose tastes seem to have favored such verse,[14] could have asked for no richer banquet of meaning.

In an effort to suggest the characteristic movement of the poem, my first chapter is closely concerned with the episodic structure of Book I. The primary purpose of that chapter is to demonstrate the constant presence of a theme contrary to the epic program enunciated in the Proem and embodied in the quest of Redcross. The muted pastoral motifs in Book I, which contrast with the explicit pastoral of Book VI, stress the insufficiency of human nature to attain holiness without divine intervention; but the complexity of those motifs serves to introduce the terms in which the very premises of heroic action will be modified as the emphasis moves in subsequent books from a transcendent mental victory over the forces of darkness to progressively more Pyrrhic victories over humbler but more persistent foes. Book I can therefore be taken as an embryonic

13. Cf. Edgar Wind, *Pagan Mysteries in the Renaissance* (New Haven, Yale University Press, 1958), pp. 158–75; A. C. Hamilton, *The Structure of Allegory in "The Faerie Queene"* (Oxford, Clarendon Press, 1961), pp. 13–14.

14. Harry Levin's extended analysis of the Player's Speech, in *The Question of Hamlet* (New York, Oxford University Press, 1959), pp. 139–64, demonstrates the relevance of Ovidian *copia* to Hamlet's meditations on the relation of poetry to reality.

version of the larger poem: it implies not only the infection of man's fallen nature, but also the positive lessons to be derived from the Book of the Creatures. The leitmotif of the pastoral garland, for example, enriches our understanding of Redcross' fall and looks forward to subsequent versions of pastoral.

My second chapter tries to locate historically the genre of a narrative poem so extensively concerned with the dialectical manipulation of character and milieu. Ariosto and Tasso are considered as Renaissance precedents for the ironic examination of the chivalric premise; they also offer striking similarities in their gross episodic structures and their tendencies to substitute a narrative viewpoint for the classical unities of action and/or character. In reference to Spenser's intricate use of erotic imagery to present the conflicting claims of Nature and Art, the interwoven strains of Petrarchan and "anti-Petrarchan" lyric provide a rich vocabulary for the poet to draw on. Citation of precedent in this fashion may diminish some of the sense of novelty in my approach to *The Faerie Queene:* the Elizabethan reader, at least, was not unprepared for Spenser's poem, and one test of any interpretation must be its adaptability to other works which appear to be in the same tradition.

The remaining chapters of this study are devoted to specific problems of interpretation arising from the general approach which I have outlined above. In discussing the various episodes of the poem, I have slighted the central books, not because they are less concerned with Nature than the others—their erotic subject matter indicates that the opposite is true—but simply because they have been more thoroughly and in my opinion more adequately treated by recent critics. Though the dissertation on which this book is based was submitted in 1961, I have tried to keep abreast of studies published subsequently and to avoid useless duplication. Furthermore, my desire to demonstrate the integrity—perhaps it should be called more simply the symmetry—of the poem as it now stands has led me to focus on its opening and closing books. The relatively extensive comparison of Books V and VI, in which I argue for a parallelism of structure akin to what has been urged for Books I and II, expresses this concern for symmetry in showing how the contrast of "hard" and "soft" pastoral (the worlds of the Wild Man and the Shepherd) constitutes a restatement— in purely "natural" terms—of the poem's earlier contrast of epic and pastoral in terms of an analogy with the realms of Grace and Nature.

A coherent reading of the entire action of *The Faerie Queene,* one which will reconcile its apparent inconsistencies in terms relevant to the literary theory of the present day, is still unrealized, partly because of the inadequacy of current literary terminology to cope with the rapidly shifting allusions characteristic of Spenser's technique. If the present study is to have any value as a preparation for such a reading, it will be as a result of its attempt to see Spenser's treatment of pastoral motifs in the context of a series of contrasts which inform all levels of the poem, from the individual image to the concept of Fairyland itself. What I am trying to suggest is not so much a completely integrated pattern of Pythagorean complexity, as an employment of language and situation in such a way as to evoke a sense of such immanent order. The resonance of Spenser's poem derives not from any single dichotomy or dilemma or dialectic, but from infinitely expandable series of such contrasts. The two images of Wild Man and Shepherd, therefore, seen as complementary halves of man's relation to the natural world, are emblematic of the delicate balance of opposing forces which is felt throughout *The Faerie Queene.* If there is any common source or nexus for these contrasts, it may lie in that paradoxical linkage of action and suffering central not only to the Christian ethic but to the classical view of the human condition as well.

1. Plowman and Knight:
The Hero's Dual Identity

The opening lines of *The Faerie Queene*, echoing as they do the introduction to the *Aeneid* as the Renaissance knew it,[1] explicitly turn from pastoral poetry to the higher demands of an epic subject:

> Lo I the man, whose Muse whilome did maske,
>   As time her taught in lowly Shepheards weeds,
>   Am now enforst a far vnfitter taske,
> For trumpets sterne to chaunge mine Oaten reeds,
> And sing of Knights and Ladies gentle deeds;
> Whose prayses hauing slept in silence long,
> Me, all too meane, the sacred Muse areeds
> To blazon broad emongst her learned throng:
> Fierce warres and faithfull loues shall moralize my
>   song.

(I.Pr.1)

The poet of the *Shepheardes Calender*, like Virgil before him, sees himself as reaching poetic maturity only when he faces the

1. Merritt Y. Hughes, *Virgil and Spenser*, University of California Publications in English, 2 (Berkeley, University of California Press, 1929), 318.

realities of his own world and ceases to linger in an imagined paradise of rural simplicity. It may be objected that such a development is in fact an argument of pastoral poetry itself: that Colin Clout has already seen his year come full cycle and, in the "December" eclogue, has resignedly hung up his pipes after experiencing all the torments of his pastoral life.[2] But what is more to the point here is that the pastoral poet's conclusion is the epic poet's premise. If the pastoral impulse leads the poet to mask himself in humble garb and flee to a simplified world which then, on closer examination, is revealed to be a microcosm of the world of daily involvement he had abandoned, epic proposes to follow an opposite course. The poet, with due apology for his weak wit and dull tongue, petitions the Muse for a "high" style with which he can confront his bewilderingly complex world from its full historical and topographical perspective.

In Spenser's poem, however, it is not only the poet or narrator who is represented as abandoning the pastoral mode; it is the hero as well. Perhaps a parallelism of narrator and protagonist is not surprising in a poem which repeatedly evokes the quality of a dream vision, with its unnamed or riddlingly named figures in a self-referential landscape: many of Spenser's most eloquent passages gain their fullest effects from a fluid setting in which more naturalistic criteria of decorum are abandoned and characters dissolve into one another as they face similar crises or explore avenues of choice ignored by earlier heroes. But this lack of naturalism must be distinguished from that of a naïve allegory[3] concerned simply with a discursive anatomizing of the author's (and reader's) world. Here, by contrast, we have a poem which explores the relationship of that "real" world

---

2. A. C. Hamilton, "The Argument of Spenser's *Shepheardes Calender*," *ELH*, 23 (1956), 171–82; S. K. Heninger, Jr., "The Implications of Form for *The Shepheardes Calender*," *Studies in the Renaissance*, 9 (1962), 309–21.

3. A better term might be "naïvely read allegory": I am not eager to measure Spenser's poem against any of the traditional examples of allegory —*Everyman* or *Pilgrim's Progress,* for instance—since all can be read more

to projected worlds of desire and fear; and it is in the context
of such a relationship that the Proem and opening stanzas of
Book I enunciate Spenser's subject matter.

The second chapter of this study attempts to identify the
tone and the mode of reference of *The Faerie Queene* by discussing its ancestry, its self-conscious position in the line of
Renaissance epic; but for the present my concern is with the
structure of Books I and II, and with the relevance of Nature
and natural settings to the definition of the individual—as a
combination of Holiness and Temperance—which these Books
develop. Since it is by means of a constant insistence upon the
ambiguity of his images that Spenser holds before the reader an
awareness of the need for such a combination, while he analyzes
the operation of individual virtues, it seems preferable to begin
with a close reading of the opening cantos of Book I. Before
demonstrating the historical precedents for a literary phenomenon, it is wise to assemble one's evidence for the existence
of that phenomenon.

At the beginning, then, *The Faerie Queene* juxtaposes the
pastoral masks of the early Spenser and the naïve rusticity of
the youthful St. George. "Immerito," the anonymous "new
Poete" of the *Shepheardes Calender,* becomes the narrator of
a poem whose hero (as the Letter to Ralegh informs us) had
himself first appeared at Gloriana's court in the guise of "a
tall clownishe younge man" and had "rested him on the floore,
vnfitte through his rusticity for a better place." It is only after
Una has seen him dressed in the armor of a Christian knight,
which she has brought with her to Fairyland, that he seems "the
goodliest man in al that company" and wins her approval as
the champion of her cause. In fact, it is at once apparent from
the poem itself, without reference to Spenser's letter, that the

---

or less profitably as works of fiction. It is not necessary to find a scapegoat,
however; perhaps none in fact exists. What does exist is the habit of reading
works reductively, of precipitating a didactic content which is then taken to
be the sole "meaning."

symbolic appropriateness of the armor to its wearer has yet
to be fully established:

> A Gentle Knight was pricking on the plaine,
>   Y cladd in mightie armes and siluer shielde,
>   Wherein old dints of deepe wounds did remaine,
>   The cruell markes of many' a bloudy fielde;
>   Yet armes till that time did he neuer wield:
>   His angry steede did chide his foming bitt,
>   As much disdayning to the curbe to yield:
>   Full iolly knight he seemd, and faire did sitt,
> As one for knightly giusts and fierce encounters fitt.
>
>   . . .
>
>   Right faithfull true he was in deede and word,
>   But of his cheere did seeme too solemne sad;
>   Yet nothing did he dread, but euer was ydrad.
>
> (I.i.1–2)

The knight is known only in terms of this armor until the tenth
canto, when at the House of Holiness he learns that he is English
and hears his name of George attributed to his childhood upbringing "in ploughmans state" (I.x.66). To be sure, there is
no question of a mystery as to his identity: the reader is surely
expected to recognize the tableau of knight, lady, ass, and lamb
described in the first stanzas of the Book. But the tableau, like
the red cross which identifies the knight for the rest of the
poem, is not a riddle to be solved and then discarded by the
reader; rather, it is what the Renaissance found in the Egyptian
hieroglyph and tried to create through its chivalric imprese: a
means of stressing the visual image as the unit of poetic discourse and of arresting the tendency of language to translate
image into metaphor and metaphor into dead metaphor or
"name." Even when for the sake of convenience we refer to
the knight as "Redcross," we are naming him where Spenser
characteristically points to him, giving him only as much of an
epithet as identifies him or serves the emphases of the moment:

"the youthfull Knight," "that Elfin knight," "that Redcrosse
knight." Spenser's periphrastic treatment of Redcross is an extreme instance of a tendency shown elsewhere in the poem,
whereby he repeatedly gives his characters names symbolic of
their roles but announces those names only after showing them
in action, so that the names themselves become capsule sum-
maries or mottoes. His more extended emphasis on Redcross'
anonymity is directly related to the plot of Book I, however,
which in seeking to define Holiness is concerned with the nature
of the hero and the sources of his strength. As an unproved
knight, Redcross is therefore only potentially St. George: Book
I traces the steps by which he is to gain his identity. The
ambiguities of Redcross' position, and the resultant tension between the sense that his armor is at first a mere protection, or
even a disguise, and the promise that it may come to be an
image of his inner nature, are presented by means of the poem's
opening incidents, in which the ambiguities of natural settings
are stressed. An extended analysis of the first part of Book I
will show the ways in which Spenser defines his poem's problems—and tries to protect himself against the reductive reading
which he has too frequently received. If the following remarks
seem at times to dwell in tedious detail on the minutiae of tonal
ironies, it is because Spenser has been widely criticized (or
more damningly, praised) for a relaxed, ornamental style which
evades any direct confrontation of the complexities of life.
Or, alternatively, as a sage and serious preceptor he has seemed
constitutionally incapable of that manipulation of imagery more
readily attributed to the Metaphysical poets. The corrective to
these assumptions must come from an examination of Spenser's
poem in the order of its presentation, for the individual concerns of commentators have too often led them to reassemble
motifs from various parts of the poem and to neglect those
elements of meaning which depend upon the poem's own sequence.

The first challenge to Redcross comes as a consequence of
a sudden shower which drives the knight and lady into the

Wood of Error. Though the storm is called a "tempest dred" in stanza 8, possibly in an ironic allusion to the knight who dreads nothing (stanza 2), its suddenness and its bluster are set against the ominous, prideful security of the wood:

> . . . Thus as they past,
> The day with cloudes was suddeine ouercast,
> And angry *Ioue* an hideous storme of raine
> Did poure into his Lemans lap so fast,
> That euery wight to shrowd it did constrain,
> And this faire couple eke to shroud themselues were fain.
>
> Enforst to seeke some couert nigh at hand,
> A shadie groue not far away they spide,
> That promist ayde the tempest to withstand:
> Whose loftie trees yclad with sommers pride,
> Did spred so broad, that heauens light did hide,
> Not perceable with power of any starre:
> And all within were pathes and alleies wide,
> With footing worne, and leading inward farre:
> Faire harbour that them seemes; so in they entred arre.
>
> (I.i.6–7)

In fleeing the shower, they have abandoned one kind of nature for another. On the plain they are exposed to the elements and almost ludicrously unprepared to confront them. To see how far this is from the "tempest" of epic or tragedy—in the sense of the hostile environment which tests man's capacity to endure —one need only compare this shower with the storm which confronts Aeneas in Book I of the *Aeneid*. Spenser makes no attempt here to develop a theme of divine wrath—his allusion to "angry *Ioue*" seems the shallowest of epithets for the darkened sky—and the abruptness of the rain is such that everyone has fled before the question of any possible resistance to it can arise. If there is any similarity here to a Virgilian storm, it is more likely to the shower that drives Dido and Aeneas together,[4] for in Virgil too the absence of any extended description of that later storm suggests the instinctive nature of the lovers' flight from it. Redcross and Una do not hesitate to take cover, and they find themselves in a wood which they seem to know all too well: willfully shrouding themselves from the light as well as the rain, they praise the trees in a catalogue which reflects man's confident moral dissection of his universe. In such a context it is ominously appropriate that the foliage of the trees should be their "sommers pride," and that the birds whose song "seemd . . . to scorne the cruell sky" provide the background for the human praise of the trees: man seems to share with the lower creatures this false sense of a security which ignores the changing seasons. The catalogue does not merely provide another link with Chaucer through the similar catalogue in the *Parlement of Foules,* establishing Spenser's position in the English tradition; it finds its deeper and more resonant origins in the Dantesque dark wood of a narrow preoccupation with the things of this world to the exclusion of broader concerns.[5]

Since they have abandoned the sunlight as well as the storms of the plain, it is significant that Una and her knight together

4. *Aeneid* 4.160 ff.
5. William Nelson, *The Poetry of Edmund Spenser* (New York, Columbia University Press, 1963), p. 159, discusses the relationship of Spenser's wood to the allegorical glosses on Virgil's *sylva* (especially as found in *Aeneid* 1 and 6) proposed by Servius and his Renaissance followers. Hamilton, *The Structure of Allegory,* pp. 30–43, discusses the episode as an initiatory "shrouding" of the knight. E. R. Curtius, *European Literature and the Latin Middle Ages,* tr. W. R. Trask, Bollingen Series, 36 (New York, Pantheon Books, 1953), 194–95, classifies examples of this "mixed forest" as a subspecies of the idealized landscape, while recognizing that they may belong instead under the heading of the Homeric or Hesiodic "catalogue." This *topos* does in fact bring together a number of classical forms; and to these may be added in Spenser's case a possible echo of Genesis 2:9: "And out of the ground made the Lord God to grow every tree that is pleasant to the sight, and good for food; the tree of life also in the midst of the garden, and the tree of knowledge of good and evil."

"beguile the way" in describing the functions of the individual elements in the wood. It is only when they have realized that they are lost, and have come upon the hollow cave of Error, that Una belatedly recognizes their position. Until then, they are content to identify the trees and append the appropriate moral or emblematic tags to each: "The sayling Pine, the Cedar proud and tall,/ The vine-prop Elme." Each of these epithets presupposes a congruence between man's world and that of nature. Even when the allusion is to the violence and suffering of man's world, as with "The mirrhe sweet bleeding in the bitter wound," the pain has been beguilingly transformed by such a sense of congruence. Only the final Alexandrine strikes a discordant note with its mention of "the Maple seeldom inward sound," where the sense of anticlimax is turned against the presumption of the human compilers of such a catalogue.

The entire first canto in fact depends for much of its irony upon a careless stockpiling of aphorisms which, for all their individual merits, tend when taken together to dissipate the hero's understanding of his position in a given episode. Thus when Una urges caution at the mouth of Error's den, such an accumulation of proverbs is nicely suggestive of perplexity:

> Be well aware, quoth then that Ladie milde,
>   Least suddaine mischiefe ye too rash prouoke:
>   The danger hid, the place vnknowne and wilde,
>   Breedes dreadfull doubts: Oft fire is without
>   smoke,
>   And perill without show: therefore your stroke
>   Sir knight with-hold, till further triall made.
>   Ah Ladie (said he) shame were to reuoke
>   The forward footing for an hidden shade:
> Vertue giues her selfe light, through darkenesse for
>   to wade.
>
>   (I.i.12)

The rapid exchange of comments, with each aphorism generating its own imagery without reference to its neighbors' and

with the syntax and verbal echoes contributing to a sense of
frenzy, reaches its climax when the Dwarf is moved to interject
his own comment: "Fly fly (quoth then/ The fearfull Dwarfe:)
this is no place for liuing men." It is an ironic comment on the
knight's confidence in the illumination cast by his virtue that
when he looks into the cavern's mouth,

> . . . his glistring armor made
> A litle glooming light much like a shade,
> By which he saw the vgly monster plaine . . .
>
> (I.i.14)

Such a transition from complacent philosophizing to a frantic
search for the appropriate tag-ends of philosophy makes abundantly clear the nature of the Error which Redcross defeats
at this first trial. It is the sort of Error which the knight's gloom-
ing light is capable of discerning plainly, Error in its crudest
and most obviously repellent form: "Most lothsom, filthie, foule,
and full of vile disdaine." Her serpentine form—her most
potent weapon, since her method of attack is that of the boa
constrictor—recalls the labyrinthine paths of moral commentary that have led the knight to her; and though she must be
fought on her own terms, she can be overcome only when faith
reinforces the knight's human powers: "Add faith vnto your
force," Una urges, "and be not faint:/ Strangle her, else she
sure will strangle thee" (I.i.19).

Various elements in the description of Error are suggestive
of broader contexts. As a combination of woman and serpent,
she anticipates Duessa's foul nether parts and may point toward
Adam's fall.[6] At the same time, and with more obvious relevance to the structure of Book I, she provides Redcross with
practice for his climactic battle with the dragon. With respect

6. Virgil K. Whitaker, "The Theological Structure of the *Faerie Queene,
Book I*," in W. R. Mueller and D. C. Allen, eds., *That Soueraine Light* (Baltimore, Johns Hopkins Press, 1952), p. 75. Cf. John M. Steadman, "Spenser's
Errour and the Renaissance Allegorical Tradition," *Neuphilologische Mit-
teilungen, 62* (1961), 22–38.

to all these relationships, it is important to note how the present incident serves to define more closely the range of the Book's action. Error is handily defeated by Redcross with Una's assistance; her offspring die quickly when they drink her poisonous blood in a vain effort at "Making her death their life, and eke her hurt their good." Error's limitations are apparent from this grotesque parody of the traditional comparison of Christ to the dying pelican, giving mankind eternal life through His blood. No such communion is possible to the creatures of Error: in fact, the only way of destroying them definitively is through a resolute attack on their poisonous source.

The crudity of Spenser's characterization of Error may seem to discourage too prolonged a meditation on her implications; perhaps it would be sufficient to read the incident, with Ruskin, as a straightforward statement that "Reverence and Religion must always vanquish . . . this first open and palpable form of Error."[7] The importance of this battle for the present study, however, lies in its relationship to the wandering wood of discontinuous meanings which lead the knight and his lady to Error's den. Their inability to see the forest for the trees— more specifically, for the isolated virtues which they ascribe to each of the trees—is here a prelude to crisis. Their delight in praising the trees as emblems of various virtues becomes suggestive of a human weakness as soon as it leads them to a degree of involvement in this *selva oscura* from which honorable retreat is impossible. They must go forward with no sounder criterion than their decision to follow the beaten path; and it is only after defeating the monster that Redcross can follow this same beaten path back to the light.

If this wandering wood is suggestive of a naïve and disjunctive reading of nature, it remains to ask how much it presents an obstacle definitively overcome and how much a continuing threat to hero and lady. On the one hand, Error is clearly dead, the more clearly so since her brood die with her, by the very

7. John Ruskin, *Stones of Venice* (3 vols. London, Smith, Elder, and Co., 1851–53), quoted in *Variorum 1,* 422.

terms of their being. But her setting, the dark wood, and her mixture of human and subhuman forms contribute to overtones of menace which continue in subsequent incidents. The hazards of natural settings, and of physical appearances in general, become the focus of the scene which immediately follows, when the knight passes from his open challenge by Error to the hidden menace of Archimago. Once again in this second part of the first canto, the two take refuge in a pastoral setting; and here it is Una who persuades Redcross to take this dangerous rest:

> Now (sayd the Lady) draweth toward night,
> And well I wote, that of your later fight
> Ye all forwearied be: for what so strong,
> But wanting rest will also want of might?
> The Sunne that measures heauen all day long,
> At night doth baite his steedes the *Ocean* waues
>   emong.
>
> Then with the Sunne take Sir, your timely rest,
> And with new day new worke at once begin:
> Vntroubled night they say giues counsell best.
>   (I.i.32–33)

Throughout Book I the night will be felt as a time of menace, when the powers of darkness assert their dominance; and in urging Redcross to imitate the sun in going beneath the waves, Una is introducing in all innocence an image which will become increasingly evocative both of spiritual danger and of the need to confront that danger through symbolic death. Her reference to the ocean waves in connection with sleep is immediately echoed in the description of the hermitage's setting—"Thereby a Christall streame did gently play,/ Which from a sacred fountaine welled forth alway"—and by the repeated association of water with oblivion, isolation from care, and sensual surrender in the stanzas which follow. Redcross and Una are "drownd in deadly sleepe" when Archimago begins his enchantment. Una's last recorded word to Redcross before their separation, the aphorism quoted above, seems conspicuously inappropriate in view of the troubles which this night is to bring. Archimago is quick to support Una, adding with a fine ambiguity that "the way to win/ Is wisely to aduise" (I.i.33). Dinner at the hermitage becomes, then, a combination of temperate diet and smooth pieties:

> Arriued there, the little house they fill,
>   Ne looke for entertainement, where none was:
>   Rest is their feast, and all things at their will;
>   The noblest mind the best contentment has.
>   With fair discourse the euening so they pas:
>   For that old man of pleasing wordes had store,
>   And well could file his tongue as smooth as glas;
>   He told of Saintes and Popes, and euermore
> He strowd an *Aue-Mary* after and before.
>
> (I.i.35)

The narrator's tone and his insistence on Archimago's Romish habits make the hypocrisy clear enough to the reader;[8] but Redcross and Una go to their sleep suspecting nothing, lulled by easy platitudes and the appearance of a cloistered virtue.

Archimago's temptations bring into clear focus the present state of Redcross' spiritual health: the combination of strength and weakness implicit in his active conscience and his dependence on reason and the evidence of his senses. It is helpful here to examine these temptations in some detail. Morpheus, the source of Archimago's erotic dream, is first seen like Redcross himself "drowned deepe/ In drowsie fit" (I.i.40), in an atmosphere which combines the elements of darkness, water, and careless isolation already associated with the hero's sleep:

> And low, where dawning day doth neuer peepe,
>   His dwelling is; there *Tethys* his wet bed

---

8. C. S. Lewis, *The Allegory of Love* (London, Oxford University Press, 1936), pp. 321–24.

Doth euer wash, and *Cynthia* still doth steepe
In siluer deaw his euer-drouping hed,
Whiles sad Night ouer him her mantle black doth
    spred.

.   .   .

And more, to lull him in his slumber soft,
A trickling streame from high rocke tumbling
    downe
And euer-drizling raine vpon the loft,
Mixt with a murmuring winde, much like the
    sowne
Of swarming Bees, did cast him in a swowne:
No other noyse, nor peoples troublous cryes,
As still are wont t'annoy the walled towne,
Might there be heard: but careless Quiet lyes,
Wrapt in eternall silence farre from enemyes.

(I.i.39–41)

This passage has been justly praised for its assimilation of traditional presentations of Sleep, its use of onomatopoeia and
personification, and its realistic humor in describing the grum-
bling sleepiness of Morpheus; but what must be stressed here
is its relevance to the condition of Redcross. Morpheus, wholly
removed from the world of day, is in a condition of passivity
which seems diametrically opposed to the active commitment
of Redcross seen earlier in the poem. Against the energy which
had gone into numbering the trees of Error's wood is set a
negative *vis inertiae* which determinedly banishes Care and
"takes keepe" of nothing. The dreamless sleep which Morpheus
seeks and to which he returns after satisfying Archimago's
demands is seen as the pole toward which the water imagery is
directed; a sleep troubled by dreams is significantly associated
with a "dryer braine."[9] The water here takes the forms of trickling stream and drizzling rain, providing an hypnotic murmur

9. R. E. Neil Dodge (*Variorum 1*, 195) relates the passage to traditional
physiology.

to lull the sleeper and to drown out the "troublous cryes" of others.

Yet even for Morpheus total oblivion is impossible, as the presence of these troubling and troubled cries suggests to the reader (the image of the walled town further hints that the disturbance is as likely to be within the walls as without, and hence that there is no clear boundary between dreamer and dream), and as his rude awakening makes explicit. Spenser has been careful in his presentation of sleep to insist on the "wakeful dogges" which protect Morpheus, as well as the other forms of care which are devoted to ensuring his carefree rest. The humor in this personification of Morpheus is ultimately related, therefore, to the ironic sense that not even the god of Sleep can get an uninterrupted night's rest, for all the effort directed toward this goal. And, more generally, it is seen that in the world of sleep dreams reflect the cares of day rather as the moon reflects the sun: indirectly and changeably. In the case of Redcross, the images which come in his sleep are a direct challenge to his interpretation of his waking world. The chaste Una first appears, to complain "how that false winged boy,/ Her chast hart had subdewd, to learne Dame pleasures toy." Venus seems to bring her to his bed, accompanied by the full machinery of a pastoral vision like that of Calidore in Book VI:

> And eke the *Graces* seemed all to sing,
> *Hymen ιō Hymen,* dauncing all around,
> Whilst freshest Flora her with Yuie girlond crownd.
> (I.i.48)

The image of the pastoral garland will be repeated throughout the Book as a mocking reminder of an erotic motive which lies hidden beneath the conscious level of the quest—a motive which is accommodated only at the end when Una is crowned, "twixt earnest and twixt game," at the time of her betrothal to Redcross (I.xii.8). Against this first, dreaming vision, when "nigh his manly hart did melt away,/ Bathed in wanton blis and wicked ioy," Redcross is able to oppose his active will. But the source of his rescue is ambiguous: he wakes in a "great passion of vnwonted lust,/ Or wonted feare of doing ought amis." Either he is shocked out of sleep by the novelty of this lust or he forces himself to consciousness in an habitual response to his scrupulous conscience. As the sequence of his temptations makes clear, these alternatives are more closely related than might appear at first. Both are expressions of that excessive solemnity alluded to in the first lines of the canto: the single-minded concentration on the narrow demands of his quest which blinds him to its broader implications. It is in this sense that he has yet to make his armor fully meaningful, fully a part of himself. His naïve dependence on a literal reading of the *visibilia* of his experience makes him an easy victim not only of the deceptive visions fashioned by Archimago, but also of the conflicting responses provoked by a single image—here that of his lady.

In this instance, it is in the former area that Redcross succumbs: not until his surrender to Duessa in Canto vii will he let himself "melt away" under the influence of the enervating fountain, where he will be found by Orgoglio "Pourd out in loosnesse" (I.vii.7). For the moment, his manly heart resists the explicit incitement to lust which he finds in his dream. The second stage of his temptation takes the form of a waking vision of the false Una created by Archimago, and here he is able to temper his first impulse of anger at her "shamelesse guise," and to hear her complaint. Ominously, though, he is chiefly concerned "To proue his sense"; it is in this continuing dependence on the evidence of his senses that his susceptibility to Archimago consists. When he chooses to put the more honorable construction on the false Una's confession of love, it becomes apparent how closely related are his scrupulousness and his sexual innocence. What faith in his lady remains at this point seems largely a result of his willed effort to repress the sexual overtones of the speech he has just heard. When he returns to bed to muse on her apparent lightness, it is clear that, although he may be no closer to succumbing to lust, he is substantially closer to repudiating Una. Significantly he is chiefly bothered by this evidence of unworthiness in someone "For whose defence he was to shed his blood" (I.i.55).

It is supremely appropriate that Archimago's assault should be directed toward the sexual sphere, for here the very solemnity of the young knight's preoccupation with his quest becomes at once his strength and his weakness. His naïve idealism is most effectively challenged in an area where his faith in a reality contrary to appearance is most difficult. He has overcome Error by following Una's advice to add faith to his force; but when in the third and final phase of his temptation Archimago presents him with the apparent evidence of Una embracing a "young Squire," such a faith becomes impossible, since it would mean denying not only the objective evidence of his senses but also (as subsequent events verify) the subjective evidence of a motive he has not yet reckoned with. The final stage in his fall comes when he yields himself totally to Duessa and presents to Orgoglio the compromising spectacle which Archimago now prepares for his sight: the image of this false Una in the arms of her companion sprite,

> Like a young Squire, in loues and lusty-hed
> His wanton dayes that euer loosely led,
> Without regard of armes and dreaded fight.
>
> (I.ii.3)

As is so often the case in *The Faerie Queene* (Verdant in Acrasia's bower is the most conspicuous example), lust is here presented as primarily a dereliction of chivalric duties, a "looseness" which is opposed to the rigors of the quest. For the present, Redcross' response to this spectacle is merely described, rather ambiguously, as "bitter anguish of his guiltie sight"; he is driven to fly "from his thoughts and gealous feare;/ Will was his guide, and griefe led him astray" (I.ii.6,12). Spenser is less concerned here with rendering realistically his hero's psychological state than with suggesting the implications of the

split between Redcross and Una. But the terms of this schism
are such as to invite (though not wholly to support) an interpretation of Redcross as an adolescent squire who is diverted from
his quest by an inability to reconcile his idealistic goals with the
demands of his senses, with the limitations of his fallen human
nature.

The chief faults of such a psychological reading lie in its
tendency to focus on Redcross to the exclusion of Una and to
exaggerate the sexual element in Redcross' fall.[10] The distracted
departure of Redcross at this point is only incidentally related,
if at all, to a fear of his own sexuality. But, although he is fleeing the imagined lust of his chaste lady, he runs unhesitatingly
toward an erotic involvement of his own with Duessa. Spenser's
technique here as elsewhere in the poem is one of symbolic
counterpoint: the parallel stories of Una and Redcross complement each other and together define the "divided personality" produced by the separation of knight and lady. In the
present discussion I hope to demonstrate that the motion of
Book I is toward a meaningful return to the tableau shown at
the beginning of the first canto: a return symbolized by the
killing of the dragon (the formal "blazoning" of the knight's
armor) and by the betrothal scene (the solemnization of the
union of knight and lady). Such actions are possible only after
the natural world, with all its limitations, has been reconciled
with the transcendent goals of the quest.

The necessity for such a reconciliation gives particular meaning to Una's earlier advice to Redcross, when she had impressed
upon him the need for "Untroubled rest." In the terms of the
imagery of Book I, it is more than a commonplace to say that
one cannot fight well without sleep. Throughout the poem a
recurrent theme is the human need for rest: the heroes of the

10. Such tendencies seem present in the otherwise helpful articles by
Linwood E. Orange, "Sensual Beauty in Book I of *The Faerie Queene,*"
Journal of English and Germanic Philology, 61 (1962), 555–61, and John W.
Schroeder, "Spenser's Erotic Drama: The Orgoglio Episode," *ELH, 29* (1962),
140–59.

poem repeatedly succumb to this need (Redcross and Guyon
in the seventh cantos of their respective Books), and the inevitable dangers of such relaxation indicate that without assistance man cannot maintain the eternal wakefulness demanded
of him. Sooner or later the forces of darkness will catch him in
an unguarded moment. In the case of Book I, with its emphasis
on the integrated individual (holiness being seen less as a distinct virtue than as a more generalized spiritual health or
wholeness), the moment will come when Redcross has exhausted the resources of this intense preoccupation with his
chivalric career. The pattern of Book I stresses the repetition of
scenes in which he overcomes a clear and present threat only
to fall prey to a hidden danger. In the first canto he overcomes
Error but is fooled by Archimago's deceptive appeal to the
evidence of his senses. In the second, he can vanquish the clearly labeled Sans Foy (rising to the full strength of his "natiue
vertue" when the Saracen curses the Cross), but at the same
time uncritically accepts Duessa when she calls herself Fidessa.

Throughout the first half of Book I repeated emphasis is
placed on the youth and naïveté of Redcross. When he leaves
Una he moves into a world of artifice where he is ludicrously
unprepared to read images that are immediately recognizable
to the narrator and the reader. Duessa seems to him no scarlet
lady but an irresistible object of admiration; her elaborate account of her sufferings is scarcely needed since he barely listens,
"More busying his quicke eyes, her face to view,/ Then his
dull eares, to heare what she did tell" (I.ii.26). His response to
her provides a clear example of the tone with which Spenser
presents him in these cantos:

> Henceforth in safe assuraunce may ye rest,
>   Hauing both found a new friend you to aid,
>   And lost an old foe, that did you molest:
>   Better new friend then an old foe is said.
>   With chaunge of cheare the seeming simple maid
>   Let fall her eyen, as shamefast to the earth,

And yeelding soft, in that she nought gain-said,
So forth they rode, he feining seemely merth,
And she coy lookes: so dainty they say maketh derth.
                                                        (I.ii.27)

The narrator's proverb in the last line wryly caps Redcross'
attempt to sum up the situation in the first half of the stanza:
"they say" echoes the inanity of "is said," while the metrical
awkwardnesses and verbal repetitions of the fourth and ninth
lines direct attention to the feebleness of the knight's aphorisms.
And Redcross' desire to please Duessa drives him to a "seemely
merth" which, in view of his characteristic solemnity, is as much
a product of artifice as Duessa's modest glances. Even the apparent aimlessness of Redcross during these central cantos is
in keeping with the picture of him as a naïve knight, too preoccupied with the details of chivalric behavior to meditate on
his own abandoned quest.

The extent to which Redcross has lost what limited defenses
he first possessed may be measured by his response to Fradubio,
whose grove resembles the Wood of Error in offering an apparent escape from the rigors of the quest. But here it is explicitly the heat of day rather than a sudden shower which drives
the knight and his lady to seek refuge, and this grove is described in terms of a menace which the humbler shepherd can
avoid:

Long time they thus together traueiled,
    Till weary of their way, they came at last,
    Where grew two goodly trees, that faire did spred
    Their armes abroad, with gray mosse ouercast,
    And their greene leaues trembling with euery blast,
    Made a calme shadow far in compasse round:
    The fearfull Shepheard often there aghast
    Vnder them neuer sat, ne wont there sound
His mery oaten pipe, but shund th'vnlucky ground.
                                                        (I.ii.28)

The apparent non sequitur in the seventh line demands a reconsideration of the contrast between the green, trembling leaves and the calm shadow which they throw; and in the implication that one man's pastoral refuge may be another's prison is introduced the first in a series of reassessments of the natural setting. The elaborate antitheses of Fradubio's speech—he is one of Spenser's most euphuistic characters—dramatize the sense of stalemate, of a helpless subjection to contradictory insights, which his name implies. He groans for "My tender sides in this rough rynd embard"; he is acutely aware that in the very act of providing shade for others he is himself exposed "in open plaines" to the sun and the north wind, "For though a tree I seeme, yet cold and heat me paines." In telling his story, he displays mixed emotions toward Fraelissa, "my dear loue,/ O too deare loue, loue bought with death too deare," and his two views of Duessa are juxtaposed through the unfolding of a single phrase: "a like faire Lady by his side,/ Like a faire Lady, but did fowle *Duessa* hyde" (I.ii.31–35). The verbal style of Fradubio's narrative expresses a sense of paradox far removed from the simplistic moral readings given to the trees in the Wood of Error, or from the naïve aphorisms characteristic of the knight to this point. When one of the trees speaks for itself, it demonstrates an Ovidian sensitivity to the poetic justice of its metamorphosis. Fradubio's human reason is the first to fail him when he chooses Duessa; and after learning his error, he further fails to use his animal faculty of motion, being content to "refraine, in minde to slip away,/ Soone as appeard safe oportunitie" (I.ii.41). What remains is a vegetative state which contains its own punishment.

Fradubio's role as an emblem of man trapped by the flesh has been generally recognized by readers, and more recently critics have adduced a variety of analogous uses of the tree image which point suggestively toward the incident's position in the plot of Book I. The figure of "Despair," who sings from an oak tree during Elizabeth's entertainment at Woodstock in 1575, reinforces our sense of Fradubio's continuing relevance

to Redcross' condition through all the stages of his decline until
his arrival at the House of Holiness.[11] Suggestions of Adam's
fallen condition are implicit throughout the episode, emerging
most clearly in Fradubio's statement that he and Fraelissa cannot be liberated from this "death" until they are "bathed in a
liuing well."[12] Fradubio's relationship to Redcross is far from
simple. It is at this point that Redcross has made a first gesture
toward enacting the scenes of his erotic visions at Archimago's
house, in preparing for Duessa a pastoral crown like the one
Flora had placed on the false Una's head:

> And in his falsed fancy he her takes
> To be the fairest wight, that liued yit;
> Which to expresse, he bends his gentle wit,
> And thinking of those braunches greene to frame
> A girlond for her dainty forehead fit,
> He pluckt a bough . . .
>
> (I.ii.30)

The limbs of Duessa's earlier victim make a fitter garland than
Redcross is able to realize. The details of Fradubio's narrative
both assert his resemblance to Redcross and by so doing help
to clarify the reader's sense of the direction in which the other
is moving. Fradubio has won Duessa in battle, and his award
of a "Rosy girlond" to her in preference to Fraelissa represents
an explicit choice of false beauty over true. Like Redcross, he
is barely restrained from killing his true love in a fit of revulsion,
and he is induced to leave her "where she now is turnd to treen
mould." And, again like Redcross, he is "drownd in sleepie
night" when Duessa works her final change on him.

From his prison Fradubio speaks with an acute awareness of
his condition. But knowledge, far from setting him free, is an

11. Nelson, *The Poetry of Edmund Spenser,* p. 162; see also Frances A.
Yates, "Elizabethan Chivalry: The Romance of the Accession Day Tilts,"
Journal of the Warburg and Courtauld Institutes, 20 (1957), 12–13.
12. Nelson, ibid.; Hamilton, *The Structure of Allegory,* p. 66.

index of his inability to act. His name, his manner of speaking, and his history all emphasize the extent to which his contradictory impulses have negated one another. It is toward this emphasis that the differences between him and Redcross are directed. He is first seen as the typical young knight,

> In prime of youthly yeares, when corage hot
> The fire of loue and ioy of cheualree
> First kindled in my brest . . .
>
> (I.ii.35)

But though he lacks the excessive solemnity of Redcross and rejoices in the erotic aspects of the chivalric life, he is all the more rapidly driven to a crisis which the other reaches only after much indirection. When Fradubio is challenged by Duessa's champion, the challenge is explicitly formulated in erotic terms. When he has won the pyrrhic victory which brings Duessa as a more insidious challenge to his faith in Fraelissa's beauty, he recognizes within himself the challenging doubt which had previously appeared outside him, where it could be overcome more easily. Finding himself now "So doubly lou'd of Ladies vnlike faire," he cannot resist the temptation to compare the two ladies. And it is because in his eyes the choice hangs in "doubtfull ballaunce" that Fradubio finds himself caught between an extreme loathing for Fraelissa and a subsequent, equivalent loathing for Duessa. It is significant that Fradubio is imprisoned not within a complacent sensuality (the animalism of Gryll in Book II, for example), but within a cycle of sexual attraction and revulsion. The two states of loathing suggest clearly enough that he is first blinded by lust to Fraelissa's "shining ray" (easily dimmed by Duessa's "foggy mist"), and then later brought in due time to a recognition of the beastliness of his new mistress. When he views the disfigured Duessa, he responds intuitively:

> Her neather partes misshapen, monstruous,
> Were hidd in water, that I could not see,

But they did seeme more foule and hideous,
Then womans shape man would beleeue to bee.

(I.ii.41)

Fradubio's besetting sin (if such a term is relevant here) is that
of Lechery; and the description of that sin in the procession at
the House of Pride (I.iv.24–26) similarly emphasizes the
"greene gowne" of vegetative function which covers the in-
constant spirit filled with "reprochfull paine." In this respect
Fradubio is contrasted with Redcross, who is moving toward a
more inclusive Pride in his self-centered concern for his quest
and the glory which attends its fulfillment. In serving as an antithesis to the hero as well as a token of the hero's fate, Fradubio's
role becomes all the more evocative of the inevitability of
crisis. In subsequent episodes the immediate causes of Redcross' downfall will be associated with his prideful joylessness:
images of Sans Joy, Lucifera, Hippolytus, and Orgoglio will
illuminate the specific weaknesses of his character. Yet the point
is not that Una should have chosen a less solemn champion,
one who, like Fradubio, might have been less resistant to Archimago's earlier incitements to lust. It is rather that any champion
from Gloriana's court would have fallen as surely as does Redcross, though he would have fallen to different forces.

What seems to be involved here ultimately is Spenser's evaluation of the chivalric milieu within which his action is set. As
I shall try to show in the second chapter, Spenser borrows from
the Italians the concept of an ironic projection of human impulses into a simplified world of chivalric values as a means
both of demonstrating the inadequacy of those values when
naïvely formulated and of suggesting the extent to which the
contradictions inherent in those values may, in the long run,
be their most valuable asset, since they lead back to illuminate
the dialectical process operative in the unsimplified world of
poet and reader. And it is toward such a repudiation of "naïve
allegory" that Spenser's technique of "symbolic parody"[13] is
directed: toward the sense that all images, and all actions in

13. Northrop Frye, "The Structure of Imagery," p. 119.

fact, are ambivalent and demand an ability not only to comprehend their various implications but, when necessary, to step outside such a comprehension in order to take a decisive action.

In the present case the dual emphasis of the chivalric ethic upon both love and glory is at the heart of the combined image of Redcross and Fradubio. The latter seems to have responded to this ethic on a relatively low level of abstraction. His interest is focused on his lady, and his role as knight seems largely directed toward defending her beauty as an extension of his own reputation. For him the lady is not a symbol but an object sought in and for herself. Consequently, his "faith" is subject to a challenge on the level of his faith in her beauty. Fraelissa is frail in the sense that all flesh is frail: it is subject to the varying desires of the beholder. Redcross, in contrast, conceives his quest on a far higher level of abstraction; the repeated superlatives in the following quotation emphasize the transcendent terms in which he views his goal:

> Vpon a great aduenture he was bond,
>   That greatest *Gloriana* to him gaue,
>   That greatest Glorious Queene of *Faerie* lond,
>   To winne him worship, and her grace to haue,
>   Which of all earthly things he most did craue;
>   And euer as he rode, his hart did earne
>   To proue his puissance in battell braue
>   Vpon his foe, and his new force to learne;
> Vpon his foe, a Dragon horrible and stearne.
>
> (I.i.3)

Such transcendence implies a consequent lack of concrete definition. A recent discussion of the poem remarks upon the abruptness with which Spenser introduces the betrothal of Redcross and Una, when their relationship until the twelfth canto has shown Una as simply "the pure object of his assigned championship."[14] Far from indicating any slackness in Spen-

---

14. Graham Hough, *A Preface to "The Faerie Queene"* (London, Duckworth, 1962), p. 141.

ser's control over his narrative, however, this is clearly designed
to indicate the knight's limited understanding of the meaning
of his quest. From the beginning he is prepared to view his
armor as symbolic, but it is the extent of the symbolism which
he has not yet grasped. Where he differs from Fradubio is in
viewing "faith" in broad, abstract terms: not simply—or even
primarily—as faith in his lady, for he has already abandoned
her before he tilts against Sans Foy. Accordingly, it is not the
person of Una but the abstraction—faith—which is challenged
by the knight; and Duessa presents herself as "Fidessa" and
adapts her tale to echo Una's.

Yet a further ironic complication becomes apparent at this
stage in the narrative. Duessa's tale falls on deaf ears, since
Redcross' very act of separation from Una has brought him
closer to Fradubio's condition; the same force which makes
him flee the tarnished ideal which he sees in Una drives him
to a new receptivity to sensual temptation. For the moment
Duessa's wiles seem a step behind the changes in Redcross himself, as he feigns mirth and sets out to court his temptress. Even
the cautionary tale of Fradubio's undoing is powerless to halt
him. The canto ends with a stanza whose verbal antitheses are
reminiscent of Fradubio's own and whose ambiguities of reference dramatize the implications of the kiss being described:

> Her seeming dead he found with feigned feare,
>   As all vnweeting of that well she knew,
>   And paynd himselfe with busie care to reare
> Her out of carelesse swowne. Her eylids blew
> And dimmed sight with pale and deadly hew
> At last she vp gan lift: with trembling cheare
> Her vp he tooke, too simple and too trew,
>   And oft her kist. At length all passed feare,
> He set her on her steede, and forward forth did beare.
>
>   (I.ii.45)

Redcross has turned away from the tree, thrusting the bleeding
bough into the ground and stopping the wound with clay, "That

from the bloud he might be innocent." The gesture is one of
piety, yet it also suggests the repression of unwelcome knowledge. The naïve "innocence" which he seeks will bring its own
guilty knowledge; the busy care with which he tries to wake
Duessa will bring him to a careless swoon; her hue is "deadly"
in two senses; his "trembling cheare" is an echo of Fradubio's
own emotional state, seen earlier in his trembling leaves; it is
not clear who is "too simple and too trew" as the two kiss.

These ambiguities reverberate throughout the poem, for Redcross is here close to assuming the role of an Adonis: compare
the relevant passage in Shakespeare's version of the myth
(*Venus and Adonis,* 463 ff.). In terms of the quests of Books I
and II, these versions of Adonis appear as fatal temptations,
destructive of that integrity of the individual which Holiness
and Temperance assert in their respective ways. For Shakespeare and Spenser, as for Ovid and his Renaissance commentators, the story of Adonis represents a myth of man's precipita-
tion through lust into the world of time, into the combination
of personal mortality and racial immortality which is man's fate
as a part of nature. Only by recognizing the full force of his
human condition, only by falling through the successive stages
of his decay, can Redcross come to an understanding of the
logical impossibility of independently fulfilling his quest, and
thereby to a recognition of the true meaning of the armor which
Una has given him. In kissing Duessa he is like Adonis unconsciously committing himself to a pattern of fall and trans-
formation, though his later career will show that he is unlike
Adonis (and unlike the elves of Spenser's fairyland) in being
fortunately fallen out of Eden and into a Christian dispensation.

Yet, although the movement of Redcross toward the House
of Pride is clear enough at this point, the pattern of the poem's
development echoes the episodic counterpoint of the chivalric
poem. Spenser interrupts the story of his hero to turn to Una's
experiences. These experiences, which occupy the third and
sixth cantos in their entirety, have received relatively little attention from recent critics. There are probably several reasons

for this neglect. Una seems to belong to a different level of reality than Redcross. As her name suggests, she is not subject to change and hence to the developmental history seen in the adventures of the young hero. Although the full range of her significance is progressively displayed to the reader through a series of oppositional relationships,[15] it is through these relationships that she functions as a touchstone by which the nature of the hero is to be further examined.[16] Throughout her wanderings she is continually in the position of a heroine in search of her knight; and it is chiefly instructive to observe the variety and nature of the substitutes for Redcross which present themselves to her. For it is as a means of illuminating those characteristics of Redcross which eventually permit him to slay the dragon—his combination of clownish plowman and Christian knight—that Spenser shows Una exploring the resources of a natural setting, "In wildernesse and wastfull deserts strayd,/ To seeke her knight" (I.iii.3). As she works her way back to Redcross, she is successively dependent on a lion, a band of satyrs, Satyrane, and Arthur.

Her first defender, the lion, is explicitly compared to Redcross as a symbol of the proud beast mastered by beauty. Una's meditation on this emblem of "yielded pride and proud submission" stresses the defect of Redcross' love which has separated the two:

> The Lyon Lord of euerie beast in field,
>   Quoth she, his princely puissance doth abate,
>   And mightie proud to humble weake does yield,
>   Forgetfull of the hungry rage, which late
>   Him prickt, in pittie of my sad estate:
>   But he my Lyon, and my noble Lord,

15. Edwin Honig, *Dark Conceit: The Making of Allegory* (Evanston, Northwestern University Press, 1959), p. 63; Hamilton, *The Structure of Allegory*, p. 88.

16. M. Pauline Parker, *The Allegory of "The Faerie Queene"* (Oxford, Clarendon Press, 1961), pp. 69 ff. Note that Una is called "true as touch" at I.iii.2.

> How does he find in cruell hart to hate
> Her that him lou'd, and euer most adord,
> As the God of my life? why hath he me abhord?
>
> (I.iii.7)

The metaphoric sense in which Redcross is Una's "Lion" gives particular relevance to the historical allusion which is presumably implicit in this episode. Redcross is too little the lion: he possesses the proud rage but lacks the intuitive capacity to recognize and pay homage to virginity. As a rational being he is divorced from those same intuitive powers which would have defended him against Archimago's lying visions. Henry VIII, by contrast, the first English champion of the Protestant faith, is in a sense too much of a lion. Given the obvious abuses of Corceca, Abessa, and Kirkrapine, he can act forcefully and decisively against the powers of hypocrisy and false piety by suppressing corrupt institutions and helping Una as she "Marres blind Deuotions mart" (I.iii.Arg.). But the lion is frail in two senses: he is as incapable of recognizing Archimago's new deceits as Una herself, and as Redcross had been the night before (when the Roman church had masked itself in Archimago's glib pieties and had avoided the bestial obviousness visible during this second night); and he is, finally, a victim to Sans Loy. Henry VIII sets in motion a violence which, from an Elizabethan perspective, lacks the guiding intelligence of a statecraft which can consolidate its achievements. The champion of Protestantism must ultimately be prepared to cope with a Saracen enemy whose bestial lust, like that of Sans Loy, is informed by an understanding of "feates of armes." In appealing to his audience's sense of recent history, Spenser underscores the necessity of a holiness which goes beyond the natural piety of an instinctive alliance to virtue.

Spenser explicitly warns the reader that the historical allusion is not completed by the action of Book I alone. Redcross' victory is not that of Elizabeth over Spain, as the prelude to his battle makes clear; and it will be reserved for a later (unwritten) Book to sing of "Briton fields with Sarazin bloud bedyde,/ Twixt that great faery Queene and Paynim king" (I.xi.7). In general, Una's adventures raise issues which can be resolved only temporarily within the framework of the first Book. Only the lion is killed outright: Archimago, Sans Joy, Satyrane, and of course Arthur will reappear in subsequent Books; and the complexities of tone with which these pastoral scenes are presented become fully meaningful only as the poem develops.

One example of such a complexity is seen in the treatment of Archimago, the malevolent creator of false images. As an old man, physically frail and unflaggingly energetic in his pursuit of futile (and rather obscure) goals, he inherits some of the ambiguous stature of the wizards of romance; but Spenser directs his emphasis in particular toward the suggestion of a demonic figure of the artist. He is repeatedly the victim of his own art:

> He then deuisde himselfe how to disguise;
>   For by his mightie science he could take
>   As many formes and shapes in seeming wise,
>   As euer *Proteus* to himselfe could make:
>   Sometime a fowle, sometime a fish in lake,
>   Now like a foxe, now like a dragon fell,
>   That of himselfe he oft for feare would quake,
>   And oft would flie away. O who can tell
> The hidden power of herbes, and might of Magicke
>   spell?
>
> (I.ii.10)

Archimago's lack of personal dignity can be explained in various ways. It may be that the Hypocrite is by nature an object of ridicule: his evil cannot enjoy a public triumph. And perhaps by making Archimago less of a serious evil in his own right Spenser focuses more sharply on the weaknesses of the hero: all the scenes of menace in Book I suggest an internal battle against one's personal limitations. But particularly interesting with regard to the poem's repeated insistence on the ways in which nature is to be read is the fact that Archimago's assumption of the appearance of Redcross invites the reader to reassess his own earlier interpretation of the reality predicated in the poem:

> In mighty armes he was yclad anon,
> And siluer shield: vpon his coward brest
> A bloudy crosse, and on his crauen crest
> A bounch of haires discolourd diuersly:
> Full iolly knight he seemde, and well addrest,
> And when he sate vpon his courser free,
> *Saint George* himself ye would haue deemed him to be.
>
> But he the knight, whose semblaunt he did beare,
> The true *Saint George* was wandred far away,
> Still flying from his thoughts and gealous feare . . .
>
> (I.ii.11–12)

After a description which stresses the cowardice of this false knight, and even scorns the material of the armor (the bunch of hairs is not colored but "discolourd"), the force of the verb "seemde" has altered strikingly in the phrase repeated from the original description of Redcross, "Full iolly knight he seemde." Here it is no longer equivocal, but frankly directed to the contrast between being and seeming. Similarly, the use here (and only here until canto x) of Redcross' "true" or precipitated name reminds the reader of the act of judgment he had performed when first confronted by the tableau of knight, lady, ass, and lamb in the opening scene of the Book. There are perhaps two senses in which, by the second canto, Archimago can consider his guests to be "diuided into double parts" (I.ii.9): Una and Redcross are literally separated from one another, and Redcross himself is metaphorically divided (beside himself, so to speak). By leaving Una he has become diverted from his progress toward the state of "being" St. George. The ironies

attached to the spectacle of Archimago outwitting himself by
deceiving not only Una but Sans Loy as well (he quickly rights
himself: when he next appears in canto vi he is in his more
customary guise of an aged pilgrim, and turns the story of his
own defeat into an account of the death of Redcross at Sans
Loy's hands) emphasize anew the perils of images for their
creator, as much as for the casual spectator. Spenser's repeated
allusions to the misunderstandings and offences which his poem
has occasioned make the same point.

Each of the first three Books concludes with the binding of
a "demonic allegorist" (to borrow in an extended sense Berger's
useful term[17]). In Books II and III this binding constitutes the
achievement of the hero's main goal—Guyon's destruction of
the Bower of Bliss, Britomart's destruction of the House of
Busyrane. In Book I it occurs incidentally and anticlimactically,
as a reminder of continuing dangers that survive the definitively killed Dragon. Though Death has lost his sting, man
must continue to watch and ward against the powers of darkness. Archimago tries to disrupt the betrothal of Redcross and
Una,

> But they him layd full low in dungeon deepe,
>   And bound him hand and foote with yron chains.
>   And with continuall watch did warely keepe;
>   Who then would thinke, that by his subtile trains
>   He could escape fowle death or deadly paines?
>   (I.xii.36)

But of course he does. Though Duessa will meet her death in
Book V, Archimago and his colleagues continue to abuse men
with their misleading images. Their victims are those who are
predisposed to a naïve reading of the *visibilia* presented to them.
Yet Guyon and Britomart are able to act decisively and vio-
lently against their adversaries, not because their understanding
transcends the argument of the temptations, but because they

17. Berger, *The Allegorical Temper,* pp. 211 ff.

are able to deny it or repress it. Whenever Guyon seems to falter, his Palmer is at hand to rouse that "tempest of his wrathfulnesse" (II.xii.83) which is the only means of denying the Bower; Britomart's chastity keeps her from understanding the fearsome lessons of Busyrane. It is in ironic anticipation of the crises of Books II and III that in the third canto Archimago is struck down by the uncontrolled violence of Sans Loy. Possibly Spenser intended the synoptic quality of Book I to extend to certain details of symmetry: the third canto shows the violent penetration of the enchanter's mask (the theme of the first three Books); and the sixth canto shows Satyrane returning to his natural origins (the theme, in a rather looser sense, of the second three Books). Whether or not such symmetry exists (it would argue for a consistent vision of the poem's structure which the various studies of its "evolution" would deny[18]) is of course unanswerable in view of our ignorance of the poem's second half. But it is possible in any case to see how the continually recurrent imagery of Spenser's argument increases the chances of suggestive repetitions of this sort.

Una, the helpless maiden wandering in the wilderness, is subject to the alternation of menace and assistance which she finds in the savage figures who confront her. In the third canto we see one such cycle completed when the friendly lion is killed by Sans Loy; the end of the canto falls as she is carried off by this new, inimical figure of bestial lust. The two cantos that describe her adventures frame the fourth and fifth cantos, in which Redcross visits the House of Pride and encounters Sans Joy; the gentle maiden's experiences in an uncivilized setting thus provide a backdrop for her youthful knight's similarly passive role in a sophisticated world. Lucifera's relationship to the chivalric norm is clear enough to the reader: her house is built on the sands, and her diabolic ancestry is seen in her name and retinue. But while the reader is being shown the

---

18. Josephine Waters Bennett, *The Evolution of "The Faerie Queene"* (Chicago, University of Chicago Press, 1942); Janet Spens, *Spenser's "Faerie Queene"* (London, Edwin Arnold, 1934).

operations of a Pride which dominates all other sins and is in
turn upheld by them, Redcross is responding with tragic naïveté
to a social situation which he reads as a naturalistic imitation
of courtly life. His only negative responses to Lucifera's court
are ironic tokens of his own pride:

> Yet the stout Faerie mongst the middest crowd
> Thought all their glorie vaine in knightly vew,
> And that great Princesse too exceeding prowd,
> That to strange knight no better countenance allowd.
>   (I.iv.15)

When Lucifera and her counselors go out "To take the solace
of the open aire," Redcross again stands on his dignity, dis-
daining to leave the House of Pride, "Him selfe estraunging
from their ioyaunce vaine,/ Whose fellowship seemd far vnfit
for warlike swaine" (I.iv.37). It is no wonder that the third
of the Saracen brothers arrives at this point. Sans Joy is repeatedly presented in terms which suggest his similarities to
Redcross. Both knights are fighting for Sans Foy's shield (a
curious emblem for Redcross to defend), and their battle is
described in a weaving alternation of phrases (I.v.7: "The
Sarazin was stout, and wondrous strong . . . The knight was
fiers, and full of youthly heat . . . Both stricken strike, and
beaten both do beat.") which obsure distinctions while pretending to stress them. The repeated phrase, "So th'one for
wrong, the other striues for right," is mocked by the simile of
griffin and dragon competing for "rightfull rauine" (I.v.8). It
is at this point that Redcross is seen most clearly to be fatally
misguided in his concern for the acquistion of glory through
chivalric combat. Duessa's visit to Sans Joy on the eve of battle
seems to echo the false Una's appearance to Redcross earlier;
and, like Redcross, Sans Joy is confident in his unassisted
powers as he sends her back to bed. In so ambiguous a conflict
it is appropriate that Redcross should win his limited victory
after misinterpreting Duessa's shout of encouragement, and

that the descent into the underworld to cure Sans Joy should present elements of considerable relevance to Redcross' own situation.

Sans Joy is brought to Aesculapius, whom Jove has cast into hell for reassembling and reviving Hippolytus' dismembered body. Such a punishment may at first seem an arbitrary act of jealousy by a deity who fears encroachment:

> Such wondrous science in mans wit to raine
>> When *Ioue* auizd, that could the dead reuiue,
>> And fates expired could renew againe,
>> Of endlesse life he might him not depriue,
>> But vnto hell did thrust him downe aliue,
>> With flashing thunderbolt ywounded sore:
>> Where long remaining, he did alwaies striue
>> Himselfe with salues to health for to restore,
> And slake the heauenly fire, that raged euermore.
>
>> (I.v.40)

Yet Aesculapius' punishment is an ironic commentary on the nature of his offense. By destroying the powers of death, he has prepared for himself an endlessly painful life against which his salves are of no avail. His condition is similar to that in which Prometheus, the creator of the faery race, finds himself as a consequence of his similar interference with divine prerogative (II.x.70): in both cases Jove has simply presided over what might be called the merely human condition, the condition of man in the natural order. Both Aesculapius and Prometheus are painfully fixed in time, divorced from the natural cycle. In the stanza quoted above, Spenser seems to be aware that Aesculapius was eventually to return from the world of the dead. His familiar association with the emblem of the serpent, moreover, links him to the many serpents figured in Book I, among them that of Fidelia at the House of Holiness. Similarly, Prometheus' imprisonment was to end eventually through the heroic intercession of Hercules; but for the moment the world of fairyland is unredeemed by its creator.[19] In the present instance Aesculapius is to be seen in the context of the other figures in Book I—Fradubio, Despair, the Deadly Sins themselves—who are trapped within a sense of paradox. His decision to revive Sans Joy is a dramatization of his own raging pain: Duessa urges him to "shew thy famous might" precisely because he has no hope left, because "heauens king/ From hope of heauen hath thee excluded quight" (I.v.43). His despairing gesture of defiance is like that of Satan, but as a curative, redemptive act it comes so close to an imitation of Christ that it could serve as a warning to Redcross of the ambiguity of his own quest.

Similarly, the story of Hippolytus has a particular relevance to the state of the proud young knight:

> *Hippolytus* a iolly huntsman was,
>   That wont in charet chace the foming Bore;
>   He all his Peeres in beautie did surpas,
>   But Ladies loue as losse of time forbore . . .
>   (I.v.37)

Once again Spenser provides a picture of imbalance. On the literal level Hippolytus is merely the innocent victim of his stepmother's lust, but metaphorically he invites nemesis by turning all his energies to a single goal; and the form of his death seems to express this failure to control his various conscious and unconscious motives. In this variation on the image of Redcross/Sans Joy, however, the emphasis begins to move toward the larger problems of the cycle of fertility and the vari-

19. Frye, "The Structure of Imagery"; Hughes' remarks on Spenser's transformations of the Dantesque and Virgilian underworlds are relevant: "Spenser's hell is Dante's inferno atrophied . . . a pale, dying gleam of the tragic, medieval conception of hell as a place where life's seemingly deathless glories are whelmed in a real immortality of pain" (*Virgil and Spenser,* pp. 376–77). I would differ from Hughes, however, in attributing this unalloyed gloom not to the poet's immature vision, but to the special conditions of the Spenserian context. It is not the knight who visits this underworld but only his joylessness, so to speak; his own view of history is to be revealed in canto x.

ous possibilities of immortality. The mention of the boar anticipates the figure of Adonis, and the curious insistence on his
failure to leave a "moniment" explains the need for his "rebirth"
at the hands of Aesculapius.[20]

> His goodly corps on ragged cliffs yrent,
> Was quite dismembred, and his members chast
> Scattered on euery mountaine, as he went,
> That of *Hippolytus* was left no moniment.
>
> (I.v.38)

The monsters that rise from the sea to fulfill a paternal wrath
contrast with the more familiar beast that Hippolytus has hunted
in the same chariot. The motifs gathered from the daytime
quests of the poem acquire confusingly ironic overtones in
this infernal setting; but in general the descent to the underworld seems designed—here as in other epics—to dramatize
the challenge of mortality to the hero's quest for identity.
The story of Hippolytus' fall has a special relevance for a
knight whose naïve literalism has limited him to purely nominal
victories over his foes and has blinded him to Una's pertinence
to his quest. But it is a function of this same literal imagination
that Redcross should be deprived of the vision of hell given
to the reader: his own vision is sufficient to rescue him from
the House of Pride, but it leaves him vulnerable to a new
figure of pride who is more "natural" and "monstrous."[21]
Reason (to employ momentarily the conventional interpretation
of the Dwarf) is able to protect Redcross from the "civilized"

20. If Spenser is drawing on *Aeneid* 7.761–82, as well as on Boccaccio,
Genealogia Deorum 10.50, he is the more likely to have borne in mind Hippolytus' later name Virbius ("twice-born" in Servius' gloss), with its Christian
overtones. Cf. H. G. Lotspeich, *Classical Mythology in the Poetry of Edmund
Spenser,* Princeton Studies in English, 9 (Princeton, Princeton University
Press, 1932), 69–70. Douglas Bush, *Mythology and the Renaissance Tradition
in English Poetry* (Minneapolis, The University of Minnesota Press, 1932),
p. 112 n., sees Seneca's *Hippolytus* as the main source.

21. S. K. Heninger, Jr., "The Orgoglio Episode in *The Faerie Queene,*"
ELH, 26 (1959), 171–87.

world of Lucifera; and the panorama of victims in her dungeons is precisely the sort of underworld vision that the Dwarf can reveal to his master: there, Old Testament names flow into a list of Romans, "The antique ruines of the *Romaines* fall" (I.v.49), which suggest through their epithets ("Stout . . . stubborne . . . sterne . . . High minded") that the stoic virtues on which Redcross is currently depending are no better than synonyms for pride. In Spenser's poem nemesis takes the form of a balancing force that reasserts the validity of the natural cycles of time: Redcross leaves the House of Pride only to fall in weariness before the enervating fountain (commemorating, ironically, the weary nymph of Diana) where all his energetic resistance will be mocked as he falls prey to Orgoglio.

Before this happens, however, Spenser turns back to Una in the sixth canto, and by tracing her career among the "saluage nation" of fauns and satyrs provides further insight into the relationship of Redcross to his natural origins at this point. A series of lion images applied to each new arrival in turn suggests the ambiguities in Una's own condition. Previously there had been the literal lion whom she had contrasted with her own, metaphoric lion, Redcross. But that simple, instinctively respectful Defender of the Faith has been killed by Sans Loy, who represents a predatory lion from which Providence must now rescue Una—"From Lyons clawes to pluck the griped pray" (I.vi.7)—by introducing the "rude, misshapen, monstrous rablement" of fauns and satyrs. To the doubting Una, however, it seems as though she were a lamb who has been delivered from a wolf only to fall prey to a lion (I.vi.10): she fears all these animal forces equally. Yet the fauns and satyrs—like the lion in canto iv—are harmless creatures: "gently grenning," they fawn on her (the pun is Spenser's) and encourage her to a pastoral interlude which will permit her "to gather breath in many miseries" (I.vi.19).

Spenser's language is at its most complex in his presentation of this interlude; the conflicts between the apparent and the real which these lion images suggest are echoed throughout the passage. Readers have generally found guidance in an historical allegory, taking Una's adventures as a description of the early history of Christianity and/or English Protestantism, when Truth is cherished in isolated rural areas before being officially accepted by the State. In these periods of primitive worship it is reasonable to see Una as being protected and instinctively respected by beings whose intellects are as yet unable to distinguish between religion and idolatry. As John Steadman has shown in impressive detail,[22] the hieroglyph of the satyrs worshipping Una's ass is rich in specific Renaissance associations of the clergy with the *asinus portans misteria*. In its entirety, however, the passage transcends any such historical allusions, and constitutes a tightly woven knot of images which recapitulate themes introduced earlier in the poem. It will be noted, first of all, that Una receives a pastoral apotheosis similar to that prefigured in Redcross' dream of her:

> Their harts she ghesseth by their humble guise,
>   And yieldes her to extremitie of time;
> So from the ground she fearelesse doth arise,
>   And walketh forth without suspect of crime;
> They all as glad, as birdes of ioyous Prime,
>   Thence lead her forth, about her dauncing round,
> Shouting, and singing all a shepheards ryme,
>   And with greene braunches strowing all the
>   ground,
> Do worship her, as Queene, with oliue girlond
>   cround.
>
>   (I.vi.13)

It is as "Goddesse of the wood" that Una is here acclaimed; the entire passage echoes continually with the reminder that this is a "wood" into which Una has moved. The fauns and satyrs "Within the wood were dauncing in a rownd" when they hear

22. John M. Steadman, "Una and the Clergy: The Ass Symbol in *The Faerie Queene*," *Journal of the Warburg and Courtauld Institutes, 21* (1958), 134–37.

her cries resounding through "all the woodes and forestes";
while they dance "old *Syluanus* slept in shady arber sownd"
(I.vi.7). The "wooddy Nymphes, faire *Hamadryades*" feel themselves displaced by her, and Sylvanus is reminded of his own
beloved Cyparissus, who is memorialized in the cypress staff
on which he supports himself.[23]

The entire incident provides Spenser with an opportunity to
display his skills as a pastoral poet. His description of Sylvanus'
response to Una is a rich blending of traditional topics in an
elegiac mood which is Virgilian in its sense of poignant loss—
the *veteris vestigia flammae* as perceived by a figure who is
ludicrously and pathetically distant from the main concerns of
the quest. Sylvanus' kinship to Fradubio seems hinted in the
first lines; the uselessness and even the wantonness of Cyparissus' suffering do not detract from its reality as Spenser describes it:

> The woodborne people fall before her flat,
> And worship her as Goddesse of the wood;
> And old *Syluanus* selfe bethinkes not, what
> To thinke of wight so faire, but gazing stood,
> In doubt to deeme her borne of earthly brood;
> Sometimes Dame *Venus* selfe he seemes to see,
> But *Venus* neuer had so sober mood;
> Sometimes *Diana* he her takes to bee,
> But misseth bow, and shaftes, and buskins to her
> knee.
>
> By vew of her he ginneth to reuiue
> His ancient loue, and dearest *Cyparisse,*

23. Spenser's word for this staff, "stadle," is of interest in this connection.
The *OED* (s.v. *staddle,* sb.) derives the term from OE *staðol* "foundation,
trunk of tree, fixed position," and sees Spenser's usage as unique in referring
to a movable object. The editors place the usage as a subcategory of sense 2,
"A young tree left standing when others are cut down. Also *dial.* the root or
stump of a tree that has been felled." Spenser may be further suggesting here
the "rooted" condition of the satyrs, with Sylvanus being viewed as the old
tree propped up by the youthful cypress.

> And calles to mind his pourtraiture aliue,
> How faire he was, and yet not faire to this,
> And how he slew with glauncing dart amisse
> A gentle Hynd, the which the louely boy
> Did loue as life, aboue all worldly blisse;
> For grief whereof the lad n'ould after ioy,
> But pynd away in anguish and selfe-wild annoy.
>
> (I.vi.16–17)

Whatever the immediate sources of this account of Cyparissus,[24] his story belongs to a long line of *topoi* involving an accidentally killed deer: the thoughtless acts of Agamemnon or of Ascanius, for example, which involve those heroes in painful consequences. The sense of violated innocence as an inevitable part of human experience—the pastoral world turned by a sudden act of brutality into a savage wilderness—runs through the line of pastoral epicedia which is climaxed by the lament of Marvell's nymph.[25] Along with this sense of violation, however, Spenser is stressing the disproportion of Cyparissus' response. In this he echoes the treatment of Ovid (*Metamorphoses* 10.106–42), who describes Apollo as vainly pleading that the boy moderate his grief. Indeed, the entire context of Ovid's tenth book has a general relevance to Spenser's concern here, and it may be useful to summarize its contents briefly. Elsewhere in the poem Spenser alludes directly or indirectly to images contained in this section of the *Metamorphoses,* and a full understanding of the tone of Una's pastoral interlude depends in part upon a recognition of how these images relate to one another.

In his tenth book Ovid describes the lament of Orpheus at

24. Lotspeich (*Classical Mythology*, p. 51) suggests analogues in Conti and Boccaccio; but the primary source was probably Ovid, *Met.* 10.120 ff., as Sawtelle had earlier proposed (*Variorum 1*, 243).

25. Don Cameron Allen, *Image and Meaning* (Baltimore, The Johns Hopkins Press, 1960), pp. 93–114, provides a useful outline of the history of this motif.

his failure to rescue Eurydice from Hades: a failure, he seems
to suggest, of the poet's faith in his beloved:

> hic, ne deficeret, metuens avidusque videndi
> flexit amans oculos, et protinus illa relapsa est.
>
> (56–57)
>
> [Afraid that she might fail him, and eager to see her, the
> lover looked back; and at once she was lost.]

In his despair he shuns the love of women and with his music
summons a grove of trees (an arboreal catalogue like that in
Spenser's Wood of Error is climaxed by the tale of Cyparissus)
under which he sits to sing of boys loved by gods (Ganymede,
Hyacinthus) and girls overcome by unlawful lusts (Myrrha),
all of whom pay the penalty of their licentiousness. What he
is describing becomes in effect the ancestry of Adonis: an
ancestry which at every stage involves a violation of the laws
of nature and a consequent metamorphosis over which Venus
presides. Throughout these stories Ovid stresses the paradoxes
of the creative act, paradoxes which an age like the Renaissance, sensitive to the poet's role as maker and to the traffic
on Platonic and Neoplatonic ladders of abstraction, might be
expected to embrace with particular enthusiasm. Gods have
frequently descended to the love of fair mortals, Orpheus relates; Jove as sovereign can carry Ganymede back with him
despite Juno's objections; Phoebus, less fortunate in his love
for Hyacinthus, can give his beloved only a seasonal immortality ("qua licet, aeternus tamen es," 164) in which the god of the
Sun and of poets reads his own guilt. But since he cannot accompany Hyacinthus into death (unlike Orpheus in one sense,
unlike Cyparissus in another), Apollo proposes a mutual com-
memoration of their love: he will sing of Hyacinthus, and the
markings on the hyacinth (AI AI) will echo his groans. By
such means Hyacinthus passes into a qualified immortality,
and Sparta will celebrate the Hyacinthia annually.

Against the dialectic of relationships between god and man
described by this tale, in which song translates individual death

into a collective seasonal pattern of resurrection, are contrasted the impieties of the Cerastae whose slaughter of guests earns them an animal metamorphosis into bulls, and still more pertinently the obscene atheism of the Propoetides, who by their promiscuity denied the divinity of Venus:

> utque pudor cessit, sanguisque induruit oris,
> in rigidum parvo silicem discrimine versae.
>
> (241–42)
>
> [And as shame left them and the blood no longer rushed to their faces, they hardened imperceptibly into stone.]

Pygmalion, in contrast, turns away in revulsion at this reality to create an idealized beauty out of ivory, and Venus smiles on his desire to embrace his creation. The description of this metamorphosis of Galatea—which reverses that of the Propoetides—stresses the artist's role: under his caressing touch the ivory softens like wax and under the shaping influence of the lover/sculptor nature is created in the image of art ("ipsoque fit utilis usu"). Under his finger Pygmalion feels the veins throbbing; and the climax of Galatea's awakening is the blush which brings the blood to her face:

> dataque oscula virgo
> sensit et erubuit timidumque ad lumina lumen
> attollens pariter cum caelo vidit amantem.
>
> (292–94)
>
> [The maiden felt the kisses and blushed, and timidly raising her eyes to the light ("ad lumina lumen") she saw her lover at the same time as the sky.]

Against such a human triumph of requited desire further instances of destructive lust reverberate. Cinyras, the grandson of Pygmalion, is loved by his daughter, Myrrha, whose speeches are expressive of revulsion at an impulse she cannot deny: for her (as for Spenser's Fradubio) metamorphosis into a tree is a self-willed denial of the privilege of either life or death. And finally Adonis is born of this incestuous union, to bring to

Venus herself an ironic revenge for his mother's passion (524).
The goddess who has presided over the course of this family
history now descends into a mortal affair whose paradoxes not
even she can resolve. The anemone into which Adonis is
changed is in fact the shortest-lived of all these flowers: even
for Venus the joys of love are limited. Ovid's tale is famed by
reminders of Time's threat. Of the growth of Adonis: "Labitur
occulte fallitque volatilis aetas,/ et nihil est annis velocius"
(519–20). Of the equally rapid growth and decay of the flower:
"brevis est tamen usus in illo" (737).

Spenser's poem shares with the *Metamorphoses* a dependence
on verbal and situational repetitions to give continuity in the
absence of the more obvious unities of character or plot. But
these repetitions always involve subtle variations and involu-
tions, so that the effect tends toward the complication rather
than the simplification of themes. In the present example of
Ovid's tenth book, Orpheus is at once lamenting his condition
and, ironically, curing it: his song infuriates the Bacchantes
at the same time that it enthralls beasts, trees, and stones; and
once the women's music has drowned out his song (so that he
can be touched by the stones and vine-wreathed spears) he is
killed and thus reunited with his Eurydice (11.1–66). At the
same time, the tales describe a cycle of relationships between
higher and lower beings in which all the possible attitudes
toward metamorphosis are expressed. In the midst of these, and
contrasting with the complex image of Orpheus as artist, is the
simple idyll of Pygmalion; but even he is tied through his
descendants to a pattern of inescapable desire, fulfillment, and
change. In concluding with the story of Venus and Adonis,
Orpheus is indicating that gods and mortals alike are bound
to the limitations of their respective natures; and in telling
Adonis the story of Atalanta and Hippomenes, Venus herself
is indicating obliquely that she has, in her wrathful moments,
helped to create the world of violence which will destroy her
beloved. Adonis' *virtus* (10.707) will be the undoing of both of
them.

It is because Spenser's description of Una's stay among the satyrs involves a similar pattern of reverberating echoes that I have chosen to give a much fuller account of the Ovidian context than is immediately relevant at this point in *The Faerie Queene*. One of the terms which inform Ovid's stories is *usus,* which seems to carry the meaning of "fruition" in its various senses. In the context of these floral and arboreal metamorphoses this *usus* is sharply limited by time: it is a brief, blossoming stage in the seasonal cycle. In this sense it is the perennially mortal aspect of the immortality gained by these lovers. In the phrase referring to the softening of wax under the warmth of the sun and the working fingers of the sculptor—"ipsoque fit utilis usu"—it becomes a crucial term in the creative process as well: the phrase stresses that Pygmalion's idealizing love has given Galatea life.[26] Although there is no direct allusion to Ovid beyond the echo of his treatment of Cyparissus, Spenser nevertheless seems here to be making a similar point as regards the possibility of meaningful response within this "woody" context. Cyparissus' transcendent love for his deer leaves him unable to survive its death. He commits himself to joylessness, so that his metamorphosis is at heart a metaphor to describe how totally he has become a monument to grief—the cypress, which, like the other trees Spenser has shown in the Wood of Error, is an emblem of single-mindedness. He has "pynd away in anguish and self-wild annoy," and the emphasis on willfulness implies a judgment on his reduction to a tree.

Similarly, the entire throng of fauns and satyrs seem bound to their "woodborne" status. The story of their adoration of Una is one of failure to distinguish between image and idea, a breakdown of religion into idolatry. Their "backward bending knees" are at once a sign of their harmlessness and more obliquely an emblem of their tendency to "worship backwards"

26. H. Fränkel, *Ovid: A Poet between Two Worlds* (Berkeley, University of California Press, 1945), p. 83. Millar MacLure, "Nature and Art in *The Faerie Queene," ELH, 28* (1961), 7, finds an implicit reference to the Pygmalion legend in Archimago's ravishment at his own image of Una (I.i.45).

in the sense of making Una a pastoral queen rather than an image of divine beauty:

> During which time her gentle wit she plyes,
> To teach them truth, which worshipt her in vaine,
> And made her th'Image of Idolatryes;
> But when their bootlesse zeale she did restraine
> From her own worship, they her Asse would worship
> fayn.
>
> (I.vi.19)

Una's time is wasted here; the satyrs' love is bootless, however eager, for they are rooted in their sylvan environment. With the passage to the story of Satyrane, however, Spenser's stress seems to move to the positive values of the satyr's life. Satyrane too is "woodborne," and his return "To seeke his kindred, and the lignage right,/ From whence he tooke his well deserued name" (I.vi.20) is repeatedly held up as an example of filial piety. This might seem rather surprising in view of the circumstances of his birth, which involve "beastly" and "brutish" motifs on every side. Thyamis (Greek *thymós* "passion"), the daughter of Labryde (*lábros* "turbulent, greedy"), is the wife of Therion ("wild beast"),[27]

> Who had more ioy to raunge the forrest wyde,
> And chase the saluage beast with busie payne,
> Then serue his Ladies loue, and wast in pleasures
> vayne.
>
> (I.vi.21)

Here the Hippolytus theme seems to be repeated in a purely savage key. As the Book has worked through these variations on the Choice of Hercules (a choice which has a particular relevance to the chivalric ethic with its double emphasis on love and honor), there has been a consistent slipping of emphasis from the original contrast between heroic action and

27. *Variorum 1*, 245.

voluptuous delinquency in the early Redcross, to the more ambiguous contrast of Diana and Venus in the tale of Hippolytus, to this final debased triangle: here Therion's "busie payne" is morally equivalent to "other game and venery" (the pun seems likely),[28] in comparison with the lustful captivity of Thyamis to her satyr. Satyrane is thus born of a union which, for all its irregularity when considered from the viewpoint of "sacred bands of wedlocke" (a viewpoint which Spenser recognizes twice in as many stanzas, I.vi.21–22), is at the same time an assertion of the irresistibility of the sexual instinct. Satyrane inherits the capacity to dominate his bestial environment; his satyr father teaches him "To banish cowardize and bastard feare" by laying his trembling hand on the wild beasts of the forest. Soon it is the father who trembles at his son's fearlessness; Satyrane has learned to overcome all that the forest can offer, and he moves on to further conquests as a knight of Gloriana.

This progress from the satyr's world to the fairy court serves to suggest simultaneously the values of the former and the limitations of the latter. Satyrane's courage has enabled him to excel in his chivalric activities. He embodies an heroic virtue which frequently seems to embrace the entire range of Gloriana's world. He shares with a "savage" figure like Artegall (or Guyon) an Achillean or Herculean background, and in the long run he would seem to be similarly limited to exercising the classical virtues of restraint rather than the more positive, informing virtues which Spenser tends to associate with his Britons. It is appropriate that Una teaches him "her discipline of faith and veritie" (I.vi.31), for it is in terms of discipline that his "pagan" knowledge of truth must be formulated.

In the poem as it now stands Satyrane is limited to relatively neutral or normative roles. His early role in subduing animals is echoed in his shortlived binding of the witch's beast

28. The suggestion was first made by Sir Thomas Warton (cited in *Variorum 1,* ibid.).

(III.vii.29–38), and the later passage helps to define his peculiar strengths:

> It was a goodly Swaine, and of great might,
> As euer man that bloudy field did fight;
> But in vaine sheows, that wont yong knights
>   bewitch,
> And courtly seruices tooke no delight,
> But rather ioyd to be, then seemen sich:
> For both to be and seeme to him was labour lich.
>   (III.vii.29)

The filial piety that brings him back to the forest shows his recognition of a part of his nature; by recognizing it he is able to control it and avoid the tendencies toward "idolatry" which characterize his wholly savage relatives. While the satyrs are gone "To do their seruice to *Syluanus* old" (I.vi.33) he leads Una out of the wood and back to the open plains of chivalric trial. Once there, his usefulness ends; he is last seen in this Book as he fights unavailingly against Sans Loy. Similarly, in the erotic contexts of Books III and IV his role as "natural" man (*L'homme moyen sensuel,* as Osgood points out[29]) enables him to move with grace and complaisance through scenes of lust and gallantry, laughing unreservedly at the tale of the Squire of Dames (III.vii.58), entering Malbecco's house with the lecherous Paridell, and leaving it with Britomart. He can temper his mood to fit any company. Yet although his recognition of his heritage might be said to protect him against the neurotic disintegration of an Hippolytus (or a Redcross), this very well-roundedness also seems to isolate him from the possibility of assuming an heroic role, at least in the earlier Books of the poem where the virtues involve corresponding limitations of understanding and/or power. Though it is always possible that he would have become the patron of a subsequent Book, his present role is rather to point toward qualities which will be

29. *Variorum 1,* ibid.

realized in later heroes who preside over the more "classical" or restraining virtues, as do Guyon and, even more pertinently, the "savage" Artegall; or who, like Calidore, find that the completion of the quest must be preceded by a return to the natural origins which lie obscured beneath the premises of court life. It is significant of the ambiguity of Satyrane's role—and of the ambiguity of pastoral motifs as Spenser employs them—that he is alternately described as wearing the emblems both of a Satyr's head (III.vii.30) and of the order of Maidenhead (IV.iv.17).

Satyrane is thus an emphatically minor character in the action of Book I, for he stands outside the Christian dispensation which alone makes Redcross' quest possible. Nevertheless his role as the agent of Una's escape from the forest helps to locate the area of investigation which will be undertaken in subsequent Books. For the moment he serves to suggest a positive aspect of the satyr's world, as a training ground for the human hero who learns to control and hence to use his natural origins. For those who, like the satyrs, are wholly imbedded in these origins, there can be no question of an education; there is only the narrator's condescending dismissal: "In vaine he seekes that hauing cannot hold" (I.vi.33).[30] On the other hand, individuals like the early Redcross who are blind to those origins, choosing in their naïve idealism to translate every solid tree into a abstract value, must learn that their spiritual health depends on recognizing the demands of their fallen nature. Fradubio has shown the conditions under which man becomes a tree; Satyrane's history has begun to show, on the level of the natural order, the ways in which man may emerge from this "wooden"

---

30. Spenser's emphasis on the difference in kind between Una and the satyrs is expressed through these punning references to their failure to speak a common language. Una's initial reluctance to "commit/ Her single person to their barbarous truth" (I.vi.12) similarly plays on the implications of her name and of the word "truth." To keep the faith requires an understanding of that faith; and the satyrs alternate between a worship of Una as a mere woman (with pastoral garlands) and an equally distorted worship of her as a bearer of truth (as seen in their worship of her ass). Like the early Redcross they are unable to comprehend her as a fusion of image and meaning.

state. The inconclusive battle against Sans Loy which concludes
the sixth canto leaves this strand of the poem incomplete, to be
taken up at greater length in the next Book when Guyon
wrestles with the conflicting appetites of man, attempting to
overcome the uncontrol implicit in each desire by subjecting
it to an opposing force, and thereby to create a "temperance"
of balancing forces without recourse to any principle outside
the natural world. Redcross has the very different task—symbolized by the *donnée* of his armor—of rising above his natural
limitations and transcending the problems which Guyon confronts, so as to make a conclusive assault on the collective
burden of man's fallen nature as it is figured in the Dragon.

It seems clear that Spenser's parallel treatment of Holiness
and Temperance in Books I and II proceeds from a contrast
between the orders of Grace and Nature, as Woodhouse has
described in an essay of fundamental importance to this problem.[31] Redcross is driven by the logic of his experiences through
stages of despair which make his own inadequacies ever more
apparent. Not until he learns that he is a Briton and therefore
subject to a merciful God (as opposed to the merely retributive
Jove who balances accounts in Fairyland) can he complete his
quest. As an imitator of Christ and a second Adam, his pro-
gressive surrender to sin constitutes a fortunate fall which exposes him to the possibility of redemption. Contrasting with
this story of Redcross is that of Guyon, who is emphatically an
Elf throughout the Book (as the contrasting histories in II.x
stress), and who imitates classical heroes (Odysseus in particular) in his prudent resistance to temptation. Yet once we have
recognized the existence of this basic contrast between Nature
and Grace, it becomes apparent that Spenser has provided so
intricate a contrapuntal pattern in his presentation of the two
stories as to deny any simple contrast of the Christian and pagan
contexts. On the contrary, the careful parallelism of the Books
serves to stress the similarities as well as the contrasts between

31. Woodhouse, "Nature and Grace," pp. 194–228.

the heroes, and it is an ironic confirmation of the centrality of Woodhouse's thesis that it has provoked so fertile an affirmation of the relevance of Christian themes to the action of Book II.[32]

Emerging from recent scholarship on the first two Books is a sense of complementary histories assembled in all their complex interrelationships by the synthesizing powers of Christian humanism. Guyon may be sinfully curious in exposing himself to temptations, yet he is also echoing the story of Christ's temptation, and in this is as much an imitator of Christ as Redcross. But his victory is not the creation of a new Eden so much as the destruction of a false one. The mixed emotions with which narrator and reader alike view the destruction of the Bower are an index of the limited success possible in Guyon's sphere. Similarly, his faint in canto vii is far from the abandonment to sin characteristic of Redcross' fall, but it is a fall none the less; and the reader's sense that Guyon is protected by a merciful deity beyond his own comprehension is made the more ironic by the fact that he is watched over by an angel in the form of Cupid, the last figure to whom this knight of Maidenhead might expect to turn.

The ambiguities of Guyon's victory transcend his own awareness of the issues involved. Verdant in the embrace of Acrasia is on the one hand a delinquent warrior, to be ensnared like Mars with Venus and restored to his proper sphere, "His warlike armes, the idle instruments/ Of sleeping praise" (II.xii.80); but he is also an Adonis, a Spring-giver as his name and boyish grace suggest. In this latter context, to liberate him from Acrasia is to awaken him to a full consciousness of his identity and to return him to an activity which will involve the changes— against which his dalliance had been a fruitless and wasting

32. Berger, *The Allegorical Temper;* A. D. S. Fowler, "Emblems of Temperance in *The Faerie Queene,* Book II," *Review of English Studies, 11* (1960), 143–49, and "The Image of Mortality: *The Faerie Queene,* II.i–ii," *Huntington Library Quarterly, 24* (1961), 91–110; A. C. Hamilton, "A Theological Reading of *The Faerie Queene,* Book II," *ELH, 25* (1958), 155–62.

gesture—upon which the natural cycle depends for its continual renewal.[33] Books III and IV will develop the themes of the destructive and integrative aspects of love; the first two Books, with their insistence on the individual personality, have been content to stress the simultaneous inevitability and insufficiency of the erotic instinct. Man in time is subject to cycles of change—the seasons, the hours, the appetites—and to deny any part of these cycles is to invite disaster by upsetting the balance of one's human nature.

Further research into Renaissance iconography seems likely to expand our appreciation of the complexity with which Spenser interweaves psychological themes and theological imagery in Book II, in order to define the nature of fallen man and to demonstrate the relevance of classical myth in describing man's struggles to recreate within himself the order he can no longer find in his external surroundings. What I have tried to show in this chapter is the extent to which the presentation of Holiness in Book I has similarly involved from the opening lines a complementary awareness that any attempt to assert a reality beyond nature must proceed from a full recognition of man's roots within nature. For this reason Spenser has chosen to describe the coming of age of the young knight, tracing the inadequacies of his naïve idealism to cope with the ambiguous *visibilia* of this world.

In the second half of Book I, where Redcross is rescued and enabled to complete his quest, ambiguities in the terms of his rescue help to maintain this awareness of his paradoxical reliance on the forces of nature if he is to transcend that nature. The initial description of Arthur in the seventh canto provides the first and the most complex set of these ambiguities. In the eight stanzas that describe the effects of his armor (I.vii.29–36), Arthur embraces the attributes of the Book's various adversaries. Like Lucifera and her palace, "His glitterand armour shined farre away,/ Like glauncing light of *Phoebus* brightest

33. Hamilton, *The Structure of Allegory*, p. 134.

ray"; repeated references to heavenly bodies stress the degree
to which the armor's brilliance similarly strives to "attaint" the
sun.[34] These similarities are scarcely coincidental, for the language of the description insists on those details which had
earlier seemed to be the indices of evil; thus the stone in the
middle of his breastplate

> Shapt like a Ladies head, exceeding shone,
>   Like *Hesperus* emongst the lesser lights,
>   And stroue for to amaze the weaker sights;
>
> (I.vii.30)

—and the phrase, "exceeding shone," is repeated four stanzas
later. Arthur's magnificence is most relevant to the concerns
of Book I in its triumphant ability to assimilate the very forces
which have intimidated others:

> His haughtie helmet, horrid all with gold,
>   Both glorious brightnesse, and great terrour bred;
>   For all the crest a **Dragon** did enfold
>   With greedie pawes, and ouer all did spred
>   His golden wings: his dreadfull hideous hed
>   Close couched on the beuer, seem'd to throw
>   From flaming mouth bright sparkles fierie red,
>   That suddeine horror to faint harts did show;
> And scaly tayle was stretcht adowne his backe full
>   low.
>
> Vpon the top of all his loftie crest,
>   A bunch of haires discolourd diuersly,
>   With sprincled pearle, and gold full richly drest,
>   Did shake, and seem'd to daunce for iollity,
>   Like to an Almond tree ymounted hye
>   On top of greene *Selinis* all alone,

34. Hamilton, ibid., p. 85, seems to defeat his own argument for a careful
distinction between luminous and reflected light in Spenser's imagery, when
he mentions Arthur's "glitterand armour" shortly after contrasting the glitter
of the children of Night with Redcross' "glistring armor."

With blossomes braue bedecked daintily;
Whose tender locks do tremble euery one
At euery little breath, that vnder heauen is blowne.
(I.vii.31–32)

In placing the figure of the Dragon on his crest, Arthur is in
effect asserting his sense of historical destiny. As the most clearly defined in time of all the characters of the poem, this figure
of Arthur "before he was king" appears *in propria persona* (and
with his own name) in a sense that others do not. Britomart is
closest to him in her sense of manifest destiny, but her virginity
and its attendant elements of uncertainty suggest a promise
more dimly foreshadowed: only Arthur can move with confidence in the memory of a vision pledged with the pressed grass
of waking experience. Redcross accomplishes the symbolic slay-
ing of the dragon which will confirm his Christian armor, but
Arthur is already wearing that symbol of Time/Death/Sin, as
a token of his own fully attained chivalry.

The surprising echoes of earlier episodes in the description
of Arthur help to clarify the Book's level of reality. If we are
prepared to admit that these echoes are more than coincidental
—and they seem far too numerous and compact for that—then
they bring into sharper focus the personal and symbolic nature
of the action, as the psychomachia of the youthful knight.
Arthur, the complete man, moves into the various Books of
the poem to remind the reader of the limited, specialized nature
of the individual action. Here he contains the full cast of Redcross' adversaries within his armor, as it were. The bunch of
hairs on his crest (the line is repeated verbatim from the earlier
description of Archimago's impersonation, I.ii.11) tremble like
Fradubio's leaves "with euery blast" (I.ii.28); but they have
been transformed into an image of joy, a pastoral garland rather
than the pervasive image of trapped and suffering humanity.[35]

35. A similar fusion of suffering and triumph is seen in the comparison of
Redcross' hill of Contemplation to the Mount of Olives, "For euer with a
flowring girlond crownd," and to Parnassus (I.x.44).

A similar collapsing of the images of hero and enchanter is seen in Arthur's shield, which is based on that of Ariosto's enchanter, Atlante.[36] Arthur's relation to Merlin, like Ruggiero's to Atlante, provides a further basis for assessing Redcross' to Archimago. In Spenser's hands the obscure motives of the Romance magician become a means of suggesting the internal nature of the struggles involved.

By means of these ambiguous allusions in the details of Arthur's attributes, the reader is reminded of the mixture of physical and spiritual, natural and divine, in the formula of Holiness which the Book is presenting. Arthur is both the irresistible bearer of divine grace and the representative of a practical heroism which is not too proud to sidestep Orgoglio's blows (I.viii.7–8). Una rescues Redcross from Despair in similar terms, by asserting that the irresistible logic of man's self-condemnation must be evaded by a timely retreat to a trust in divine mercy. And when his education at the House of Holiness is climaxed by the revelation of his personal origins, Redcross learns that his name is simultaneously expressive of his nation, his religious dispensation, and his humble education as a plowman's foundling. With a nod probably to Langland as well as to Caxton,[37] Spenser brings his clownish youth full cycle, to a recognition of the human creature which has been hiding from itself in borrowed armor. When Redcross finally confronts the adversary, therefore, he is able to survive not only because he is a chosen vessel of grace but also because he is a child of earth. Like Antaeus, he falls to earth only to rise with renewed strength; the night is now a time of nourishing rest rather than

36. Don Cameron Allen, "Arthur's Diamond Shield in *The Faerie Queene*," *Journal of English and Germanic Philology, 36* (1937), 234–43; Nelson, *The Poetry of Edmund Spenser*, p. 143.

37. A. C. Hamilton, "Spenser and Langland," *Studies in Philology, 55* (1958), 533–48, and "The Visions of *Piers Plowman* and *The Faerie Queene*," in William Nelson, ed., *Form and Convention in the Poetry of Edmund Spenser*, English Institute Essays (New York, Columbia University Press, 1961), pp. 1–34. Spenser's indebtedness to Caxton's translation of the *Golden Legend* is discussed in this context by Susan Snyder, "Guyon the Wrestler," *Renaissance News, 14* (1961), 249–52.

of nightmare and menace. God's grace takes the form of enabling man to recapture the healthful relationship to nature which he had lost with his first fall into knowledge. Water and Tree, symbols of menace to man's fallen nature earlier in the Book, are now made the means by which Redcross can emerge reborn to prove his armor.

At the beginning of the eleventh canto, the narrator with seeming anticlimax asks his Muse to "come gently" into his breast, renouncing any intention of describing a confrontation of fully epic proportions:

> Faire Goddesse lay that furious fit aside,
>   Till I of warres and bloudy *Mars* do sing,
>   And Briton fields with Sarazin bloud bedyde,
>   Twixt that great faery Queene and Paynim king,
>   That with their horrour heauen and earth did ring,
>   A worke of labour long, and endlesse prayse:
>   But now a while let downe that haughtie string,
>   And to my tunes thy second tenor rayse,
> That I this man of God his godly armes may blaze.
>   (I.xi.7)

So deprecatory an invocation may have seemed particularly necessary in view of the nautical imagery of the Dragon's description (cf. particularly stanza 10), published at a time when readers could expect allusions to the Armada in any work, and most of all in an allegory dedicated to their Queen. But even without a topical relevance to the passage, the tone of Spenser's invocation is meaningful in terms of the issues that I have been describing. It is not simply that the "political" virtues are being saved for a second set of twelve Books, as the Letter to Ralegh promises. It is that Redcross' battle is by definition personal and ahistorical, a symbolic act in which the individual relives the history of his race and comes thereby to a mature sense of his identity. From the beginning Redcross has seen his quest as an opportunity "To proue his puissance in battell braue/ Vpon his foe, and his new force to learne" (I.i.3); and the narrator now describes it as an emblazoning of the knight's armor. Although the fight will be fierce enough in its physical details, Spenser here explicitly couches his invocation in such a way as to insist on its meaning to the knight: in a significant variation on the Virgilian formula, this part of the poem is concerned with arms *of* the man, and with the relation of God to each of these terms.

Redcross' victory over the Dragon, like Arthur's over Orgoglio, is seen as the reduction of a natural phenomenon to its proper perspective.[38] The dragon is first seen "Where stretcht he lay vpon the sunny side/ Of a great hill, himselfe like a great hill" (I.xi.4); and he falls like another Orgoglio:

> So downe he fell, as an huge rocky clift,
> Whose false foundation waues haue washt away,
> With dreadfull poyse is from the mayneland rift,
> And, rolling downe, great *Neptune* doth dismay;
> So downe he fell, and like an heaped mountaine lay.
> (I.xi.54)

With nature now in its place a pastoral diversion is possible. Redcross can see his beloved receive the garland that Archimago's dream had earlier forecast, and can see her face to face, like the morning star or the "freshest flowre in May" (I.xii.21–22). But it is a betrothal rather than a wedding which is to be celebrated at this point in the knight's career: he has proved himself, but his term of service to Gloriana has only begun. Even this limited ceremony is threatened by Duessa and Archimago, whose powers continue though they are no serious challenge at the moment. The Eden which Redcross' victory has restored is seen to be a function of the knight's self-knowledge, and the tone of the twelfth canto is precariously balanced "twixt earnest and twixt game," like Una's veneration by the maidens of the town. Only this balance of attitudes can avoid the idolatrous enslavement to nature characteristic of the satyrs in canto vi. The Book's constant concern for the imaginative faculty helps to explain the narrator's convoluted description of

38. Heninger, "The Orgoglio Episode," pp. 171–97; Hamilton, *The Structure of Allegory,* pp. 75–79.

this pastoral epiphany of Una: "Who, in her self-resemblance well beseene,/ Did seeme such, as she was, a goodly maiden Queene" (I.xii.8). Una is what she seems to be; but it is nevertheless the spectator's responsibility to recognize the two distinct levels of being and seeming as well as to note their congruence here.

The First Book has defined Holiness in terms of man's recognition of the polarities of his being. Spiritual health or wholeness is the subject of St. Paul's epistle to the Ephesians, Spenser's avowed source for Redcross' armor; and the Bishops' Bible (like the King James version) translates the Greek *panoplia* as "the whole armor" of God. The history of the integration of Redcross' personality has been tantamount to a survey of the full range of pastoral motifs employed throughout the poem. The natural setting may be a place of savagery or of ease; it may be a source of education, temptation, or punishment. The pastoral interlude may be at best a vision of human communion, achieved with difficulty and inevitably violated; at worst it may be a simple evasion of human identity. The scenes and situations presented in Book I will recur throughout subsequent Books, and their changing meanings will be a key to the varying operations of the virtues being defined.

Before continuing with an examination of these pastoral motifs, however, it may be helpful to approach the problem from a different direction and to consider the literary traditions which Spenser inherited and adapted in *The Faerie Queene*. I have briefly suggested above the extent to which the poem shares with Ovid's *Metamorphoses* a principle of organization through the symbolic counterpoint of related images. But Spenser's relationship to Ovid, as to both technique and theme, will seem tenuous and distant until we examine the bonds of literary tradition which link them. The ones which I shall discuss— others could be as easily chosen—will be the Petrarchan lyric and the Italian modifications of traditional epic forms in the loosely related body of poems which go under the title of "chivalric epic."

2. The Problem of Genre:
Some Continental Antecedents

ARIOSTO AND THE CHIVALRIC PREMISE

In his Letter to Ralegh, Spenser defines the ancestry of his poem in terms which have bearing on our own sense of its conflicting areas of indebtedness:

> I haue followed all the antique Poets historicall, first Homere, who in the Persons of Agamemnon and Vlysses hath ensampled a good gouernour and a vertuous man, the one in his Ilias, the other in his Odysseis: then Virgil, whose like intention was to doe in the person of Aeneas: after him Ariosto comprised them both in his Orlando: and lately Tasso disseuered them againe, and formed both parts in two persons, namely that part which they in Philosophy call Ethice, or vertues of a priuate man, coloured in his Rinaldo: The other named Politice in his Godfredo.

It is characteristic of Spenser's love of schemata that his list traces a carefully patterned chiasma (one of his favorite forms[1])

1. Alastair Fowler, in "Numerical Composition in *The Faerie Queene*," *Journal of the Warburg and Courtauld Institutes*, 25 (1962), 199–239 (repr.

in which two modern poets are balanced against two ancients, and the two inner positions given to single, composite heroes who contrast with the "disseuered" heroic pairs in the outer terms of the sequence. But the enforced symmetry of this scheme is likely to trouble the modern reader less than the fact that Ariosto should have been included at all. Not only does Orlando seems to have little in common with Aeneas, ethically or politically; but the ironies, buffooneries, and discursiveness of Ariosto's poem offer little ground for comparison with the high seriousness and unified plot of the *Aeneid*. Spenser's citation of Ariosto in such a context has suggested to some scholars an almost incredibly humorless reading of the Italian. Although his indebtedness to the poem for specific borrowings of character and incident has been long recognized and scrupulously recorded, source studies have been skeptical of any broader areas of kinship between the two poets. Thus R. E. Neil Dodge concluded that "However seriously . . . Spenser may at times have taken Ariosto, it is manifest that the latter can have had no real influence upon his deeper imaginative life . . . When he copies Ariosto it is almost always with a change."[2] The most

---

in *Spenser and the Numbers of Time,* London, Routledge and Kegan Paul, 1964, pp. 24–33), traces the use of quadripartite schemata in Book IV, where he sees the Book's number as a symbol of Friendship's role, to temper extremes with means. But the chiasma or tetrad occurs throughout the poem—as do triads, pentads, hexads, and other geometric patternings. Such forms seem to have less connection with the subject matter of individual Books than with Spenser's general concern for an elaborate formal texture.

2. R. E. Neil Dodge, "Spenser's Imitations from Ariosto," *PMLA, 12* (1897), 195–96. Further treatment of Spenser's indebtedness to Ariosto is found in Anna Benedetti, *L'Orlando Furioso nella vita intellettuale del popolo inglese* (Florence, Bemporad, 1914); Allan H. Gilbert, "Spenser's Imitations from Ariosto: Supplementary," *PMLA, 34* (1919), 225–32; R. E. Neil Dodge, "Spenser's Imitations from Ariosto—Addenda," *PMLA, 35* (1920), 91–92; Susannah J. McMurphy, *Spenser's Use of Ariosto for Allegory,* (Seattle, University of Washington Press, 1924); W. J. B. Owen, "*Orlando Furioso* and Stanza-Connection in the *Faerie Queene,*" *Modern Language Notes, 67* (1952), 5–8; D. G. Rees, "Italian and Italianate Poetry," in *Elizabethan Poetry,* Stratford-upon-Avon Studies, 2 (New York, St. Martin's Press, 1960), 52–69.

recent attempt to evaluate Spenser's debt to the Italian poets, though it is sensitive to the variety and richness of Ariosto and to the similar discursiveness of the central Books of *The Faerie Queene,*[3] continues to rely on De Sanctis' formula of "pure art" and Croce's of "harmony," terms which have until recently deflected Italian criticism from any consideration of Ariosto's position in the heroic tradition.[4]

This heroic aspect of the *Orlando Furioso* is one which an Elizabethan reader would single out for emphasis, at least if he were attempting a defense of the poem. Thus John Harington in the introduction to his translation (1591) similarly traces a parallel between Ariosto and Virgil, not only pointing to the opening and closing lines of the two poems but going on to assert that "there is nothing of any speciall obseruation in *Virgill* but my author hath with great felicitie imitated it, so as whosoeuer wil allow *Virgil* must *ipso facto* (as they say) admit Ariosto."[5] Harington's attempts to allegorize Ariosto, like those of the Italians from whom he borrowed, are frequently capricious and contradictory, but their very disorder is suggestive of an enthusiastic response to the poem:

> True it is I added some notes to the end of euery canto, euen as if some of my frends and my selfe reading it together (and so it fell out indeed many times) had after debated vpon them what had bene most worthie consideration in them, and so oftimes immediatly I set it downe.[6]

---

3. Hough, *A Preface to "The Faerie Queene,"* pp. 9–81.

4. Robert M. Durling, "The Divine Analogy in Ariosto," *Modern Language Notes, 78* (1963), 1–14, provides the most helpful recent commentary on Ariosto in English, including a brief summary of traditional approaches.

5. John Harington, trans.: *Orlando Furioso in English heroical verse* (London, R. Field, 1591), S.T.C. 746. Harington's Preface, from which this quotation is taken, is reprinted by G. G. Smith, *Elizabethan Critical Essays* (2 vols. Oxford University Press, 1904), *2,* 194–222. Harington makes Ruggiero the hero of the poem, parallel to Aeneas.

6. Ibid. For a discussion of Harington's use of Italian commentators, see Townsend Rich, *Harington & Ariosto: A Study in Elizabethan Verse Translation* (New Haven, Yale University Press, 1940), p. 142.

Ariosto's richness confounds any attempt to provide a systematic reading of the poem. Here I am concerned primarily with indicating that Spenser could find in the *Orlando Furioso* not only the subject matter for many of his chivalric legends, but also a precedent for the ironic evaluation of the chivalric ethic. A detailed examination of a few of Spenser's borrowings shows that he tended to borrow not so much plot sequences (as was the case with Shakespeare's use of his sources, for example), as individual situations, character relationships, tropes. *The Faerie Queene* is studded with momentary recollections of Ariosto: though characters may be "disseuered" and recombined variously in the process of translation, the postures which they strike clearly show Spenser's indebtedness.

A reading of Ariosto's opening canto in light of some of the themes discussed in the preceding chapter illuminates the problems of this indebtedness. A number of apparent parallels between the two poems are in a sense false, since both poets are concerned with defining their relationship to the epic tradition and are consequently alluding to common motifs from that tradition. Frequently, however, when Ariosto and Spenser choose a common motif of this sort, it seems likely that Spenser is building on the Ariostesque version as well as on the original in Virgil or Dante. In such an area of investigation, confident assignment of "sources" for such allusions must give way to recognition of a common attitude toward the received tradition.

Ariosto's opening lines, like Spenser's, constitute a conspicuous Virgilian imitation; not surprisingly, Ariosto's tone is that of deliberate parody, suggesting a total renunciation of epic sobriety:

> Le donne, i cavallier, l'arme, gli amori,
> le cortesie, l'audaci imprese io canto,
> che furo al tempo che passaro i Mori
> d'Africa il mare, e in Francia nocquer tanto,
> seguendo l'ire e i giovenil furori
> d'Agramante lor re, che si diè vanto

di vendicar la morte di Troiano
sopra re Carlo imperator romano.

Dirò d'Orlando in un medesmo tratto
cosa non detta in prosa mai né in rima:
che per amor venne in furore e matto,
d'uom che sì saggio era stimato prima;
se da colei che tal quasi m'ha fatto,
che 'l poco ingegno ad or ad or mi lima,
me ne sarà però tanto concesso,
che mi basti a finir quanto ho promesso.

(I.1–2)

[I sing of women, knights, arms, and loves, of chivalrous and bold undertakings, which took place at the time when the Moors crossed over from Africa and did so much damage in France, following the wrath and the youthful madness of their king Agramante, who boasted of avenging Troiano's death on King Charles, the Roman Emperor.

At the same time, I will tell of Orlando something not yet said in prose or rhyme: how love infuriated him and drove him mad, a man who had been thought so wise before; if, that is, she who has practically done the same thing to me, so that she doles out even now what little sense I have, will only grant me enough to finish what I have promised.]

The opening line of the poem arranges the two central themes in a chiasma whereby the *arma virumque* of Virgilian epic (*arma virosque* in the Carolingian romance) are swallowed up by the erotic concerns. Although the poem's historical setting is defined in terms of the larger, public problems of the war between Christians and infidels, it is clear that the distracting powers of love will dominate the private lives of the heroes on both sides.

Indeed, although the comic structure of the poem might appear to be based on a contrast of man's higher, martial ambitions with his humbler, erotic weaknesses, the phrasing of these opening lines shows that Ariosto is casting his net even more widely, and proposing to demonstrate the elements of "madness" in both the public and private areas of activity. Against Orlando's madness is balanced the madness—equally "juvenile" —of Agramante's crusade to avenge his father's death. Both martial and erotic impulses are generated by furies, Ariosto seems to suggest; and resolution of this comic situation does not consist simply of a return to the battle lines between Moors and Christians drawn up at the beginning of the poem. In fact, the conversion of Ruggiero to Christianity and the establishment of his line as the historical predecessors of the d'Este provide the basis for a pattern of reconciliation that will transcend the simple opposition of Christian and infidel, as Ariosto's dedicatory verses (I.3–4) indicate.

As for the decorum which the poem observes, these same opening lines stress the combination of heroic pretension and human inadequacy in the character of the poem's narrator, whose humiliating servitude to his own mistress threatens to frustrate the writing of the poem. This tension between martial and erotic motives on the part of hero and poet alike is suggestive of the similar tensions between epic and pastoral discussed in the preceding chapter. Both Ariosto and Spenser call attention to themselves as narrators who feel the same weaknesses as their heroes. Though the former more frequently wears the mask of the urbane manipulator of plot strands, reveling in his protean powers while the latter tends to dwell on the exhaustions and frustrations of the poet's career,[7] the result in both cases is a poem which calls attention to its own artifice: a poem which is at least partly concerned with the way a poem is conceived, a study in perspective.

The chief restraint on Ariosto's satirical wit—the "debunking" spirit which many readers have taken to be the poem's

7. From this technique comes the popular notion of Spenser's "gentleness" which has constituted the chief area of biographical extrapolation from the poems.

sole motive[8]—derives from his relationship to the d'Este. Like Virgil and Spenser, he is presenting the ancestry of his patron. In one sense or another all three of these "Poets historicall" are trying to present the elements which constitute their own culture. The relationship between the poet's world and the poem's may be different in each case. The latter may be praised or satirized to varying degrees, with a corresponding adjustment of the connections between the two worlds. But in all three poems, the relationship between the poem and its patron is explicitly formulated and permitted to give at least occasional overtones of an historical allegory.

In this connection it may be significant that Ariosto's first apostrophe to his patron, Ippolito d'Este, names him as "generosa Erculea prole" (I.3), in reference to his father, Ercole. The periphrasis obviously suggests an Herculean grandeur and heroism; it may also relate implicitly to the Herculean mixture of martial and erotic motives which the poem presents.[9] At any rate, Ippolito is urged to lower his high thoughts so that they can dwell on his poet's verses (I.4). The poem is not explicitly offered as containing what many Renaissance readers found, a portrait of a good governor and a virtuous man; but the courteous humility of the narrator is not in itself an unambiguous and trustworthy disclaimer of higher ambitions than the momentary entertainment of a prince.

The first scenes of the poem quickly move away from the picture of a stable, unified society in which Orlando and other heroes are drawn up in opposing lines of battle, Christian against infidel. The Christians are routed, and Angelica (whom Charlemagne had set aside as a prize for the hero of the day's

8. Josephine Waters Bennett, "Genre, Milieu, and the Epic-Romance," in Alan S. Downer, ed., *English Institute Essays, 1951* (New York, Columbia University Press, 1952), p. 102.

9. One of Ariosto's most recent editors, Lanfranco Caretti (*La Letteratura italiana, storia e testi, 20,* Milan and Naples, Ricciardi, 1954, p. 843) suggests that the poem's title may have derived from Seneca's *Hercules Furens.* There is no obvious or dominant pattern of explicit Hercules imagery in the poem, however.

fighting) flees into the forest. There she meets first Rinaldo, who is wandering on foot in search of his horse, and then Ferraù, who has left the battle for a drink of water and has carelessly dropped his helmet in the river. One might say that in general all movement away from the field of battle is symptomatic of the "wandering" that forms the subject of the poem and is most fully expressed in Orlando's madness.[10] Both Rinaldo and Ferraù are ludicrous in their undress: Ariosto places their losses in the context of an erotic quest where they are particularly sensitive to these affronts to their masculine pride. Throughout the poem these erotic quests of individual knights are presented as blind, fundamentally self-centered evasions of responsibility; the Petrarchan terms with which they refer to their passions are customarily contrasted with the acute practicality of their wooing. Thus Rinaldo interrupts his duel with Ferraù to ask:

> If this is taking place because the shining rays of the new sun have enflamed your breast, what are you gaining by making me delay here? For even when you kill or capture me, the fair lady will still not be yours, since she is getting away while we are delaying. (I.19)

The language of chivalric love is embedded in arguments of expediency, and the love of Angelica is far from being an incitement to valor (as Charlemagne had hoped earlier, however unchivalrous his own treatment of Angelica may have seemed).

In effect, Ariosto's sardonic allusion to Virgil at the beginning of his poem may be taken as an attempt to evaluate the goals of the confused tradition of the chivalric epic as it was received by him. The distance between Boiardo's *Orlando Innamorato* and Ariosto's continuation of it is seen first in the

10. Giuseppe Toffanin, *Il Cinquecento* (4th ed. Milan, Vallardi, 1950), pp. 180–208, provides a useful discussion of the poem's "occult symmetries" of organization.

titles of the two poems. Orlando's love becomes madness in Ariosto's view: the futility of his quest for Angelica is anticipated and reflected in the comic disintegration of chivalric ideals found throughout the poem. The ambiguity of Angelica's role is summed up in her name, her "angelic semblance" (I.53) which is ultimately incapable of being judged either true or false, since it awakens a love which by definition makes rational judgment impossible.

Ariosto's elaborate variations on themes of disguise and enchantment are frequently directed at the epistemological problems raised by the quest romance. Spenser's frequent echoes of these themes suggest one of the most important bonds between the two poets, though it is the most difficult to illustrate concisely. The events of Books I and II of *The Faerie Queene,* in which the possibilities of individual heroic action are examined, reflect Ariosto's general concern with an ironic ventilation of the heroic tradition. But it is not until Books III and IV, where Spenser is specifically treating the varied aspects of the erotic impulse, that he imitates Ariosto's diffuse plot lines, taking from him the overall metaphor of the confused "furies" of love. An example of his use of a single stanza from the *Orlando Furioso* will show the extent of his indebtedness to Ariosto's imagery in Book III.

Rinaldo and Ferraù agree to postpone their duel and make common cause in pursuing Angelica until they have her safely secured as their prize. Accordingly they ride off in pursuit of her, both of them mounted on Ferraù's horse. This example of religious tolerance provokes an ironic apostrophe from the narrator:

> Oh gran bontà de' cavallieri antiqui!
> Eran rivali, eran di fé diversi,
> e si sentian degli aspri colpi iniqui
> per tutta la persona anco dolersi;
> e pur per selve oscure e calli obliqui
> insieme van senza sospetto aversi.

Da quattro sproni il destrier punto arriva
ove una strada in due si dipartiva.

(I.22)

Or in John Harington's translation (1591):

O auncient knights of true and noble hart,
Riuals they were, one faith they liu'd not vnder,
Beside they felt their bodies shrewdly smart
Of blowes late giuen, and yet (behold a wonder)
Through thicke and thin, suspition set apart,
Like frends they ride, and parted not a sunder
Vntill the horse with double spurring driued,
Vnto a way parted in two arriued.[11]

Harington's comic use of feminine rhymes is matched in the
original by the rhyming of the adjective "diversi" with the re-
flexive verbs "dolersi" and "aversi"; and the anticlimax of the
final couplet in both original and translation gives emphasis
to the mock-heroism of the entire stanza. This comic exploita-
tion of the ottava rima (in a fashion which an English reader
recognizes as Byronic) clearly points up the conflict between
the premises of militant Christianity on the one hand and those
of nonsectarian eroticism on the other; and it does so in a
predominantly satirical tone. But Harington's version omits
the stanza's more somber tones: in Ariosto the knights ride not
simply "Through thicke and thin" but "per selve oscure e calli
obliqui." Ariosto has retained enough of the atmospheric chiar-
oscuro of Boiardo's world, and has added enough metaphysical
irony of his own, to justify our sense of a Dantesque overtone
at this point. Like Spenser's Wood of Error, Ariosto's "dark
woods" provide an apt setting for the knights-errant who move
at random in pursuit of their dimly perceived goals.

Spenser's echo of Ariosto's apostrophe seems far different
in tone:

O goodly vsage of those antique times,
In which the sword was seruant vnto right;

11. Harington, *Orlando Furioso*, p. 3.

> When not for malice and contentious crimes,
> But all for praise, and proofe of manly might,
> The martiall brood accustomed to fight:
> Then honour was the meed of victorie,
> And yet the vanquished had no despight:
> Let later age that noble vse enuie,
> Vile rancour to auoid, and cruell surquedrie.
>
> (III.i.13)

Only the first line of Ariosto's stanza has been directly imitated; for the rest, Spenser appears to be presenting in all seriousness the conventional sentiments which his predecessor was satirizing. "The conclusion is clear," Dodge remarked of this passage. "When Spenser read the *Orlando Furioso* he read it in the light of his own serene idealism."[12]

Yet if one considers the incident to which Spenser's apostrophe refers, the relationship between the two poems begins to emerge more clearly. Guyon, his own quest completed in the preceding Book, has encountered Britomart on his wanderings and has been unseated by her enchanted spear. Humiliated by an unprecedented defeat, he is determined to continue the battle on foot. His Palmer, however, recognizes the situation as Guyon does not, and sees that any continuation of the fight will be fatal. Accordingly, he and Arthur apply all their skills of diplomacy to calm the champion of Temperance:

> By such good meanes he him discounselled,
> From prosecuting his reuenging rage;
> And eke the Prince like treaty handeled,
> His wrathfull will with reason to asswage,
> And laid the blame, not to his carriage,
> But to his starting steed, that swaru'd asyde,
> And to the ill purueyance of his page,
> That had his furnitures not firmely tyde:
> So is his angry courage fairely pacifyde.

12. Dodge, "Spenser's Imitations from Ariosto," p. 172.

Thus reconcilement was betweene them knit,
Through goodly temperance, and affection
chaste . . .

(III.i.11–12)

After this instance of artful dissuasion, in which Guyon's companions carefully avoid any appeal to the true state of his
helplessness against Britomart's spear, producing a series of
specious arguments to salve his injured feelings, the reader is
scarcely prepared to accept this as a reconciliation of two
abstract virtues. Consequently, though one is surely meant to
remember that Guyon is the champion of "goodly temperance"
and Britomart of "affection chaste," one seems just as surely
meant to feel that the operative word in the last line above
is the preposition, "through." Guyon and to a lesser extent
Britomart are here being subjected to the operation of motives
which the poem's declared allegorical program would seem to
have made coterminous with them. "Allegorical inconsistency"
of this sort is too frequently found in Spenser and other writers
of allegory to be simply dismissed as an aberration; it seems
rather to be one of the most common forms of wit characteristic
of allegory.

The incident, then, suggests something beyond the relative
superiority of Chastity to Temperance in Spenser's scheme:[13]
it also points to the limitations of Guyon's perceptions, and
thereby heralds the new area of action being introduced with
Book III. As has been suggested in the preceding chapter, the
isolated "virtues" of Spenser's fairyland are presented as isolated
drives or propensities toward a single area of endeavor, unaccompanied by any broad understanding which would give
the individual hero a sense of his role in the total order of
things. It is this quality in the chivalric ethic, an overriding
self-commitment as it is epitomized by the concept of the
Quest, which constitutes one of the chief areas of Spenser's
indebtedness to Ariosto's presentation of the chivalric milieu.

13. F. M. Padelford, "The Allegory of Chastity in *The Faerie Queene*,"
Studies in Philology, 21 (1924), 367–81; cited in *Variorum 3,* 321–29.

In the present instance, Spenser's entire first canto of Book III bristles with allusions to the opening of the *Orlando Furioso*. Guyon is unseated by Britomart as Sacripante had been by Bradamante (I.63); and the comforting words of the Palmer and Prince Arthur echo those of Angelica (I.67). In Ariosto's complex action the earlier spectacle of the two knights on a single horse is echoed later in the canto when Angelica takes Sacripante onto her palfrey. To Ariosto's allegorical commentators, this insistence on his heroes' inability to control their horses or retain their armor intact was significant of the uncontrol of minds possessed by love;[14] and though the elements of burlesque may be more immediately apparent here to a modern reader, clearly this very burlesque is based on an amorous unconcern for dignity or the niceties of chivalric behavior when confronted with the practical demands of erotic pursuit.

Spenser's opening canto similarly evokes the absurd chaos of Ariosto's world. Florimell's mysterious arrival and departure draw the earlier Books' heroes away in her pursuit: Arthur, Timias, and Guyon are all moved by this spectacle of beauty in distress. Any reader who is hoping to find these characters behaving "allegorically" will lament with Cory at the confusion in which Spenser "turns sober knights into pompous clowns."[15] Britomart holds back from the chase not from any sense of her distinct allegorical mission—the climax of Book III will in fact consist of her rescue of Amoret from Busyrane's lustful designs —but from the more homely fact that she is a woman and hence unmoved by female beauty. Criteria of psychological realism become dominant at this point in *The Faerie Queene* as they have not earlier, and with the emergence of the diffuse motivations of the erotic sphere Spenser turns to Ariosto's metaphor of the furies of love.

14. Cf. *Orlando Furioso di M. Lodovico Ariosto,* con gli Argomenti di M. Gio. Andrea dell'Anguillara, Et con l'allegorie di M. Gioseppe Horologgio (Venice, Gio. Varisco, 1566), p. 3, allegory to Canto I; and Harington's remarks, *passim.*
15. *Variorum 3,* 201–02; Spens, *Spenser's "Faerie Queene,"* pp. 18–19; Bennett, *The Evolution of "The Faerie Queene,"* pp. 144–47.

Ultimately, Ariosto's chief contribution to the tradition of the chivalric romance lies in just this area of an ironic ventilation of the conventional ideals, exposing their contradictory insistence on both love and honor simultaneously. In the *Orlando Furioso* this contradiction becomes a pretext for comic situations, whereby the exalted capabilities of heroes, their supernatural strength, their enchanted weapons, their emotions larger than life, are associated with the undirected frenzies and blindness of romantic love, while the demands of the social order, the claims of a religious and military conflict and the dynastic destiny of Bradamante, are symbols of control and subordination to the larger pattern of things, of coming to one's senses. Where Pulci and Boiardo had emphasized the ribald gigantism or the ingenious variety of the old tales, with a certain amount of nostalgic admiration for the ideals which they embodied, Ariosto provides a far more thorough examination of their points of relevance to contemporary life and to the humbler motivations of everyday men. For him the chivalric milieu becomes a means of confronting the ideal with the actual; and in this respect it is impossible to disregard his influence when one is speaking of the "Neoplatonism" of Spenser.

TASSO'S MORALIZED SONG

The *Orlando Furioso* opens with an echo of the first line of the *Aeneid,* significantly changed to indicate its broader range of subject matter. It concludes with an imitation of the last lines of Virgil's epic: Rodomonte's defeat at the hands of Ruggiero is as much an expression of the forward thrust of historical destiny as is Aeneas' victory over Turnus. Yet despite these and other verbal and thematic parallels, Ariosto's poem is too securely rooted in its comic approach to appeal to any conventional sense of epic tone or plot. Tasso, on the other hand, approaches his subject with a consistent seriousness of tone, and with a concern for the structure of epic. His opening lines assert a union of Christian themes and classical structure, where Ariosto's had suggested a comic disintegration of the Virgilian form:

> Canto l'arme pietose e 'l capitano
> che 'l gran sepolcro liberò di Cristo:
> molto egli oprò co 'l senno e con la mano,
> molto soffrí nel glorioso acquisto:
> e in van l'Inferno vi s'oppose, e in vano
> s'armò d'Asia e di Libia il popol misto;
> il Ciel gli diè favore, e sotto a i santi
> segni ridusse i suoi compagni erranti.

> (I.1)

[I sing of pious arms and of the captain who liberated the great sepulchre of Christ: he labored greatly with mind and hand, and he suffered greatly in this glorious achievement: in vain Hell opposed him, and in vain the mixed races of Asia and Libya armed themselves; Heaven favored him, and he was able to collect his wandering comrades under the holy banners.]

The first stanza of the *Orlando Furioso* was limited to promising to tell of men and women and their various deeds "at the time that" the Moors had invaded Europe. That is, it indicated the historical locus of the action, and suggested that it would provide a panorama of all that was then taking place. If these lines of Ariosto's pointed toward any literary genre, it was that of the historical novel. Tasso, by contrast, has provided in his first stanza a carefully organized summary of his poem's action, following the pattern of Virgil's first seven lines but asserting significant differences at each point. Like Virgil, he is singing of arms and of a single man whose action is directed toward a single goal, to be reached at the conclusion of the poem. Like Virgil, he will attach much importance to *pietas:* he introduces this notably Virgilian term in his first line, but in a context which clearly implies his Christian adaptation of a classical theme.

It may be useful to examine in somewhat greater detail the program outlined in these first lines of the *Gerusalemme Liberata*. Spenser had probably evolved a fairly extensive and coherent idea of *The Faerie Queene* by the time he read Tasso's poem,[16] and it is undeniable that he is far more deeply indebted to Ariosto for incidents and situations; but as has been frequently observed, when he borrows from Tasso he does not feel compelled to make alterations of tone, or even of phraseology. For this reason, and because as a near contemporary of Spenser Tasso provides opportunities for comparison on the level of critical theory, some discussion of their common approach to the literary tradition is in order.

A striking parallel to the portion of Spenser's letter to Ralegh cited at the beginning of this chapter is provided by the "Allegory" which Tasso had apparently composed as early as 1576, and which he first published as a commentary to his poem in the Baldini edition at Ferrara of 1581.[17] Like Spenser's appeal to precedents for his concern with the private and public virtues of the hero, Tasso's remarks trace his poem's lineage:

> Of the Life of the contemplative Man the Comedy of *Dante,* and the *Odysses,* are as it were in every Part a Figure: but the civil Life is seen to be shadowed through the *Ilias,* and throughout the *Aeneis* also, although in this

16. Hough (*A Preface to "The Faerie Queene,"* p. 59) argues that the *Gerusalemme Liberata* "came, not too late, but just in time to be an effective influence." It is a question of finding a working definition of various kinds of influence, however.

17. Angelo Solerti et al., eds., *Gerusalemme Liberata: Poema Eroico di Torquato Tasso* (3 vols. Florence, Bemporad, 1895–96), "Bibliografia delle Stampe," *1,* 141–43. Treatment of Spenser's indebtedness to Tasso is found in E. Koeppel, "Die englischen Tasso-Übersetzungen des 16.Jahrhunderts," *Anglia, 11* (1889), 11–38, 333–62; H. H. Blanchard, "Imitations from Tasso in the *Faerie Queene,*" *Studies in Philology, 22* (1925), 198–221; Alberto Castelli, *La Gerusalemme Liberata nella Inghilterra di Spenser* (Milan, Soc. Ed. Vita e Pensiero, 1936); C. B. Beall, "A Tasso Imitation in Spenser," *Modern Language Quarterly, 3* (1942), 559–60.

there is rather set out a Mixture of *Action* and *Contemplation*.[18]

He goes on to add that the contemplative life is shown through solitary actions, as when Aeneas leaves his comrades and descends to contemplate the pains and rewards of the underworld, and that the active life is prefigured in social activity: "Aeneas is seen to be accompanied, when he fighteth, or doth other civil acts."

It is clear from such remarks that Tasso and Spenser use remarkably similar language in defining the anatomy of heroic virtue provided by the epic. Where they differ is in their concepts of narrative structure. Tasso's opening stanza is in fact radically opposed to Ariosto's promise of diversification. It reaches back through Virgil to the Homeric epics and promises to combine the linear plot of the *Odyssey* with a reunion of the hero and his comrades which was denied to Odysseus himself. Goffredo is not merely a "man" (*virum, Andra*—the subjects of the *Aeneid* and *Odyssey*) but a "captain"; and the emphasis will be on his political triumph rather than on the mere fact of his personal survival as in Homer's poem:

> Tell me, O Muse, of that ingenious hero who travelled far and wide after he had sacked the famous town of Troy. Many cities did he visit, and many were the nations with whose manners and customs he was acquainted; moreover he suffered much by sea while trying to save his own life and bring his men safely home; but do what he might he could not save his men, for they perished through their own sheer folly in eating the cattle of the Sun-god Hyperion; so the god prevented them from ever reaching home.
>
> (*Odyssey*, I.1–9)[19]

18. Edward Fairfax, trans., *Tasso's Jerusalem Delivered* (4th ed., London, J. Clark, 1749) p. 494.
19. Samuel Butler, trans., *The Odyssey* (2nd ed., London, Jonathan Cape, 1922), p. 1.

Goffredo, in contrast, succeeds in reuniting his wandering knights into a single "civil Company" which is to function as a group in accomplishing its goal. In stressing this important difference between Goffredo and Odysseus, Tasso is asserting his own view of epic achievement as a collective effort, to be seen both as a society acting in unison and as the individual man holding all his various faculties in a just relationship to one another. Significantly, too, Tasso's hero is challenged by the "lower" world (*l'Inferno*), where Aeneas had been opposed by a faction of the Olympian pantheon (*vi superum, Aeneid,* I.4). From the Christian viewpoint, the chief flaw in the classical view of man lies precisely in this concept of him as a pawn of competing higher powers, among whom he must chart a course of tactful placation, taking care not to offend the deities by a disproportionate attachment to any one of them. Taken on the next higher level of abstraction, this classical view implies that happiness is to be found in the attainment of a temperance which is to be pursued for its own sake without any sense of an ulterior goal for man. By asserting a context within which the human struggle is seen as an upward striving against man's lower nature, Christianity provides mankind with a hierarchy of values and an informing purpose. Seen in this light, the action of the *Gerusalemme Liberata* restates the Virgilian concept of imperial destiny, itself an answer to the individualism of the *Odyssey,* as a Christian view of man's struggle toward the Kingdom of Heaven.

Spenser sees Goffredo and Rinaldo as representatives, respectively, of the good governor and the virtuous individual: in the terms of Tasso's "Allegory," Rinaldo's "Return, and Reconciliation to *Godfrey,* noteth Obedience, causing the *irefull* Power to yield to the *reasonable.*"[20] Described in this manner, Rinaldo's characteristics suggest those of Spenser's two "classical" heroes, Guyon and Artegall; and Spenser makes use of Tasso in Books II and V in presenting the temptations faced by these heroes.

20. Fairfax, p. 499.

Spenser's most famous single borrowing from the *Geru-salemme Liberata* is found in canto xii of Book II, where the description of the Bower of Bliss follows Tasso's presentation of Armida's isle, in considerable detail and at great length. A less frequently mentioned indebtedness to Tasso, but one which is of importance in relation to this more substantial one, is seen in Book V when the captive Artegall, forced by Radigund to abandon his knightly trappings and do women's work, is compared to Hercules submitting to Iole. The unorthodox mythological allusion may refer ultimately to Boccaccio, as Lotspeich suggests;[21] but certainly the immediate source is a stanza taken from the midst of the scene on Armida's isle:

> Mirasi qui fra le meonie ancelle
> favoleggiar con la conocchia Alcide.
> Se l'inferno espugnò, resse le stelle,
> or torce il fuso; Amor sel guarda, e ride.
> Mirasi Iole con la destra imbelle
> per ischerno trattar l'armi omicide;
> e'n dosso ha il cuoio del leon, che sembra
> ruvido troppo a sí tenere membra.

(XVI.3)

In Edward Fairfax's translation:

> *Alcides* there sat telling Tales, and spun
> Among the feeble Troops of Damsels mild;
> He, who the fiery Gates of Hell had won,
> And Heav'n upheld; false *Love* stood by, and smil'd:
> Arm'd with his Club, fair *Iole* forth run,
> His Club with Blood of Monsters foul defil'd,
>   And on her Back his Lion's Skin had she,
>   Too rough a Bark for such a tender Tree![22]

21. Lotspeich, *Classical Mythology*, pp. 72–73.
22. Fairfax, p. 352. It should be noted that Fairfax's translation is apparently influenced by Spenser's version in a few of its details.

Spenser's comparison is introduced as an explicit allusion—
either to Tasso or to other versions of the myth—and stresses
the iconography of this visual spectacle, rather in the manner
of an inscription from an emblem book. In this respect he is
closer to the repeated *mirasi* of Tasso than is Fairfax's later
translation:

> Who had him seene, imagine mote thereby,
>   That whylome hath of *Hercules* bene told,
>   How for *Iolas* sake he did apply
>   His mightie hands, the distaffe vile to hold,
>   For his huge club, which had subdew'd of old
>   So many monsters, which the world annoyed;
>   His Lyons skin chaungd to a pall of gold
>   In which forgetting warres, he onely ioyed
> In combats of sweet loue, and with his mistresse
>   toyed.
>
> (V.v.24)

Within the context of Book V this comparison with Hercules
is part of a larger pattern of Spenser's definition of Artegall's
capacities and limitations in terms of mythical comparisons;
what is especially significant in the present instance is that
Spenser recalls Tasso's description of Armida's isle with regard
both to Acrasia, the enemy of temperance,[23] and to Radigund,
the "reckless woman"[24] who opposes her own intemperance
in the way of Artegall's passion for justice. Books II and V of
The Faerie Queene share a common concern with virtues which
might be called either "pagan" or "Aristotelian," depending on
the precise weight one wishes to give the "Christian Platonism"
with which these virtues are contrasted in Books I and VI. At
any rate, Temperance and Justice, as Spenser conceives them,
imply self-restraint, a balance of opposing drives which constitutes the negative or circumscribed aspect of problems that

23. Berger, *The Allegorical Temper*, p. 66.
24. John W. Draper, "Classical Coinage in the *Faerie Queene*," *PMLA*,
47 (1932), 103.

are treated in their transcendental aspects as Holiness and Courtesy. It is significant, therefore, that the chief temptations represented in Books II and V do not take the form of false appearances but rather are seen as incitements directed at the appetites.

Tasso's own comments on the two areas of temptation represented by his demons make a similar distinction:

> The Devils, which do consult to hinder the Conquest of *Jerusalem,* are both a Figure, and a Thing figured; and do here represent the very same Evils, which oppose themselves against our civil Happiness, so that it may not be to us a Ladder of Christian Blessedness. The two Magicians, *Ismen* and *Armida,* Servants of the Devil, who endeavour to remove the Christians from making War, are two devilish Temptations, which do lay Snares for two Powers of the Soul, from whence all other Sins proceed. *Ismen* doth signify that Temptation, which seeketh to deceive, with false Belief, the Power (as a Man may call it) *opinative; Armida* is that Temptation, which layeth Siege to the Power of our Desires: so from that proceed the Errors of *Opinion,* from this those of the *Appetite.*[25]

Tasso's "Allegories" are helpful in providing an initial perspective for Spenser's scenes of temptation in Books II and V. They furnish a conceptual framework which might be considered as the first stage of Spenser's presentation; in this sense they might be taken as the first, most general area of Spenser's indebtedness to Tasso. But however accurately they may or may not describe the "meaning" of the *Gerusalemme Liberata,* they quickly fail to account for the developing complexities of Spenser's scenes. As Robert M. Durling remarked of Spenser's Bower of Bliss: "He is not describing like Tasso, and Ariosto before him, the illusions of beauty by which the senses over-

25. Fairfax, p. 496.

come the unwilling reason, but rather the way in which the mind shapes actual objects in order to corrupt the appetite."[26] In this sense the distinction between opinative and appetitive is blurred and the two are seen to involve one another. Archimago and Busyrane project images of lust to undermine the reason; Acrasia's garden of delight is orchestrated to the tune of a false logic.

Paradoxically, therefore, the second main area of Spenser's indebtedness is seen in the close imitations of individual passages, where Spenser captures the brooding, rather Virgilian melancholy of Tasso's scenes and uses it as an index of these complexities of perspective. Spenser could never have found this moody sensuousness of tone in Ariosto, nor could he have found the sober earnestness of theme: that the two elements seem to work at cross purposes seems puzzling until one considers the extent to which the one serves as a counterpoise to the other.

Tasso's concern for a unity of action and his conscious attempts to realize an epic form while incorporating Christian themes in a chivalric setting restrict his usefulness to Spenser with respect to actual imitations of incident or situation. But the two poets see in the world of chivalry a reflection of the most insistent problems confronting them: the human struggle as a pressing toward the Ideal which must be constantly alert to the truth and falsehood mixed in all images of that Ideal; and above all the problem of releasing the powers which will enable man to follow his higher nature, while yet retaining enough control over these powers to keep them from being estranged from his reasonable faculty. Their common debt to Ariosto is evident from the fact that they turn to the chivalric romance for a presentation of these problems.

One is led to suspect that *The Faerie Queene* might have been a far simpler poem if Spenser had not had the example of the *Gerusalemme Liberata* on which to build. Tasso's an-

26. Robert M. Durling, "The Bower of Bliss and Armida's Palace," *Comparative Literature*, 6 (1954), 346.

nounced program as well as his more complex mixtures of will and imagination in individual scenes provided Spenser with one of those versions of epic to which his own poem could point. In striving to combine and overgo Homer and Virgil, Ariosto and Tasso, Spenser aspired to a poem which was to be organized by no unity of character or of plot, but rather by its continuing concern with the shaping imagination. "Who had him seene, imagine mote thereby . . ." The similes throughout *The Faerie Queene* which begin with such a periphrasis constitute only one means by which Spenser calls attention to the function of vision in his poem. Another is the extensive network of explicit allusions to earlier epics. Source study is important to an understanding of Spenser precisely because it is for the most part a study of such allusions. Similarly, one of the most important respects in which Spenser changes his sources is that he uses them *as* allusions: the images of past epics are presented as part of the landscape of his poem.

By now it is apparent that the reading of *The Faerie Queene* which I am proposing entails a close attention to continually shifting ironic perspectives. Even within a single Book, the poem is not predominantly concerned with the adventures of a single protagonist. Its narrative is discontinuous; and though in some cases Spenser borrows his diversity from Ariosto he is not principally interested in an elaborate web of ingeniously woven plot lines. Nor is there a wholly continuous expository structure of allegorical meaning, even in the first Book where Ruskin's famous summary[27] works fairly well to describe the adventures of Redcross but less well for those of Una. Rather, the poem relies for its unity largely on a pattern of imagistic repetition, a dreamlike evocation of vaguely familiar scenes which confront successive heroes and give the illusion of a continuity of theme. Although it would be possible to find precedents for this quality in the romance tradition, and even in the sophisticated treatment of this tradition by Ariosto and

27. *Stones of Venice, 3,* 205–09. Reprinted in *Variorum 1,* 422–24; and by Hough, *A Preface to "The Faerie Queene,"* pp. 145–48.

Tasso, it may be more helpful at this point to speak briefly of
Spenser's place in the traditions of lyric poetry. For what is
unique to *The Faerie Queene* in the line of heroic poems is the
Spenserian stanza, with its constant curb on narrative flow, its
relentless tendency to transform every statement to its own
characteristic rhythm, to take every narrative step forward and
turn it around and inside out, making all participate in the same
dance of meter. In this sense the poem comes close to the form
of a sequence of Spenserian stanzas rather like a sonnet sequence in its loose assumption of a narrative context while
relying primarily on a varied presentation of lyrical postures.

Clearly no reader could assimilate a sequence of lyrics so
lengthy as *The Faerie Queene;* Spenser must appeal to conceptual and narrative continuities if he is to keep his audience.
Yet to rely exclusively on such continuities is to miss the poem's
most conspicuous rhythm. Moreover, the richness of Spenser's
vision is largely based on a mixture of attitudes which he had
learned as the pastoral "new Poete" before discarding his oaten
reeds. A closer look at the structure of Spenser's imagery may be
in order.

ANTI-PRIMITIVISM AND ANTI-PETRARCHANISM
IN SPENSER'S IMAGERY

A recurrent motif in *The Faerie Queene* is the failure to interpret correctly the physical images presented to the various
characters. In some cases this failure comes as a result of the
consciously deceptive appearance of an object, as when a
malevolent imagination creates a false image to compete with
the true. Archimago's and Duessa's imitations of Una and the
witch's image of the False Florimell are examples. At other
times it is the beholder who is at fault for failing to see that
physical beauty is an image of spiritual beauty and should be
an incentive to virtue rather than a temptation to self-indulgence. Both cases involve a statement of the incomplete and
potentially misleading quality of the physical object. As a mix-

ture of beast and angel, man realizes his higher nature in his capacity to recognize beauty in the physical object; to recognize, that is, the presence of a natural order and symmetry which are images of God's order. Failing to recognize beauty in this sense, he exists on the level of the beasts. But what is more, he is not only able to choose between using or not using his rational faculty: he may also abuse that faculty, and in that event his actions represent a perverse, demonic parody of the angelic function, which is to contemplate and praise the divine.

Within the presentation of conventional metaphors, Spenser frequently uses the device of an expanded comparison to suggest the problems relating to attitude. Consider for instance two examples of the image of the Rose as a symbol of virgin beauty. In Acrasia's Bower the anonymous male singer presents the argument of *Carpe diem* traditional to erotic poetry. Here Spenser is imitating most directly Tasso's description of Armida's isle (where this song is recited by one of the birds[28]), and indirectly Ariosto as well, who gives the song to Sacripante:[29]

> Ah see, who so faire thing doest faine to see,
> In springing flowre the image of thy day;
> Ah see the Virgin Rose, how sweetly shee
> Doth first peepe forth with bashfull modestee,
> That fairer seemes, the lesse ye see her may;
> Lo see soone after, how more bold and free
> Her bared bosome she doth broad display;
> Loe see soone after, how she fades, and falles away.

> So passeth, in the passing of a day,
> Of mortall life the leafe, the bud, the flowre,
> Ne more doth flourish after first decay,
> That earst was sought to decke both bed and
> bowre,

28. *Gerusalemme Liberata*, XVI.13–16. The bird is male in Tasso; female in Fairfax's translation.
29. *Orlando Furioso*, I.42–44. Sacripante is not identified until he has finished his song.

> Of many a Ladie, and many a Paramowre:
> Gather therefore the Rose, whilest yet is prime,
> For soone comes age, that will her pride deflowre:
> Gather the Rose of loue, whilest yet is time,
> Whilest louing thou mayst loued be with equall crime.
>   (II.xii.74–75)

The surprising reference to "equall crime"[30] at the end of the song has the effect of underscoring the sense of melancholy with which it is pervaded. Though readers are generally agreed that the Bower is evil, every attempt to assign its weakness to a specific element has been met with objections. The difficulty seems to be that its evil is one of imbalance rather than of specific content: if Acrasia's name suggests an intemperate, unbalanced or unmixed attitude, her Bower is similarly an image of nature in disequilibrium. Though the bathing girls may represent a disproportionate emphasis on visual entice-ment, as Lewis suggested,[31] it is clear that lust in action is also a part of the Bower; and though the generative aspects of sexuality are conspicuously absent, it would be equally absurd to read the passage as an allegorical assault on birth control.

It is rather the mood of stagnation which dominates the passage as a whole, the sense of futility, which argues most conclusively for Guyon's decisive action. And in the image of the rose, it is an easy step from a view of man as the plucker of a short-lived flower to a more pervasive sense of the preda-tory guilt of lust. The essential joylessness of the singer's argu-ment has subverted the rhetoric of his appeal to pleasure; and the phrase "equall crime" conveys the sense less of "mutual enjoyment (and hence no crime at all)" than that of "a repro-

---

30. Tasso's phrase is "amiamo or quando/ esser si puote riamato amando." Spenser elsewhere uses the word "crime" in ways which seem imprecise to a modern reader: as when he refers to *The tree of Life,* the crime of our first fathers fall" (I.xi.46). And "time" and "crime" (along with "slime") are frequent rhyme words for Spenser. Whatever may have induced the use of the word, however, its effect on the tone of the passage is striking.

31. Lewis, *The Allegory of Love,* p. 331.

bate guilt to be shared by all." The singer's exhortation is a counsel of despair.

Spenser's use of this highly conventional motif is thus seen to involve an alteration in meaning which is part of the significance of the whole episode. The song is addressed to the person "who so faire thing doest faine to see"; and the possible double meaning to "faine"[32] reinforces the emphasis on the tendentiousness of the speaker's argument. The flirtatious bashfulness of the bared bosom has been anticipated a few stanzas earlier in the bathing girls; and here as there the rising and "falling" rhythm appears. By placing this emblem of the rose as a climax to this network of repeated motifs, Spenser conveys a sense that the pursuit of love in such a context is in effect a pursuit of death. Similarly, the allusions to Venus and Mars and to Venus and Adonis in the trapping of Acrasia and Verdant serve to dramatize the negative aspects of myths which appear elsewhere in the poem as symbols of positive value.

A similar complexity of tone may be seen in Spenser's next use of this image of the rose, in the fifth canto of Book III. In praising Belphoebe, he shows her in the relationship of gardener to her "rose":

> That dainty Rose, the daughter of her Morne,
> > More deare then life she tendered, whose flowre
> > The girlond of her honour did adorne:
> > Ne suffred she the Middayes scorching powre,
> > Ne the sharp Northerne wind thereon to showre,
> > But lapped vp her silken leaues most chaire,
> > When so the froward skye began to lowre:
> > But soone as calmed was the Christall aire,
> She did it faire dispred, and let to florish faire.

$$(III.v.51)$$

This eulogy comes at a point when Belphoebe's role in the action demands a peculiar subtlety of balance. Her nursing of

32. Empson, *Some Versions of Pastoral*, pp. 136–38, discusses the use of this pun in Shakespeare and Spenser.

Timias' wounds has awakened his love. Consequently, she is at once a figure of highly laudable chastity and unconsciously a type of the cruel mistress:

> But that sweet Cordiall, which can restore
> A loue-sick hart, she did to him enuy;
> To him, and to all th'vnworthy world forlore
> She did enuy that soueraigne salue, in secret store.
>
> (III.v.50)

This is not to suggest that she receives any of the criticism directed against Mirabella in Book VI: even without a reminder of her role as an image of the virgin Queen (and Tudor rose), it is clear that she is guiltless in this matter. The world *is* unworthy. Yet the juxtaposition of this praise with the story of Timias' love does provide an ironic context which illuminates the limitations of Belphoebe. From the viewpoint of Timias she possesses a gift which can restore him, one which her self-willed virginity denies to the world. Belphoebe's point of view, however, is simply one of cultivating her own garden. It might be noted that her care is quite well adapted to a precious rose, but is not clearly meaningful if the rose is equated with her virginity. Virginity is a rose which may be plucked or left to wither on its stem, as the earlier passage has demonstrated: there is no precise equivalent to the threats of midday sun or northern wind. Her concern for her rose *qua* rose is thus an index of her invulnerability to the arrows of love: for her the rose is a rose, not a euphemism.

We have already seen in Book I some of the ambiguities attaching to the pastoral garland, especially when it is self-gathered. In the present instance, Belphoebe is not precisely erring in her self-absorbed care for "the girlond of her honour"; but it does seem that a certain narcissistic obtuseness to the concerns of others is the price which she pays for her immunity to lust. She is even rather pathetic in her glorious isolation. Virginity such as hers is a "heauenly coronall,/ Such as the Angels weare before Gods tribunall"; she stands "on the highest staire/ Of th'honorable stage of womanhead" (V.v.53–54).

Spenser's praise of Belphoebe, therefore, points to two complementary views of her. On the one hand, the image of the rose unites her roles as romantic heroine, religious virgin, and virgin queen.[33] But at the same time, this very elevation of her to an iconic status is expressive of her inability to cure Timias, whose love is destined to lead him through an extensive agony. Not only is she above Timias; she is also ignorant of his situation, here and in his later fall from favor when he is found consoling Amoret (IV.vii). Even her acts of bounty appear fundamentally to be in fulfillment of her own private nature. The ambiguities of Spenser's imagery constitute a means of tempering and informing our approval of the individual figures of the poem. Love for an object is lust when it is not controlled by a firm sense of its meaning. Similarly, any metaphor which fails to illuminate the significance of the object to which it is applied constitutes a temptation to contemplate the physical for its own sake, without reference to any broader standard which might attach a proper, relative value to the physical. As with the satyrs who worshipped Una in their backward fashion, a failure to recognize the metaphorical nature of statements constitutes idolatry.

A further examination of Spenser's use of conventional erotic imagery will show his emphasis on the essentially neutral quality of the physical object, which achieves value only with the recognition of its significance and its proper use. Critics have frequently recognized the incongruencies in Spenser's similes; but they have rarely been willing to see these incongruencies as part of a consistent and far-reaching concern to show the limits of metaphorical discourse. Most have preferred to emphasize what *is* relevant and to suggest reasons (usually historical ones) why Spenser may have disregarded the disparities between the

33. Padelford, *Variorum 3*, 326; Thomas P. Roche, Jr., *The Kindly Flame: A Study of the Third and Fourth Books of Spenser's Faerie Queene* (Princeton, Princeton University Press, 1964), pp. 139–42.

two objects being compared.[34] But an understanding of Spenser's allegorical technique, and a recognition of the emphasis on problems of human responsibility and control which motivates that technique, will indicate that the Spenserian metaphor must be taken seriously as a double-edged evaluation of its subject. Since what is in question here is the attitude Spenser adopts toward the natural world, a discussion of his imagery is essential to an appreciation of the role of "nature" in the milieu of *The Faerie Queene*. Furthermore, Spenser's treatment of love in its personal aspects (uncomplicated by dynastic implications, for example) is infused with an awareness of its limitations. The decorum which this awareness entails has certain affinities with pastoral, in its suggestion of a personal truancy from one's higher obligations to society: a truancy, however, that may help to strengthen and restore one to a renewed dedication to those obligations.

One of Spenser's most conspicuous uses of Petrarchan terms in an ironic context appears in canto viii of Book VI, when Serena is menaced by a "salvage nation" of marauding cannibals. In the context of the Book's concern with Courtesy, their cannibalism is presented as a logical consequence of their refusal to participate in any productive activity—agriculture, cattle raising, commerce—

> But on the labours of poore men to feed,
> And serue their owne necessities with others need.
>
> (VI.viii.35)

This predatory relationship to human society is thus summarized by their "monstrous cruelty gainst course of kynde." Spenser's cannibals are ultimately derived from the "wild men" of classic and medieval texts, symbols of man's fallen nature and of the tendency toward uncontrol which society must repress.[35] The statement that they prey on "straungers . . . which

34. My debt to Berger (*The Allegorical Temper,* pp. 120 ff.) is obvious.
35. Richard Bernheimer, *Wild Men in the Middle Ages* (Cambridge, Mass., Harvard University Press, 1952); Frank Kermode, ed., *The Tempest,* Arden Shakespeare (6th ed. London, Methuen, 1958), Introduction.

on their border/ Were brought by errour, or by wreckfull wynde" (VI.viii.36) suggests not only the misfortunes of Elizabethan voyagers, but also those of Odysseus among the Lestrygonians. Possibly too, as C. S. Lewis suggests,[36] the incident as a whole owes something to Boiardo's description of Orlando's encounter with the "Lestrigoni" in the *Orlando Innamorato*.

Yet the comparison with Boiardo suggests certain important differences at the same time that it points to one significant area of similarity. The comedy of Boiardo's treatment is readily apparent, for it is based on the familiar ambiguity of the visitor's role at the cannibal feast. When savages are shown eating at table with silver plates and golden cups, their actions become a burlesque of polite society, made the more comic by their civilized guest's slowness to recognize that he is the subject of their conversation:

> Now the count heard one of them whispering to another: —He's nice and fat.—and the other replied:—I don't know; once I see him roasted, or for that matter when I have a taste of him, I'll know better whether I'll want a full helping.—Orlando wasn't paying attention to this conversation . . .
>
> (*O.I.*, II.xviii.39–40)

Spenser's description of his cannibals shares with this Italian analogue a similarly comic parody of civilized society, but his satire becomes more pointed by virtue of his presenting the ambiguities of polite compliment:

> So round about her they them selues did place
> Vpon the grasse, and diuersely dispose,
> As each thought best to spend the lingring space.
> Some with their eyes the daintest morsels chose;
> Some praise her paps, some praise her lips and
> nose;

36. C. S. Lewis, "Spenser's Irish Experiences and the *Faerie Queene*," *Review of English Studies*, 7 (1931), 84; cited in *Variorum 6*, 233.

Some whet their kniues, and strip their elboes bare:
The Priest him selfe a garland doth compose
Of finest flowres, and with full busie care
His bloudy vessels wash, and holy fire prepare.

(VI.viii.39)

Spenser's wit is based on linking the cannibals' confusion of
the two appetites of hunger and lust with the language of a
love-religion. The linkage is the more significant since the action of Book VI will stress similar pastoral glorifications of the
mistress in later cantos: both Pastorella (VI.ix) and the poet's
lady (VI.x) will be presented in the midst of their admirers,
crowned literally and symbolically with garlands of flowers.
Before this occurs, however, Spenser presents a warning of the
abuses possible in such celebrations. Both the marauding cannibals and the vacationing courtiers intrude on the rustic world
and exploit its riches. The dance of the Graces symbolizes the
exchange of gifts, the give and take of courtesy by which society's bonds are strengthened. Here, by contrast, the savages
recognize only the predatory principle, worshipping gods
created in their own cannibalistic image.

Thus Spenser differs from Boiardo in abandoning the simple
parallelism by which the cannibals share with Orlando a common conversational repertory while retaining a set of motives
which are theirs alone. The Lestrigoni are only interested in
cannibalism; consequently their imitation of polite society holds
no satirical implications for that society. Serena's cannibals,
on the other hand, are motivated by lust as well as by hunger,
and in stripping her of her clothing their two appetites begin
to be confused:

But all bootes not: they hands vpon her lay;
    And first they spoile her of her iewels deare,
    And afterwards of all her rich array;
    The which amongst them they in peeces teare,
    And of the pray each one a part doth beare.
    Now being naked, to their sordid eyes

The goodly threasures of nature appeare:
Which as they view with lustfull fantasyes,
Each wisheth to him selfe, and to the rest enuyes.

Her yuorie necke, her alablaster brest,
Her paps, which like white silken pillowes were,
For loue in soft delight thereon to rest;
Her tender sides, her bellie white and clere,
Which like an Altar did it selfe vprere,
To offer sacrifice diuine thereon;
Her goodly thighes, whose glorie did appeare
Like a triumphall Arch, and thereupon
The spoiles of Princes hang'd, which were in battel
won.

Those daintie parts, the dearlings of delight,
Which mote not be prophan'd of common eyes,
Those villeins vew'd with loose lasciuious sight,
And closely tempted with their craftie spyes;
And some of them gan mongst themselues deuize,
Thereof by force to take their beastly pleasure.
But them the Priest rebuking, did aduize
To dare not to pollute so sacred threasure,
Vow'd to the gods: religion held euen theeues in
measure.

(VI.viii.41–43)

The "temperance" to which their religion enjoins them is clearly of scant consolation to Serena; there is no substantial difference between the "beastly pleasure" of the savages and that of their hungry gods. It is difficult to accept Upton's comment that "our truly theistical and Christian Poet exclaims, 'Tantum religio potuit suadere bonorum.' "[37] Spenser's echo of Lucretius' description of the sacrifice of Iphigenia confirms rather than refutes the Roman's argument.

Discussions of Spenser's imagery have seen in stanza 42 an

37. John Upton, *Variorum 6*, 235.

instance of an "oriental" strain, characterized by a comparison
on the level of symbolic value rather than on that of physical
resemblance, and deriving perhaps from the *Song of Songs* (e.g.,
"Thy necke is as the tower of Dauid built for a defence; a thousand shields hang therein, and all the targates of the strong
men.").[38] But however accurately such commentary may locate
the sources of individual similes, and may assist in the typo-
logical classification of Spenserian imagery, it remains to determine the significance of the simile at this point in the poem.
The imagery of this entire incident functions in a rather complicated manner, for it is directed toward the union of two attitudes which at first glance appear to be diametrically opposed.
For the sake of brevity they might be called anti-primitivism
and anti-Petrarchanism; but these terms will need a good deal
of definition. The cannibals misuse Petrarchan metaphors by
aping the forms of a love-religion while ignoring the spiritual
analogies which constitute the sole basis of such a religion.
They misuse nature by imitating the qualities of beasts rather
than its freedom from the corrupt aspects of civilized society.
In both cases there is a perversion of the imagistic faculty—
man's capacity to argue from the natural, concrete semblance
to the supernatural, abstract essence. Any understanding of
Spenser's employment of pastoral motifs must therefore involve
a recognition of the threat represented by these cannibals. It
is a threat from which not even Calidore is immune: he must
abandon his courtly manners before he can address himself to
his pastoral mistress (VI.ix.35).

The role of Serena in Book VI suggests a number of parallels
with that of Amoret in Book IV; the chief of these lies in the
striking similarity between this episode and that of Amoret's
kidnapping by the "wilde and saluage man" (IV.vii.4 ff.), who
finds her in the forest when she is "of nought affeard" (she

38. *Song of Songs* 4:4 (Bishops' Bible, 1568). Cited by Israel Baroway,
"The Imagery of Spenser and the *Song of Songs*," *Journal of English and
Germanic Philology*, 33 (1934), 35. Cf. Carl Robinson Sonn, "Spenser's
Imagery," *ELH*, 26 (1959), 156–70.

shares with Serena an unjustifiable confidence in her security when wandering alone through the woods), and who proposes to rape her and then to eat her. The fact that Amoret is menaced by an individual and Serena by a "saluage nation" complete with its own ideas of communal worship may probably be traced to the nature of the virtues being defined in the respective books: Chastity and Friendship refer to relationships between individuals, while Justice and Courtesy involve the individual's relationship to his society. But despite this difference, and despite the differences in social and allegorical rank between the two women, both may be seen to represent a passive, easily menaced femininity which clearly contrasts with the confident, invulnerable chastity of a Belphoebe or a Britomart. Where the latter are Amazon types,[39] linked mythologically to Diana in their self-reliance, Amoret and Serena are associated with the ways of Venus and love (though not an unchaste love: Spenser is not primarily concerned with a simple opposition of lust and chastity). The emotion of love may ennoble or degrade, depending on whether one is able to control its physical aspects and subordinate them to the spiritual (or, in the case of the knights, depending on whether it interferes with one's work). The wild men are symbols of uncontrol: *"Amoret rapt by greedie lust . . ."* is the way the Argument to IV.vii summarizes the incident. In the context of these issues the imagery of love assumes an extraordinary prominence, for the use or abuse of love is ultimately stated as a question of understanding the conventional terms of love poetry. And since at the basis of the allegorical structure of *The Faerie Queene* the concerns of Christian Platonism—Actual vs. Ideal, image vs. referent—involve similar problems of use or abuse, it is of general importance to come to an understanding of Spenser's imagery as it functions in the action of the poem.

The incident of Serena among the cannibals therefore provides a convenient pretext for a study of these larger problems.

39. Rosemond Tuve, "Spenser and Some Pictorial Conventions," *SP, 37* (1940), 149–76.

For in its presentation of the abuses of love in terms of a savage bestiality that perverts all of man's attempts at civilization, it points to a useful way of examining Spenser's attitude toward the conventions of courtly love, considered in its personal, social, and religious implications. To begin with the putative ancestor of many of these conventions, the goal of Petrarch's *Rime* is relatively simple: to present a view of human love which by a process of gradual accretion of connotations comes to be understood as an image of divine love. The figure of Laura stands constantly at the center of the poet's field of vision. Unlike Dante's Beatrice, she makes no direct comment, but serves as a focus for the poet's meditations on the natural order and ultimately on the divine order as well. In keeping with this goal, the terms of Petrarch's imagery are vague and ambivalent, inclusive rather than exclusive; the syntax is periodic, and the technique is one of an accumulation of minor revelations all directed toward the major revelation of an exalted love. Spenser's poem has a far more complex subject. It is only partially and indirectly concerned with a presentation of human love as an analogue of and an incentive toward the divine. More generally its concern is with the intricate patterns of relationship traced by the combination of ethical impulses in man's nature. The Books of the poem are arranged in pairs, and for each "positive" or outgoing virtue there is provided a corresponding impulse of control and restraint. Holiness and Temperance, Chastity and Friendship, Justice and Courtesy: this principle of contrast and qualification, seen here in the largest structural units of the poem, is visible in the smallest units as well, in the implications of the individual image or simile. If the physical image is capable of providing a just imitation of true form, it is also capable of distorting truth. Since the image mediates between object and beholder, the error may lie in the failure of the image to conform to the nature of the object, or it may lie in the failure of the beholder to interpret rightly the images with which he is confronted. It is in this latter realm of error that Spenser's use of simile may be seen at its most complex.

Spenser's *Amoretti* provide a convenient link between Petrarch and the treatment of love imagery in *The Faerie Queene.* Unlike the *Rime,* they celebrate a happy courtship, one which concludes with the marriage seen in the *Epithalamion.* This distinction may seem to account for the difference in tone between the two works. The poet is confident of his ultimate success, and consequently his courtship has some of the complacency of the merchant who feels that his efforts are well invested:

> So euery sweet with soure is tempred still,
>   that maketh it be coueted the more:
>   for easie things that may be got at will,
>   most sorts of men doe set but little store.
> Why then should I accoumpt of little paine,
>   that endlesse pleasure shall vnto me gaine?
>
> (*Amoretti* 26)

Even more than complacency, however, humor appears as one of the most striking characteristics of these sonnets: a humor which is constantly present to temper any tendency of the imagery to make the poems more exalted than decorum will permit:[40]

> Ye tradefull Merchants that with weary toyle,
>   doe seeke most pretious things to make your gain:
>   and both the Indias of their treasures spoile,
>   what needeth you to seeke so farre in vaine?
> For loe my loue doth in her selfe containe
>   all this worlds riches that may farre be found,

---

40. C. S. Lewis, *English Literature in the Sixteenth Century* (Oxford, Clarendon Press, 1954), p. 372; and more importantly, Louis L. Martz, "The *Amoretti:* 'Most Goodly Temperature,' " in Nelson, ed., *Form and Convention,* pp. 146–68, 180.

if Saphyres, loe her eies be Saphyres plaine,
if Rubies, loe her lips be Rubies sound:
If Pearles, hir teeth be pearles both pure and round;
if Yuorie, her forhead yuory weene;
if Gold, her locks are finest gold on ground;
if siluer, her faire hands are siluer sheene:
But that which fairest is, but few behold,
her mind adornd with vertues manifold.

(*Amoretti* 15)

The inventory of the lady's features is a commonplace of love poetry. Normally, however, as in the description of Serena quoted earlier, the climax of the sequence is in "Those daintie parts, the dearlings of delight,/ Which mote not be prophan'd of common eyes." Surely the first thirteen lines of the present sonnet lead the reader to expect a similar conclusion; and the unexpected appearance of a Neoplatonic moral is more than a little anticlimactic. Such anticlimax provides a gentle repudiation of a love poetry which employs the "Petrarchan conventions" while moving stealthily toward an elegant and euphemistic celebration of physical love. In this sense the sonnet quoted above may be termed "anti-Petrarchan."

Conventional erotic imagery is thus seen as a potential threat to one's proper understanding of the love relationship. This fact may help to shed light on Spenser's use of "oriental" imagery. In commenting on the present sonnet, Baroway argues that the incongruity of stressing the roundness of the pearls to which the lady's teeth are compared can be justified only in terms of Spenser's "desire to direct the reader's attention to the standards of value rather than to the members of the body, to the interfusing connotations of the high symbols rather than to the eyes, the teeth, the locks, the forehead, and the hands themselves."[41] But perhaps Spenser is consciously alluding to the physical disparity between image and object at the same time that he is asserting their similarity as regards value. Such an interpreta-

41. Baroway, "The Imagery of Spenser," pp. 34–35.

tion seems the more reasonable in view of the final couplet, with its deliberate rejection of the physical aspects of the imagery, and it is reinforced by an examination of the rhyme words in lines 7–12. Each of these lines concludes inconsequentially: the images are all completely stated if we disregard the last word or two of each line. Perfect jewels may be plain, sound, or round; fine gold comes from the ground; silver is sheene: but these final qualifications have no pertinence to the qualities of the lady. Similarly, the verb "weene" in line 10 maintains the anticlimactic tendencies of the individual lines. What seems to be suggested here is that although all intimations of the Ideal must result from our capacity to progress from the physical to the spiritual, by means of an understanding of the comparisons of value implied by metaphor, nevertheless the metaphor must never be permitted to exalt the physical *as such*.

This is, after all, one of the meanings which anti-Petrarchanism is constantly asserting. Shakespeare's Sonnet 130 ("My mistress' eyes are nothing like the sun . . .") does not minimize the power of the speaker's love, even though it disparages the physical beauty which provokes that love. In contrast Spenser expresses his awareness of the incongruity between image and object by stressing the logical absurdity of the image; but his meaning is essentially similar.[42] The imagery of the *Song of Songs*, with its characteristic disregard for physical congruity,

---

42. In this respect Spenser's technique is closer to the anti-Petrarchan device of mixing attributes, as in Berni's parody of Bembo's sonnet, "Crin d'oro crespo e d'ambra tersa e pura . . ." (Pietro Bembo, *Opere in volgare*, ed. Marti, Florence, Sansoni, 1961, Rime 5, p. 456), as "Chiome d'argento fine, irte ed attorte . . . occhi di perle vaghi . . . ciglia di neve," etc. (Francesco Berni, *Poesie e Prose*, ed. Chiòrboli, Geneva and Florence, Olschki, 1934, *Rime* 23, p. 79). Cf. Sidney's sonnet from the old *Arcadia* (ed. Ringler, *Poems of Sir Philip Sidney*, Oxford, Clarendon Press, 1962, p. 12), where Mopsa is said to be "Like great god *Saturn* faire, and like faire *Venus* chaste:/ As smooth as *Pan*, as *Juno* milde, like goddesse *Isis* faste." The existence of such a tradition of parody provides additional evidence, if any is needed, that the Renaissance poet was unlikely to adopt "oriental" imagery without remaining acutely aware of its incongruities.

is well suited to his ends; the important thing to notice, however, is that he employs this imagery as a Western poet, with
an evident awareness of physical connotations. This is particularly apparent in another sonnet, where the indebtedness to
the *Song of Songs* rests in the comparison between the loved
one and the banquet table:[43]

> Was it a dreame, or did I see it playne,
>   a goodly table of pure yvory:
>   all spred with iuncats, fit to entertayne
>   the greatest Prince with pompous roialty?
> Mongst which there in a siluer dish did ly
>   twoo golden apples of vnualewed price:
>   far passing those which Hercules came by,
>   or those which Atalanta did entice.
> Exceeding sweet, yet voyd of sinfull vice,
>   That many sought yet none could euer taste,
>   sweet fruit of pleasure brought from paradice
>   by Loue himselfe and in his garden plaste.
> Her brest that table was so richly spredd,
>   my thoughts the guests, which would thereon haue
>   fedd.

(Amoretti 77)

Even without reference to the similar description of Serena, it
seems apparent that two appetites are merged in this image,
and that the contemplation described in the final line has
physical as well as spiritual overtones. This is made emphatically clear by the nature of the mythological allusions attached
to the image of the apples. The two allusions, to the apples of
the Hesperides and to the golden apples used to entice Atalanta,
are similarly paired in Spenser's description of the Garden of
Proserpina (II.vii.54); in both cases the myths emphasize the
tempting or distracting properties of the apples. In both passages there is also an implicit allusion to the apple of the Fall.

43. Baroway, p. 41.

In the Garden of Proserpina, the comparison arises from the fact that the apples grow on a single tree and all serve to tempt mortals. In the sonnet, on the other hand, the statement that the apples are "brought from paradice," and the shift from a plural noun to the ambiguous "sweet fruit," help to suggest the single apple of Eve's temptation. But the apples are said to be "voyd of sinfull vice," and the allusion to the Fall is not made explicit; Spenser is careful to avoid blaming either physical beauty or physical love for its capacity to appeal to the lower as well as the higher nature of the beholder or the agent. Love and marriage, properly used, are valid means to man's higher ends. This is no forbidden fruit; but it must be taken for nourishment rather than mere cannibalistic "gurmandize."

The decorum of the *Amoretti* is most clearly expressed in the eightieth sonnet, where the poet apologizes for his truancy from the concerns of Fairyland, and describes the "personal" poetry of these sonnets as a kind of relaxation which will enable him to return to the remaining books of *The Faerie Queene* with renewed vigor:

> Till then giue leaue to me in pleasant mew,
>> to sport my muse and sing my loues sweet praise:
>> the contemplation of whose heauenly hew,
>> my spirit to an higher pitch will rayse.
> But let her prayses yet be low and meane,
>> fit for the handmayd of the Faery Queene.
>
> *(Amoretti* 80)

These lines are strikingly similar to those in which Spenser apologizes for the pastoral truancy of Calidore (VI.x.1–4), and subsequently for his own exaltation of Gloriana's "poore hand-mayd" in the description of Calidore's vision of the Graces (VI.x.28). In both instances more is at stake than the tactful apology of a poet who has intruded his own interests before those of his sovereign. Rather, the contrast between the two kinds of poetry, personal and public, frivolous and serious, is reminiscent of the opening lines of *The Faerie Queene,* where

the "Oaten reeds" of the pastoral poet are exchanged for the
heraldic trumpets of the poet of fierce wars and faithful loves.
Indeed, if it were not that an overextension of the term "pastoral" might lead to more confusion than illumination, it would
be helpful to consider the *Amoretti* as a pastoral mode, one
in which the myth of the simple, uncomplicated life is presented
in the image of the humble poet—a pastoral of personal allusion. By whatever name one may choose to describe this technique, however, it it important to note that Spenser consistently
employs the suggestion of autobiographical reference as a pretext for a more detached and critical examination of the relationship between image and object, between the specific and
the ideal, than would be appropriate if he were presenting a
more inclusive and less "private" view of society.

To return, finally, to the figure of Serena among the cannibals
which provoked the foregoing discussion, it may be noted that
the "oriental" similes describing her body serve admirably to
illustrate both the true nature of the object and simultaneously
the cannibals' idolatrous misinterpretation of the image. The
comparison of Serena's belly with an altar "To offer sacrifice
diuine thereon" (VI.viii.42) points to the sacramental overtones
of a reverent love; at the same time it foreshadows the monstrous impiety of the sacrifice envisioned by the savages.
Whereas the physical incongruities found in the imagery of the
Song of Songs, and the ambiguities of Petrarch's imagery, are
both directed toward the ends of a larger synthesis of values, a
broader sense of significance, the incongruity and ambiguity
of Spenser's simile operate as a check against too easy a fusion
of meanings. Similarly, the fact that the actions of the cannibals
are in accordance with the forms of a religion that even succeeds
in restraining their lust provides a reminder that the religious
impulse can be perverted and made an expression of man's
bestiality. The savagery represented by the cannibals is appropriately seen as a mixture of "primitivism" and "Petrar-
chanism"; for both motives, at their worst, constitute an abuse
of nature.

3. Gardens of Adonis:
Man in the Cycle of Generation

In its present state, *The Faerie Queene* contains no direct presentation of Cleopolis. The poem's action takes place in the undefined, neutral terrain familiar to chivalric legend: a series of open spaces serving as battlefields, bounded by wilderness and linked by devious and perilous paths. The heroes are far from home, in that other country of challenge and response. If the various palaces, cottages, and caves scattered over this terrain are sometimes presented as miniature social units, they refer specifically and primarily to the concerns of the poem's action at the time of their appearance. At most these microcosmic societies may demonstrate the ideal working of an individual virtue; but they do not pretend to be total images of the societal impulse, as does the perpetually offstage court of Gloriana.

Similarly, the "natural" settings found in the poem—the gardens, groves, and other images of retreat—offer a picture of the natural order which is always relative to the persons visiting them: they cannot be abstracted from their narrative contexts. The present chapter will examine these settings in an effort to define the images of nature and the natural order which they imply, but it will be ultimately concerned with the relevance of these images to the poem's larger purpose: a presentation of human responsibility in a world where the Golden Age is at most a distant memory of a society that can never be literally restored, one in which mankind enjoyed an easy communion with the rhythm of a friendly nature. For fallen and redeemed man, Love has taken on a new meaning beyond that attributed to it in the scheme of nature. In its more complex role as an organizing principle of society and the central factor in man's search for divine enlightenment, the physical aspects of love will be of assistance only in proportion as the individual succeeds in recognizing the place of nature in the Christian order of values.

Of the various natural settings described in *The Faerie Queene,* the Garden of Adonis offers the most prolonged and comprehensive meditation on the natural order. Consequently, the following discussion will consist chiefly of an examination of the Garden and its relevance to the contrast between Belphoebe and Amoret in Book III. But it is not enough to consider the description in its narrative context alone. The passage itself (III.vi.29ff.) focuses on the narrator's conflicting attitudes toward Nature. Readers who have regarded it as a conveniently quotable statement of Spenser's philosophy may have been guilty of critical fallacies, and they have usually been indiscreet in exposing themselves to the challenge of opposing statements drawn from other passages in the poem; but they have been responding to an undeniable mode of personal reference visible in the shifting tones of the description. The narrator is trying to "locate" the Gardens with reference to his own, human experience;[1] and in his attempts to be true to their sympathetic and unsympathetic aspects alike (their "hard" and "soft" aspects, in the terms used by Lovejoy and Boas[2]), he describes

1. Cf. Harry Berger, Jr., "Spenser's Gardens of Adonis: Force and Form in the Renaissance Imagination," *Toronto Quarterly, 30* (1961), 128–49.
2. Lovejoy and Boas, *Primitivism and Related Ideas in Antiquity.*

what amounts on the visual level to no single garden but to a series of Gardens of Adonis. The very discontinuity of the topography—the problems which it raises as to Time's presence or the meaning of "in" and "out" in stanza 32, for example— suggests that the passage is dialectical rather than descriptive in its structure. It also suggests one reason for the especial futility in this instance of the conventional source study that tries to identify Spenser's point of view: the poet is trying to assimilate the full range of possible attitudes toward the seasonal cycle of generation.

One expression of the paradox under examination here is seen in the very title given to these gardens. The phrase in antiquity refers to a potted plant or forcing bed in which the brevity of the seasonal cycle is accentuated:

> *Socrates:* . . . Now tell me this. Would a sensible husband-
> man, who has seeds which he cares for and which he
> wishes to bear fruit, plant them with serious purpose in
> the heat of summer in some garden of Adonis, and delight
> in seeing them appear in beauty in eight days, or would he
> do that sort of thing, when he did it at all, only in play and
> for amusement? Would he not, when he was in earnest,
> follow the rules of husbandry, plant his seeds in fitting
> ground, and be pleased when those seeds which he had
> sowed reached their perfection in the eighth month?
>
> (Plato, *Phaedrus* 276 B)

> "What do you mean . . . by gardens of Adonis?" "I mean,"
> said Silenus, "those that women plant in pots, in honour
> of the lover of Aphrodite, by scraping together a little
> earth for a garden bed. They bloom for a little space and
> fade forthwith."
>
> (Julian, *The Caesars* 329 C)[3]

3. I have followed the Loeb Classical Library translation: Plato, *Works, 1,* ed. H. N. Fowler (London and Cambridge, Mass., Wm. Heinemann Ltd. and Harvard University Press, 1914); Julian, *Works, 2,* ed. W. C. Wright (London and Cambridge, Mass., Wm. Heinemann Ltd. and Harvard University Press,

Spenser's Garden would seem at first to have little in common
with these ephemeral plants. On the contrary, the principal
force of the description as a whole is toward a celebration of
permanence in the midst of and through the mutability of
individual flowers: the climax, and the most memorable lines
of the passage, assert triumphantly that "There is continuall
spring, and haruest there/ Continuall." The negative view
of Adonis as flower seems more adequately suited to the
Tassesque melancholy of the singer at the Bower of Bliss,
whose apostrophe to the rose similarly stresses its mortality.
Yet an identical ambiguity is inherent to both gardens, Spenser's
and those of the celebrants of Adonis. For in proportion as a
flower's characteristic life-span is shortened it becomes a more
convenient symbol not only of the brevity of human life but
also of its capacity for a racial immortality through successive
generations. Or to put it differently, the chief hindrance to an
acceptance of human mortality lies in the relative length of
the individual life: a perspective in which the cycle is accelerated
reduces the significance of the individual biography and hence
neutralizes the threat of time to man's sense of value. It is
toward such a perspective that the poet is working in his description of the Gardens, struggling against a pessimism like that
urged by Acrasia, who can only see futility in heroic endeavor
when confronted with the example of vegetable nature. In
Book II, it may be recalled, Acrasia's rose translates into tones
of despair the more lighthearted dalliance with which Phaedria
perversely invokes the lilies of the field in her appeal to Guyon
(II.vi.16).

It may be useful, therefore, to note the negative connotations
of the Gardens of Adonis as they emerge from the classical
sources quoted above, for Spenser's gardens are contrasted,

1913). Cited by Josephine Waters Bennett, "Spenser's Garden of Adonis,"
PMLA, 47 (1932), 46–80; despite my different approach, I am indebted to
this study, and to the scholarly debate which arose out of it, for much pertinent
information.

explicitly or implicitly, with a number of other settings in the poem. In terms of the action of Book III, the Gardens are challenged by the House of Busyrane. The fact that Amoret is educated in one and menaced in the other, together with the location of the two descriptions, one at the middle of the book and the other at its end, should make this comparison inevitable. Secondly, as the terrestrial abode of Venus, the Garden is opposed to the wilderness where Diana and her nymphs roam, the environment in which Amoret's twin sister, Belphoebe, is educated. And as a natural setting that celebrates physical love, it is further contrasted with the incitements offered in Book II by Acrasia's bower and Phaedria's isle. Readers have frequently mentioned this last contrast, though they have debated the problems of comparing scenes which occur in different books and are consequently directed to different emphases.[4] And finally, as an evocation of a pre-lapsarian Paradise to which the Faeries enjoy a ready access denied to fallen mortals, the Garden of Adonis must be compared with the poem's more limited versions of pastoral, the groves and humble bowers that refresh the flagging spirits of those visitors to Fairyland who are bound to the responsibilities of their historical roles. In the light of these comparisons, Spenser's Garden of Adonis will be shown to have retained some of the connotations which were traditionally associated with its name, even before it was expanded to denote a full-scale mythological garden. The cycle of seasonal birth, death, and rebirth celebrated in the worship of Adonis finds an expression in both kinds of garden, in the forcing-beds scorned for their ephemeral products as well as in the terrestrial paradise envisioned in *The Faerie Queene*. The present chapter will discuss the relationship between love and the natural order as it is expressed through the four areas of

4. Cf. Lewis' oft-quoted and oft-disputed distinction between the Garden and the Bower, based on the latter's alleged "voyeurism" (*The Allegory of Love*, pp. 330–33). Note, incidentally, that the descriptions of Phaedria's isle and Acrasia's bower occur respectively in the sixth and twelfth cantos, the positions held in Book III by the Gardens of Adonis and Busyrane's house.

comparison mentioned above, and will explore the concept of "chaste affection" which directs the poem's complex of attitudes toward nature.

Although Socrates' objection to the precocious development fostered by gardens of Adonis is not precisely that implied by Spenser, the very fact of Busyrane's ability to kidnap and transfix Amoret does suggest an inadequacy of some sort in her education. In Book III Spenser is dealing freely with the material of romance, material that affords extensive precedent for rather hazily or ambiguously motivated erotic quandaries; and his account of Amoret's difficulties manages to be generally credible without providing much specific ethical definition. Readers continue to debate the precise label to attach to Busyrane's challenge.[5] But instead of attempting to decide, for example, whether he represents Amoret's lust, or Scudamour's, or that of some third party, it is more profitable to begin by taking him simply as a vile enchanter in his own right, like Archimago, and to ask in what way Amoret's training has been so onesided as to have left her unable to break free from his enchantments, at the same time that it has given her the strength to resist his temptations. The answer to this question concerns the inadequacy of the natural order in itself—the "course of kynde"—to account for the role played by courtly love in the organization of human impulses. Amoret is educated in a place where Cupid is thoroughly domesticated, subordinated to the reproductive goals of Nature, and himself a family man. It is not until she has left the Garden and come to the Fairy court that she learns of his role as a source of civil strife, a force for disorder which is at variance with his role in the Garden. Busyrane introduces her to this new picture of Cupid, through the "mask of loue" which he brings in at her bridal feast and

5. Padelford, "The Allegory of Chastity," p. 376 (cited in *Variorum 3*, 326); Bennett, "Spenser's Garden of Adonis," p. 78 n.; Thomas P. Roche, Jr., "The Challenge to Chastity: Britomart at the House of Busyrane," *PMLA*, 76 (1961), 340–44 (reprinted in Roche, *The Kindly Flame*); A. Kent Hieatt, "Scudamour's Practice of *Maistrye* upon Amoret," *PMLA*, 77 (1962), 509–10.

employs as a device to kidnap her while her companions are "Surcharg'd with wine" and assume that what they are watching is "By way of sport, as oft in maskes is knowen" (IV.i.3). On the one hand this incident provides a dramatic illustration of the dangers inherent in the situation of the banquet, where the drinking of wine is both a means to social integration and a potential cause of disorder. At the same time, it is specifically Amoret who is unprepared for these images of love which constitute the currency of a courtly society; she has been trained to a love which is natural, purposeful, monogamous (and hence chaste in Spenser's sense of a chaste marriage), but by the same token physical.

In the Garden of Adonis love has no meaning apart from this physical context. The frankness of love there, its freedom from rancor or envy (III.vi.41), is accompanied by a similar freedom from the stratagems by which the erotic impulse is made a means to power. Busyrane is not simply introducing Amoret to the discovery that Cupid is no respecter of marriage bonds (and hence indicating that adultery is implicit in the language of the court); he is also capitalizing on the fact that as the darling of Venus she has been deprived of those defenses which enable her twin sister to enjoy all the social dominance characteristic of the Petrarchan mistress.[6] Amoret's naïveté takes the form of an inability to handle the abstracted language of courtly love in isolation from the physical context in which she has been educated, and toward which she is destined through her marriage with Scudamour, whose name significantly is as reminiscent of Cupid as her own. Busyrane may be seen as offering the knowledge of Good and Evil to one who has till now led her life in a Paradise free from such knowledge; but both the names of the principal characters and the nature of the action make clear that a specific area of knowledge is involved.

6. Belphoebe's role as courtly mistress is not only seen in her relationship to Timias, but is anticipated as well in the language of her original description, II.iii.21 ff.; cf. Berger, *The Allegorical Temper*, pp. 115–60.

The image of Cupid is central to Spenser's presentation of this problem, and it is within the context of erotic mythology that Amoret's history is contained. Just as it is in love's wound ("her dying hart,/ Seeming transfixed with a cruell dart," III.xii.31) that Busyrane will dip his pen, so it is as a result of a fruitless search for Cupid that Venus comes to adopt Amoret in the first place. Cupid is generally associated with the goadings of sexual desire, and with the physical and emotional appetites which inspire to love. Venus is closer to the figure of Mother Nature, and represents the larger natural principles of generation which lie behind the sexual desires of animals and humans: she is appropriately the "mother" of Cupid. If Cupid embodies the erotic appetite, Venus is concerned with actual fruition: as she remarks to Diana, "my delight is all in ioyful-nesse,/ In beds, in bowres, in banckets, and in feasts" (III.vi.22). Ideally, mother and son live together in harmony, and Cupid's "wanton parts" are accessory and instigatory to the enactment of Venus' rites. But when he runs away from home, irked by his mother's chidings, his actions cease to be subordinated to the demands of the natural order, and become instigations to chaos.

This runaway Cupid may be described in the terms of Latin poetry as a capricious and undisciplined boy whose indiscriminate sport wreaks havoc on all levels of society: this is the presentation found in the description of Venus' search for him (III.vi.11ff.). Or he may take on the attributes found in medieval love poetry, where he is a full-scale deity, presiding over the courts of love and enforcing submission to the principles of courtly love.[7] He is most clearly seen in this latter role in the description of Mirabella's trial (VI.viii.32ff.); but the tapestries at the House of Busyrane and more importantly the Masque of Cupid there (III.xii.1ff.) show him in this context as well. In one sense these two roles are not strictly distinguishable, since both are expressions of his traditional function and differ

7. Lotspeich, *Classical Mythology,* pp. 48–50.

only in the degree of seriousness attached to his disruption of the harmonious and rationally controlled relationships between individuals. But it is inevitable that a view of human society which sees love as the central organizing principle—as is true in different senses of both courtly and Christian love—should tend to regard Cupid in a much more serious light than had the antique tradition.[8] The relatively lighthearted treatment of Cupid's ravages as they are seen by Venus in her searches through court, city, country, and wilderness is symptomatic of his classical role: the fact that his ravages are viewed in order of descending importance—ranging from the woeful Ladies and Lords and the view of him as "the disturber of all ciuill life," to the plaints of shepherds which provoke only smiles from Venus, to the apparently untouched haunts of Diana— reinforces the sense that Cupid is little more than a naughty child. Venus' selection of Amoret to serve as his replacement ("in her litle loues stead, which was strayd,/ Her *Amoretta* cald, to comfort her dismayd") stresses his diminutive status, and suggests at the same time that this change in domestic arrangements cannot fail to represent an improvement.

Most noteworthy in the entire scene leading up to Spenser's presentation of the Gardens of Adonis is its suggestion of apparent triviality. Its idyllic and playful tone, the hearsay quality of all its evidence for Cupid's misbehavior, the tact with which Venus quickly placates Diana's annoyance, all work against any suggestion of a basic opposition between the principles of Love and Chastity. As Venus is quick to point out, she and Diana are no more than civil servants, heads of their respective departments but by no means autonomous: "We both are bound to follow heauens beheasts,/ And tend our charges with obeisance meeke" (III.vi.22). Spenser's imitation of Moschus' idyll, with its relaxed narrative and absence of intricate allusion, gives overtones of a social harmony that is actually at odds with

8. Erwin Panofsky, "Blind Cupid," in *Studies in Iconology: Humanistic Themes in the Art of the Renaissance* (New York, Oxford University Press, 1939), pp. 95–128; Lewis, *The Allegory of Love,* passim.

the situation being described. Later incidents will demonstrate
the significance of Cupid's behavior, and of the distinction between "perfect Maydenhed" and "goodly womanhed," the goals
which Diana and Venus establish for their respective charges.
But for the moment all is calm. The poet alludes to Cupid with
complaisance, and in describing the Gardens of Adonis his
immediate concern is with the problem of mutability. The
Cupid who reappears at the end of the canto has (as least temporarily) set aside his "sad darts" to play the role of husband
and father. The problem of love's wounds (the subject of so
much of Book III) has been adroitly, if ominously, repressed.

The richness and compression of Spenser's treatment of the
Gardens, beginning with stanza 29, contrast with the looseness
of this preceding scene; but there is no interruption of the
continuing sense of a natural order which is thoroughly under
control. The logical inconsistencies in the description cannot
be explained away. But the fluent transitions minimize one's
awareness of them, by continually diverting the reader's attention away from the physical, topographical status of the garden
itself, toward an emphasis on the narrator's reactions. Actually,
several distinct attitudes to Garden-of-Adonis myths are presented in succession; the overriding notion of Permanence in
Mutability embraces them all and lends them the appearance
of compatibility. First there is the myth of the Garden as a kind
of conservatory,

> . . . the first seminarie
> Of all things, that are borne to liue and die,
> According to their kindes.

(III.vi.30)

This Garden is a place distinct from the actual world, set off
from it by gold and iron walls. "All that to come into the world
desire" are fitted with "sinfull mire" and sent out to live in the
world, returning after death to the Garden, via the "hinder
gate." "All" of what, though? To equate Spenser's "naked

babes" with human souls[9] is to overlook the fact that animals and fishes are sent out as well (stanza 35). And the infinitely varied shapes of creatures bred here include among them "Some fit for reasonable soules t'indew": the inference is that the shapes are themselves something apart from the souls.

Yet these stanzas do seem, at least to a modern reader, to suggest that the image of birth represented by the passage of the naked babes from the Garden into the world is in some sense an image of the body-soul relationship. There is much talk of the union of the immortal part and the mortal. But even more importantly, one senses throughout that as a generation myth, purporting to describe the way in which God's creatures come into the world and leave it, obeying the command to increase and multiply, this description must be a complete one; and to be complete it must at some point contain an image of the human soul.

Actually, however, it does not. Spenser is concerned here with a portrayal of the *natural* order; to emphasize the absence of the soul from this order would be neither necessary nor consonant with the sense of the completeness and integrity of this order, considered in itself. Probably the Elizabethan reader would not have been tempted to confuse natural and supernatural, and to expect to find the soul in this context. For him the allusion to "reasonable soules" cited above would be readily understood as indicating the precise point—man—at which the natural world accommodates a supernatural element derived elsewhere.

Recognition of the fact that the Garden of Adonis is an expression of the natural order helps to clear away much of the confusion which has resulted from attempts to reconcile its distinctions between forms and substance with the transcendent, Platonic senses of these terms. The stumbling block has been that Spenser's forms are transitory and his substances perma-

9. Bennett, "Spenser's Garden of Adonis," p. 51 passim.

nent, where in Platonic terms the opposite would have been expected:

> The substance is not chaunged, nor altered,
> But th'only forme and outward fashion;
> For euery substance is conditioned
> To change her hew, and sundry formes to don,
> Meet for her temper and complexion:
> For formes are variable and decay,
> By course of kind, and by occasion;
> And that faire flowre of beautie fades away,
> As doth the lilly fresh before the sunny ray.
>   (III.vi.38)

Confronted with this statement, the reader who has taken the Garden of Adonis as an otherworldly abode of souls and "Platonic forms" must judge either that Spenser has unaccountably reversed his terms, or that the Garden is ambidextrous, growing both souls and at the same time the mortal "forms of other things." To reject both of these alternatives is to reject as well the notion that the Garden contains any suggestion of personal immortality. What is immortal in nature is the "huge eternall *Chaos*" where the substance is unchanging precisely because it is undifferentiated. In the hothouse atmosphere of the Garden, with its sundry beds each devoted to a different kind of being, the Sun/Adonis (the parallels between the description of Adonis here and the preceding description of the Sun's impregnation of Chrysogone make this identification unavoidable) begets forms in the recipient substance of the Earth.

Since these forms—aptly imaged as flowers, the commonest of all emblems of mortality—are themselves destined to die, it is logically appropriate that they should be menaced by the figure of Time with his scythe. What does seem inconsistent, however, even when we recognize the impermanence of these flowers, is that Time should be actively present in a Garden described as a nursery or "seminarie" whose walls set it apart from the "mortal state" of the world outside. Surely the wicked Time described in stanza 39 is a full-scale image of mortality:[10] he represents a force more inclusive than Abortion or Infant Mortality or Unscientific Gardening; and he cuts down plants which are already flowering and in their full glory. The image of the Garden of Adonis would be blurred indeed if we were being asked to imagine Venus as producing her vast array of forms for export at the same time that she retained some of these forms as a part of her private landscaping plans. But Spenser does not superimpose one image on another: rather, the earlier image fades away and no further mention is made of Genius, the outer walls of the Garden, or the endless ranks of flowerbeds.

The poet's first presentation of the Garden has stressed the immutability of the physical substance which supplies the endless round of generation and decay. From the first union of form and substance in the womb of the earth (and there is surely an image of the womb in the walls of this first Garden), the life history of the creatures is followed as they emerge into the world and reach maturity. At this point, beginning with stanza 39, the first garden-of-Adonis image is supplanted by another, by which the Garden is an image of the natural world itself. This Paradise bears a striking resemblance to Eden: it is a place in which the natural order is wholly observed, so that the only hindrance to "immortall blis" is the fact that mortality is a necessary factor in that order:

> But were it not that *Time* their troubler is,
>   All that in this delightfull Gardin growes,
>   Should happie be, and haue immortall blis:
>   For here all plentie, and all pleasure flowes,
>   And sweet loue gentle fits emongst them throwes,
>   Without fell rancor, or fond gealosie;
>   Franckly each paramour his leman knowes,

10. His "flaggy wings" recall those of Redcross' Dragon (I.xi.10), as Mr. Robert Tully has helpfully pointed out to me.

Each bird his mate, ne any does enuie
Their goodly meriment, and gay felicitie.

There is continuall spring, and haruest there
Continuall, both meeting at one time:
For both the boughes doe laughing blossomes
    beare,
And with fresh colours decke the wanton Prime,
And eke attonce the heauy trees they clime,
Which seeme to labour vnder their fruits lode:
The whiles the ioyous birdes make their pastime
Emongst the shadie leaues, their sweet abode,
And their true loues without suspition tell abrode.
                                                     (III.vi.41–42)

These two stanzas describe the society to which Amoret is educated in the Garden. The contrast between this natural society
and the civilized world represented by the fairy court is indica-
tive of the weaknesses in her upbringing, which leave her unable
to combat the enchantments of Busyrane. In the Garden of
Adonis love is sweet, and throws gentle fits; merriment is unconstrained, unenvied, freely admitted, and fruitful. Spring and
harvest are simultaneous and continual: love is not dissociated
from its generative goal. The "true feminitee" to which Amoret
is educated in this environment is radically defenseless; for it
participates spontaneously in the cycle of life without fear of
any challenge to personal identity. In this natural order love is
so wholly a part of generation that marriage rites are as superfluous as any other intrusion of Art: it is only in a less innocent
world which has learned good and evil that human community is no longer natural and becomes a perilous and fleeting
achievement.

It is in the middle of this Paradise, so conceived, that a
third Garden of Adonis is found: a grove located on the top
of a "stately Mount," representing Nature on a higher level
of abstraction, the allegorical and mythological focus of Spenser's presentation of the Garden. This third image is an inclu-

sive one, in the sense that it assumes the two preceding views of nature—its permanence in the midst of mutability, and its spontaneous assimilation of love to this larger rhythm. But it is also detached from Time in a way that the two preceding Gardens had not been: its concern is with the permanence of the generative principle, which is something quite different from the permanence of undifferentiated substance asserted at the beginning of the presentation of the Garden. Here the union of Venus and Adonis is described as an everlasting moment, transcending the inevitable mortality of the forms which it begets. It is important to recognize the progression of imagery leading up to this passage.

In the first vision of the Garden the basic image is that of the flower, which is sown in the ground, fertilized by the Sun, brought to maturity, and then cut down by Time. Not surprisingly, the imagery of the second view of the Garden is concerned with forms of life which have a more conspicuous sexuality: the birds playing among the shady leaves, the trees with their combination of colorful blossoms and heavy fruit. The third view of the Garden combines these two strands of imagery. First there are described the myrtle trees which enclose the grove and perfume the ground with their sweet gum:

> And in the thickest couert of that shade,
> There was a pleasant arbour, not by art,
> But of the trees owne inclination made,
> Which knitting their rancke braunches part to part,
> With wanton yuie twyne entrayld athwart,
> And Eglantine, and Caprifole emong,
> Fashiond aboue within their inmost part,
> That nether *Phoebus* beams could through them throng,
> Nor *Aeolus* sharp blast could worke them any wrong.
> (III.vi.44)

This natural arbor affords protection against the extremes of sun and wind, ensuring a temperate climate suitable for the

unhampered enjoyment of love. Curiously enough, the language
of this description echoes an earlier stanza describing the care
with which Belphoebe protects the "faire flowre" of her
"chastity and vertue virginall":

> That dainty Rose, the daughter of her Morne,
>> More deare then life she tendered, whose flowre
>> The girlond of her honour did adorne:
>> Ne suffred she the Middayes scorching powre,
>> Ne the sharp Northerne wind thereon to showre,
>> But lapped vp her silken leaues most chaire,
>> When so the froward skye began to lowre:
>> But soone as calmed was the Christall aire,
> She did it faire dispred, and let to florish faire.

> (III.v.51)

Belphoebe has been trained to protect herself against the elements. Amoret, on the other hand, has been brought up in an
environment where nature has taken care of this matter for her.
Small wonder, then, that she is unprepared for the intemperate
weather outside the Garden.

A more complicated problem is raised by the next element in
the description of the mount:

> And all about grew euery sort of flowre,
>> To which sad louers were transformd of yore;
>> Fresh *Hyacinthus, Phoebus* paramoure,
>> And dearest loue,
>> Foolish *Narcisse,* that likes the watry shore,
>> Sad *Amaranthus,* made a flowre but late,
>> Sad *Amaranthus,* in whose purple gore
>> Me seemes I see *Amintas* wretched fate,
> To whom sweet Poets verse hath giuen endlesse date.

> (III.vi.45)

Some of the uncertainty attaching to this stanza is in connection
with its textual history. The fragmentary fourth line was added
in 1609 to what had been an eight-line stanza in the editions of

1590 and 1596. Whether or not to accept this addition is not in question here;[11] but the existence of a textual alteration which is relatively unusual in the case of *The Faerie Queene,* together with the fact that "of yore" in the second line seems to imply that all the flowers cited will be classical examples, suggests that the allusion to Amintas is possibly an afterthought, provoked by events occurring after the original draft of this stanza had been composed. Recent studies have recognized this as an allusion to Thomas Watson's Latin *Amyntas* (1585), translated into English by Abraham Fraunce (1587); the ambiguous "Poets verse" may refer to one or both of these poets, but there can be no doubt that Spenser is providing further testimony to the quite extraordinary popularity enjoyed by this poem.[12] Recognition of the appropriateness of the literary al-

11. Smith's arguments in favor of the emendation seem to me persuasive. Spenser has broken lines elsewhere, presumably in imitation of Virgil; for an editor to add one seems improbable (J. C. Smith, ed., *Spenser's Faerie Queene,* Oxford, Clarendon Press, 1909, Introd., I.xix).

12. Fraunce's 1587 translation was reprinted in 1588 and 1589, before becoming incorporated, with changes, into his *Yuychurch* of 1591. The popularity of Amintas as a pastoral hero is further attested not only by Fraunce's pastoral anthology in the 1592 *Yuychurch,* but also by a lyric attributed to "T. W. Gent" and included by "R.S." in his *Phoenix Nest* (1593), entitled *"Amintas for his Phillis";* and by an anonymous lyric in MS. Bodl. Rawl. Poet. 85, f. 84v: "Verses made in manner of argument upon : 11 : lamentationes of Amintas."

The desire for a prior history of Amintas to accompany Watson's original "Funerals" led Watson to write his own Latin *enfance, Amintae Gaudia* (1592), and Fraunce to translate Tasso's *Aminta,* with appropriate alterations and additions, as the first part of his *Yuychurch.* Cf. W. W. Greg, "English Versions of Watson's Latin Poems," *Modern Language Quarterly* (London), 6 (1903), 125–29; and Norma Rose, *"Amintae Gaudia* by Thomas Watson: edited, with translation, introduction, and notes," an unpublished Ph.D. dissertation (May, 1944) in the Yale University Library.

To the present day, scholars have persistently confused Watson's two poems with one another or with Tasso's *Aminta,* to which they bear no relationship whatsoever. It seems safe to assert that in England the reputation of Amintas had been fully attained before Tasso's drama became known. Cf. William Ringler, "Spenser and Thomas Watson," *Modern Language Notes,* 69 (1954), 484–87; Harry Morris, "Richard Barnfield, 'Amyntas,' and the Sidney Circle," *PMLA, 74* (1959), 318–24.

lusion which these lines constitute may remove some of the
urgency of determining the precise nature of the personal allusion that may have been intended.

The allusion to Hyacinthus continues the motif suggested in
the preceding stanza. Hyacinthus was loved by Apollo and the
West Wind: caught between their conflicting loves he is an
innocent victim when the discus thrown by Apollo is caught
up by the wind and made the instrument of his death (*Metamorphoses* 10.162ff.). It is not surprising that he should now be
located in a place sheltered from the blasts of sun and wind.
Narcissus, on the other hand, is a victim not of powers outside
his control but of his own delusions. Spenser, like Ovid (*Metamorphoses* 3.432), calls him "foolish"; Natale Conti judges him
more harshly:

> These are the things that have been said of Narcissus in
> the fables. But what is contained in this story that is use-
> ful to human life, and that would have justified handing
> these parables down to posterity? They signified that re-
> venge follows the imprudent, and lustful, and criminal
> man, just as one's shadow follows the body.
>
> (*Mythologiæ,* IX.xvi)

Imprudence, then, is the central fact of Narcissus' character:
his love for his own reflected image is taken as a symbol of all
love which is directed fruitlessly against insubstantial images.
In making him and Hyacinthus into flowers the gods have
shown their pity by reducing the "sad louers" into forms which
are apt expressions of their true natures. Now they belong to a
level of creation where sexual identity and active love are un-
necessary. Merely by flowering and withering and falling to
earth, they achieve their own immortality of kind. It should be
noted that Spenser's flower imagery has by now undergone a
significant change in emphasis. Where in his more generalized
presentation of the natural cycle the flower had been a symbol
of all natural creation, individually subject to mortality but
participating in the larger immortality of Nature, it is now a

symbol of a more limited range of creatures, those involved passively in the vegetative cycle without having achieved personal identity through a normal sexual career.

The presence of Amintas/Amaranthus seems at first glance to run counter to these implications of sexual abnormality. To be sure, he is like Hyacinthus and Narcissus a sad lover turned into a flower; but as Watson tells his story he is a victim neither of the gods nor of his own delusions. Rather, his death is self-inflicted after twelve days of lamenting the untimely death of his fiancée, Phyllis. Here is a fitting elegiac hero: Abraham Fraunce, after presenting translations of Tasso's *Aminta* and Watson's *Amyntas* in his *Countesse of Pembrokes Yuychurch* (1591), establishes him as the subject of an annual "Amyntas Day" to be held in the part of Pembrokiana's Ivychurch where the amaranthus has been found growing; "Amyntas Dale" is in fact the subject of the pastoral anthology found in *The Third Part of the Countesse of Pembrokes Yuychurch* (1592). In deciding to include at this point the flowery remains of one of the great tragic lovers of the decade, Spenser expands the implications of his statement, and thereby minimizes certain moral overtones that are basically irrelevant at this point.

From the viewpoint of the natural order, it does not much matter why a lover is cut down in the flower of his youth, without having participated directly and actively in the reproductive cycle. Homosexuality (Hyacinthus was the first object of homosexual desire on the part of gods and humans alike[13]), narcissism, or noble grief at the death of a loved one, are all the same when they keep one from the central fact represented by the Garden of Adonis. In another context Amintas received a different kind of celebration; here he is linked indiscriminately with other examples of sterile love, considered unsentimentally in terms of the physical order.

13. Apollodorus, *The Library* I.iii.3; Ovid, *Metamorphoses* 10.162 ff. It should be noted that Ovid does not consider metamorphosis into a flower to constitute a particularly desirable form of immortality: "Qua licet, aeternus tamen es . . ." (10.164).

Sexual union constitutes the subject of this part of the description of the Garden. Just as Adonis has been considered from the beginning "the Father of all formes," Venus has by implication been seen as the mother of all things; the identification of Adonis with the Sun has led to a similar identification of Venus with the Earth; and a parallel between the earth and the female body has been hinted with the mention of the womblike walls which surround the first image of the Garden. Although this metaphor does not approach the schematic detail of the anatomy of Alma's house in Book II, there is a general heightening of the erotic imagery as the description is climaxed by a meditation on this *mons Veneris*. The emphasis is on the feminine protectiveness within which Adonis is preserved and enjoyed in accordance with the will of Venus, whenever it is time to engender more forms:

> There wont faire *Venus* often to enioy
> Her deare *Adonis* ioyous company,
> And reape sweet pleasure of the wanton boy;
> There yet, some say, in secret he does ly,
> Lapped in flowres and pretious spycery,
> By her hid from the world, and from the skill
> Of *Stygian* Gods, which doe her loue enuy;
> But she her selfe, when euer that she will,
> Possesseth him, and of his sweetnesse takes her fill.
> (III.vi.46)

Spenser's treatment of the myth, like Shakespeare's, shows Venus in the dominant role, reaping pleasure from a lover who is described throughout in passive terms: her maternal quality is further stressed by the equation of Adonis with her own "wanton boy," Cupid. Venus has so ordered things that the Boar (identified with Winter in Conti's discussion of the seasonal myth[14]) is held prisoner, and the daily and seasonal cycles entail a regular rebirth of Adonis in accordance with his role.

14. Conti, *Mythologiæ* V.xvi, cited by Lotspeich, pp. 32–33.

The passivity of Adonis (recalling perhaps the sleeping Verdant in Acrasia's bower) suggests the ambiguity of the flowery lovers who attend him. On the one hand his role as fertilizing agent contrasts with the sterility of Hyacinthus, Narcissus, and even Amintas as human individuals. Yet Adonis himself is an object of floral metamorphosis,[15] and Venus' enjoyment of him suggests a vegetable rather than an animal mode of sexuality. Spenser's Adonis seems almost as reluctant a lover as Shakespeare's, to judge from the tapestries at Castle Joyous; in the context of Book III such reluctance invites comparison with the other examples of futile attempts to resist love. Like Britomart, or like Hippolytus and Redcross in Book I (and unlike the Verdant of Book II), Adonis is too preoccupied with the pursuit of his Boar to devote himself to the enjoyment of his love. But with his death and metamorphosis he is translated to a state in which the Boar roams no longer and enjoyment is perfect and continual, without the intervention of death—either sexual or literal.

In postulating this existence of Adonis, Spenser has clearly moved beyond the view of the Garden in which Time was still operative, into a world created by the will and hedged about by appeals to the authority of common consensus ("And sooth it seemes they say . . .") and logical necessity ("Therefore needs mote he liue, that liuing giues to all"). Rather like Adonis himself, the poet has begun by attempting to confront directly the challenge of Time and mutability—both in the epic program of Book I and again in meditative terms through his description of the Gardens of Adonis; in both cases he has ended by recognizing the necessity of love to define and crown his quest. This is not to suggest that the heroic impulse is erroneous, but merely that it is incomplete until complemented by the pastoral. By contrast, Verdant in Book II is a precocious Adonis who must be roused from his reverie and sent once more on his heroic path.

15. Cf. *Metamorphoses* 10.725 ff. The tapestry at Castle Joyous similarly stresses this aspect (III.i.35–38).

The view of Cupid and Psyche that concludes Spenser's presentation of the Gardens of Adonis stresses this need for suffering before the Garden can be properly attained. The Cupid who turns up here is a far cry from the wayward youth Venus had set off to find earlier in the Canto; and he is equally remote in his connotations from the winged tyrant seen at the House of Busyrane. He is wholly domesticated now, faithful to "his true loue faire *Psyche*" and no longer concerned with wreaking havoc in the world. The introduction of Psyche provides a transition from the natural order as it is embodied in the structure of the Garden to the question of the merits and drawbacks of the Garden as a training ground for Amoret. Psyche comes here with Cupid only

> After long troubles and vnmeet vpbrayes,
> With which his mother Venus her reuyld,
> And eke himselfe her cruelly exyld . . .
>
> (III.vi.50)

These sufferings are past now, for Psyche; but they are still to come for Amoret. Trained to "all the lore of loue, and goodly womanhead," she will pledge herself to a knight of Cupid, Scudamour; but before she can be united with him, she will have to undergo a cruel exile of her own, one in which Cupid himself will play a part, as the wanton god represented in Busyrane's Masque of Cupid. These sufferings, Spenser suggests, are an inevitable consequence of Amoret's education at the hands of Psyche. This education stresses the ideals of passive womanhood to the exclusion of the protections necessary in a world where one is exposed to the sun and the wind, where Cupid stalks with his bow and arrows, and where civilization has given Love a social role far more complicated than the simple contribution to the natural cycle found in the world of nature. Even for the classical world, the reconciliation of Venus and Psyche is possible only after much suffering.

Sun and Earth, Adonis and Venus, Cupid and Psyche, Scudamour and Amoret: these various pairings of sexual opposites in the Gardens of Adonis suggest a progression from the purely natural phenomenon, to the mythological and hence anthropomorphic representation of that phenomenon, to increasingly closer approximations of human figures which first are conceived as embodying and then merely parallel the relationship and function of the natural deities. Seen in descending order in this fashion, these pairs become progressively less autonomous as they become more immediately relevant to man's state. To appreciate the precise fashion in which Scudamour and Amoret relate to man, it may be helpful to recall another pair of sexual opposites whose relevance is suggested by an earlier reference to the Gardens of Adonis. In Book II, Guyon reads of the origins of the Fairy race:

> . . . how first *Prometheus* did create
> A man, of many partes from beasts deriued,
> And then stole fire from heauen, to animate
> His worke, for which he was by *Ioue* depriued
> Of life him selfe, and hart-strings of an Ægle riued.

> That man so made, he called *Elfe,* to weet
> Quick, the first authour of all Elfin kind:
> Who wandring through the world with wearie
>   feet,
> Did in the gardins of *Adonis* find
> A goodly creature, whom he deemd in mind
> To be no earthly wight, but either Spright,
> Or Angell, th'authour of all woman kind;
> Therefore a *Fay* he her according hight,
> Of whom all *Faeryes* spring, and fetch their lignage
>   right.

> (II.x.70–71)

The mixed nature of the Fairy race is apparent from this account; the reader is reminded of it at the beginning of III.vi, in the name of Amphisa ("both natures"[16]), the mother of Chryso-

---

16. Draper, "Classical Coinage," p. 99.

gone and the grandmother of Belphoebe and Amoret. Spenser's
etymology of *Fay* suggests an obvious parallel not only with
the name of Psyche but with the other aspects of the female
principle seen in the Gardens of Adonis. In fact Cupid is twice
called an *Elfe,* once in the description of Busyrane's tapestries
(III.xi.45) and once at the Masque of Cupid itself (III.xii.22)—
in both cases in the context of his cruel manifestations. It would
seem, moreover, that Spenser keeps something of this elf-fay
distinction in his discussion of subsequent generations of the
Fairy race. Although he is less consistent in this respect in later
Books, where distinctions between Elf and Briton are less important structually than in Books I and II, and where the terms
"Elf" and "Elfin" occur less and less frequently,[17] he does tend
to limit his use of these terms to contexts in which they connote
some degree of inferiority, either real or imaginary.[18] The
female members of the Fairy race, on the other hand, include
the two major images of Elizabeth, Belphoebe and Gloriana,
and these are of course treated with much less qualification. In
general, though, it may be noted that in both these creation
myths, the account of the origins of Fairyland and the more
general view of nature in the description of the Gardens of
Adonis, Spenser tends to associate the female with the enduring,
undifferentiated sensuous *given,* and the male with the goadings
of the shaping human will.

17. "Elf" occurs seven times in Book I, six in II, three in III, twice each
in IV and V, and once in VI. "Elfin" occurs ten times in I, seven in II, once
in III, three times in V, and twice in VI.

18. In Book I, "Elf" or "Elfin" is applied to Redcross exclusively, except
once when Sans Joy calls Satyrane a "misborne Elf." In nine of these sixteen
applications, the terms are in the context of the fight with Sans Joy. At the
end Redcross learns that he was kidnapped at birth by a Faery who left her
own "base Elfin brood" in exchange (I.x.65). In Book II, Guyon is the principal
object of these epithets; and here they appear in greatest profusion at Mam-
mon's cave (five of the eight cases).

In the later Books, Care, Paeana's dwarf, the Souldan, and even Pastorella
in captivity are all called elves (IV.v.34, IV.viii.61, V.viii.19, VI.xi.19). In
these later instances, therefore, the term seems to be applied more loosely,
but generally in a disparaging context.

The Gardens of Adonis are accessible only to the Fairy race. As a terrestrial paradise, an expression of a kindly Nature where the weather is always temperate and the living easy, they can be no more than a nostalgic daydream for the fallen Christian. But as an ideal they continue to hold a powerful appeal which requires serious scrutiny. In presenting the stories of Belphoebe and Amoret, Spenser is describing a classical educational experiment, of the sort that begins: Take two identical twins, A and B; separate them at birth. . . . In this case, the variable to be tested is the element of protectiveness. The twins, born under virtual laboratory conditions, are raised in atmospheres of "hard" and "soft" primitivism, respectively: Belphoebe is trained by Diana and her nymphs to the rigors of the chase, while Amoret is sheltered from the elements and trained to a passive femininity. The contrast is not unlike that developed by Socrates, in the lines from the *Phaedrus* cited at the beginning of this chapter. The results obtained by Spenser's experiment suggest a similar conclusion. The question has been the relative durability of the "flowers" cultivated by these two horticultural techniques; and it is seen that Amoret's goodly womanhood can be seriously menaced in the outside world, and requires the assistance of the hardier bloom of one trained to the sterner ideal of chastity.

Since *The Faerie Queene* is concerned with portraying the education of a prince—or more specifically, of a Queen—it may be that the education of Belphoebe and Amoret has a topical relevance as well. Elizabeth's rigorous training had served her well in the masculine role to which she was called; and in Ascham's boast of her, that "Her mind has no womanly weakness,"[19] it is easy to see a parallel to Spenser's emphasis on Belphoebe's invulnerability. In any event, Spenser's concept of chastity demands the qualification provided by Amoret's history. There is no question of evil or falsehood in the Gardens of Adonis and the natural principles which they represent.

19. Quoted by J. E. Neale, *Queen Elizabeth* (New York, Harcourt, Brace, and Co., 1934), p. 14.

What is at stake is the question of the adequacy of those principles to prepare an individual for the perils of human society. Before comparing the Gardens with any other pastoral setting in *The Faerie Queene,* two facts should be borne in mind: first, that it is presented as a training ground, in which an individual is prepared for life in the actual world; and secondly, that it is a woman who is to be educated in it. Neither of these conditions applies to the Bower of Bliss, for instance. The celebration of sexual intercourse in the Gardens is informed by an awareness of its role in the cycle of birth and death, whereas Acrasia's Bower celebrates it for its own sake, unreasoningly. But the main difference between the two settings lies in their roles: one as an image of natural order, the other as an image of human irresponsibility. The myth of Mars and Venus, which lies behind the picture of Acrasia and Verdant in the Bower, relates to the truancy of the irascible instinct, the subordination of one motive to another; in the context of Book II it is expressive of a disruption of that ordering of values which gives the individual an impetus toward his goal in life. In its less serious form, this disruption may simply delay the hero from his quest, as Guyon's Phaedria or Odysseus' Calypso seek to do; more seriously, it may subvert the reason so completely as to destroy the hero's human qualities, to enchant him as Acrasia or Circe seek to do. Acrasia's Bower presents Nature as an image of the human condition, and pretends that it is a complete picture. To do so is to deny man's superiority to the beast; and for this reason the acceptance of Acrasia's image of life leads toward an animal metamorphosis.

Any discussion of Spenser's pastoral settings must be careful, therefore, to distinguish among the various roles which they may perform. They may be designed as a preparation for human life, as is true of the Gardens of Adonis and of the forests where Belphoebe and Artegall are educated. They may be temptations to a truancy from the responsibilities of life, as with Acrasia's Bower. Or, finally, they may be places of retirement from the confusion of this life, where men who have fulfilled their duties in this world may prepare themselves for the life to come. In this case, the pastoral settings are not directly concerned with presenting images of the natural order, true or false, but offer a simple contrast to the abodes of human society, providing an individual with a humble setting where nature fulfills his barest needs and where he is free to contemplate heavenly matters without distraction. This kind of setting is seen most clearly in the home of the Hermit who cures Serena and Timias in Book VI:

> . . . towards night they came vnto a plaine,
> By which a little Hermitage there lay,
> Far from all neighbourhood, the which annoy it may.

> And nigh thereto a little Chappell stoode,
> Which being all with Yuy ouerspred,
> Deckt all the roofe, and shadowing the roode,
> Seem'd like a groue faire braunched ouer hed:
> Therein the Hermite, which his life here led
> In streight obseruaunce of religious vow,
> Was wont his howres and holy things to bed . . .
> (VI.v.34–35)

This Hermit, who is described as a retired warrior of great renown, recalls the later career predicted for Redcross, when Contemplation tells him that true holiness is to be won ultimately by prayer and meditation rather than by glorious actions. He also recalls the disguise adopted by Archimago repeatedly in Book I. He is reminiscent, on a very different level, of Sir Henry Lee, whose Retirement Tilt of 1590, with its farewell to a life of involvement in Elizabethan pageantry, carries the cult of Elizabeth to its logical conclusion, in his promise to the sovereign "To be your Beadsman now, that was your Knight":

> My helmet now shall make a hive for bees,
> And lover's songs shall turn to holy psalms:
> A man at arms must now sit on his knees,
> And feed on prayers that are old age's alms.

And so from court to cottage I depart,
My Saint is sure of mine unspotted heart.[20]

An awareness of the pageantry which attended Elizabeth will help to restrain the reader of *The Faerie Queene* from an undue emphasis on the explicitly Christian implications of such a character as the Hermit. The mixture of flattery and genuine religious fervor found in this quasi-sacred imagery of Elizabethan compliment is difficult to analyze; but it is as clearly present in Spenser's poem as in the more ephemeral entertainments of the period. Pastoral motifs are predictably dominant in the entertainments presented to Elizabeth during her progresses: a contrast between her glorious court and the rural abodes of her nobles is inevitably a major theme under such circumstances. She is saluted by the semicivilized genii of these places: nymphs, wild men, and even on occasion a Fairy Queen,[21] all pay homage to her divine radiance. In ways that can seldom be precisely and persuasively identified, the unique character of Elizabethan society, with its opposition of Town and Country in a sense unknown on the Continent, is reflected in the pastoral settings of *The Faerie Queene*.

The literally pastoral world of Pastorella and the shepherds to which Calidore retreats in Canto x of Book VI combines aspects of all the settings enumerated above. It represents a temptation to avoid the responsibilities of the quest, and is therefore a world which Calidore cannot adopt permanently: his pastoral garb is only a temporary disguise. Like the Hermit's Ivychurch, it is a world in which Nature readily yields man the bare

20. Quoted by Frances A. Yates, "Elizabethan Chivalry: The Romance of the Accession Day Tilts," *Journal of the Warburg and Courtauld Institutes, 20* (1957), 17; cf. E. K. Chambers, *Sir Henry Lee: An Elizabethan Portrait* (Oxford, Clarendon Press, 1936).

21. Note particularly the entertainments at Kenilworth and Woodstock in 1575, the Retirement Tilt of 1590 and its sequel at Ditchley in 1592, and the entertainment at Sudeley in 1592: John B. Nichols, *Progresses and Public Processions of Queen Elizabeth* (3 vols. London, J. B. Nichols, 1823), *1*, 473 ff., *3*, 136 ff.; A. W. Pollard, ed., *The Queen's Majesty's Entertainment at Woodstock, 1575,* (Oxford, H. Daniel & H. Hart, 1903).

necessities of his existence, and in which Meliboeus' contempt for wealth predicates the simple life as the basis of true contentment. Like the Gardens of Adonis, it is the setting for an education—that provided by the vision of the Graces, whose dance illuminates the action of Courtesy in human society. And like Redcross and Adonis and the Hermit, the poet is able to find in this pastoral milieu a fitting if paradoxical conclusion to his heroic quest. These pastoral episodes of Book VI depend for their full meaning, however, on the "antique image" of Artegall's Justice as it is presented in Book V. By demonstrating the distance between an ideal, spontaneously ordered natural society as it is envisioned in the myth of the Golden Age, and the harsher reality of a savagely repressive order as it is found in the fallen world of man, Spenser gives a new meaning to the pastoral impulse, and suggests the more tentative, partial and even illusory victory to be won against the forces of disorder that challenge the social unit. The patron of Courtesy is no dragon-killer; the "Grace" with which he is endowed is of a far different kind than that of Redcross. But together with Artegall, he betokens the poem's shifting frame of reference, from the individual's search for personal identity toward an increasing emphasis on the bonds by which society is defined. The natural world in its harsher and gentler aspects becomes now less an object of meditation than a setting within which man constructs his world.

4. Astraea: The Golden Age and Artegall's Savage Justice

The presentation of Justice in Book V of *The Faerie Queene* has been severely criticized for a repellent narrowness of conception, made all the more obvious by a singularly unfortunate choice of historical analogy. To anyone acquainted with Elizabethan history, the brutalities of Lord Grey's policy in Ireland have afforded few suggestions of a divine justice reestablished on earth; even within the framework of the poem itself, Spenser seems frequently to dwell on the less attractive aspects of a sternly repressive police force. Artegall's iron groom, Talus, seems far more conspicuous than his golden sword, Chrysaor, which derives from heaven and bears connotations of a "cleaner" justice. B. E. C. Davis speaks for many readers when he complains that "Neither authority nor the demands of allegory can palliate the offence of admitting this grotesque automaton, Thor with his hammer but without his humour, upon the shores of old romance. Talus is a very affront to the hero's dignity, a lapse on the part of Spenser that can only be attributed to waning power."[1]

1. B. E. C. Davis, *Edmund Spenser: A Critical Study* (Cambridge, Cambridge University Press, 1933), p. 124; quoted in *Variorum 5*, 298.

Yet the very unattractiveness of Artegall's justice might suggest that the apparent "simplicity" of Book V—the perfunctory, "mechanical" structure of its episodes[2]—is in fact a function of Artegall's limited role as the champion of earthly justice. For it is not enough for the modern reader to repress his democratic preconceptions in order to appreciate Elizabethan attitudes. It must be apparent that the trial of Duessa (V.ix.36ff.), with the conflicting emotions it provokes in Mercilla, shows that when Justice is enacted by human beings with respect to one another it is anything but a simple matter. To appreciate this complexity it is necessary to examine in greater detail the view of human history by which Astraea and Artegall are related to one another, and to comprehend the allusions to the Golden Age at the beginning of Book V in the context of Spenser's invocations elsewhere of that "antique image" of Fairyland which presents an ironic contrast to the current state of human existence.

In connection with this temporal perspective on the poem's action, it is helpful to reexamine some of those passages scattered throughout the poem in which the poet speaks in the first person as he introduces or comments on aspects of the action. Such passages, occurring for the most part in the proems to the various Books, or in brief transitional formulae between episodes, are so clearly indebted to literary precedent that one may feel it is enough to recognize their role in defining the poem's genre in relation to its antecedents. Yet these same elements have another function as well, for the use of the first person permits a commentary on the poem's action from the viewpoint of contemporary actuality. The proems, with their repeated invocations and dedications to Elizabeth, and to a less marked degree those brief passages which conclude cantos or come between two distinct episodes with a glimpse of the poet tugging

2. Cf. Kate M. Warren, ed., *The Faerie Queene* (6 vols. Westminster, Constable, 1897–1900), 5, vii–viii (quoted in *Variorum 5*, 169–70): "The Fifth Book . . . is in both form and matter the simplest of all the six Books of the poem."

his plow to a new furrow or breathing heavily as his port comes
into sight, all provide a contemporary frame for the poem's
picture of Fairyland. Such a confrontation of the fictive with the
actual is especially pertinent to *The Faerie Queene:*

> Why then should witlesse man so much misweene
> That nothing is, but that which he hath seene? . . .

> Of Faerie lond yet if he more inquire,
>   By certaine signes here set in sundry place
> He may it find; ne let him then admire,
>   But yield his sence to be too blunt and bace,
>   That n'ote without an hound fine footing trace.
> And thou, O fairest Princesse vnder sky,
>   In this faire mirrhour maist behold thy face,
>   And thine owne realmes in lond of Faery,
> And in this antique Image thy great auncestry.
>   (II.Proem.3–4)

A critic speaks of the "abruptly self-defensive tone"[3] of this
passage; but such a complaint fails to take into account the
possibility that this proem is less a defense against anticipated
objections than an introduction to the poem's milieu. The allegorist is in a sense peculiarly responsible for the truthfulness
of his work; to the extent that his images are led by their allegorical import away from a coherence based on a recognizable
portrayal of human situations, or even of human reactions to
illogical situations as in some types of fantasy, they come to depend for their coherence on the reader's capacity to interpret
them. By providing a vast array of allusions, drawn from history, religion, literature, and common life, the poet not only
increases his chance of conveying his meaning: these allusions
also constitute his evidence, and their range and variety add
plausibility to the conceptual world of his poem.

It is in this context that the proem to Book II invokes the
spirit of "hardy enterprize" by which new continents are daily

3. Edwin Honig, *Dark Conceit: The Making of Allegory,* p. 201 n.

being explored, and encourages the reader to a similar voyage of discovery in the world of the poem. Contemporary advances in man's knowledge of physical geography are advanced as an argument for exploring man's moral geography. It is no co-incidence that examples are chosen which suggest a rediscovery of the truths to be found in classical myth on the one hand, and in the cult of Elizabeth (with the Christian analogue which is never wholly absent from that cult) on the other:

> . . . who in venturous vessell measured
> The *Amazons* huge riuer now found trew?
> Or fruitfullest *Virginia* who did euer vew?
>
> (II.Proem.2)

Similarly, in the apostrophe to Elizabeth which concludes this proem, the poem is said to provide a "faire mirrhour" in which the Queen may find her image reflected. Perhaps the significance of this term will be clearer if one takes it in the sense in which it appears in the *Mirror for Magistrates,* for it is obviously no simple image of Elizabeth which the poem offers. Certainly the praise of the Queen herself is unqualified; yet there is much that is cautionary as regards those who would model them- selves on her. The poem is full of characters who appear to embody certain of her attributes, but lack the virtues to inform those attributes: the recurrent and never wholly explicit motive of the Amazon is only one instance of Spenser's attempts to deal with problems which arise, ultimately, from the nature of his allegory. For if it is true that the Idea is in its purity too brilliant to be comprehended by human intelligence, it is equally true that every attempt to filter this brilliance through the veil of concrete imagery will bring with it the risk of confusing tenor and vehicle, of mistaking the image for the thing imaged. From this danger arises the incessant conflict of Appearance and Reality which dominates so much of the poem; from the consequent need for a complex system of checks and balances attendant on every major image, one might derive the poem's principle of expansion through ironic repetition of motifs.

Specifically, the poet offers an "antique Image" to Elizabeth. Each of the six proems alludes to antiquity: the poet draws his history from "antique rolles" (Book I); he cannot point to Fairyland but must "vouch antiquities, which no body can know" (Book II); he cannot portray Elizabeth directly but must shadow her portrait "in colourd showes . . . And antique praises vnto present persons fit" (Book III); he finds that in "former ages" the works of philosophers and heroes alike were founded in love (Book IV); modern instances of courtesy seem but "fayned showes" in comparison with those of "plaine Antiquitie" (Book VI). But it is in the proem to Book V that the contrast between antiquity and the present is made fully explicit:

> So oft as I with state of present time,
>   The image of the antique world compare,
>   When as mans age was in his freshest prime,
>   And the first blossome of faire vertue bare,
>   Such oddes I finde twixt those, and these which are,
>   As that, through long continuance of his course,
>   Me seemes the world is runne quite out of square,
>   From the first point of his appointed sourse,
> And being once amisse growes daily wourse and
>   wourse.
>   (V.Proem.1)

The poet appeals to an *image* of antiquity, as opposed to the *state* of the present: one suspects that the two belong to different realms of being, and that the world of the poem is not that of any classical antiquity that can be located in time. Nor is it that of classical mythology, though gods and heroes figure in the action of the poem, alongside historical and even contemporary personages. Rather, "antiquity" refers to a past so distant that it can only be intuited by men who must base their knowledge on the distorted evidence of history. Antiquity is a state of mind; or, considered from a different viewpoint, a symbol of the Ideal as it exists before passing through the distorting lens of the Actual.

In varying forms this motif of the Golden Age recurs throughout the poem. Guyon (II.vii.16) contrasts the "antique world"
which contentedly accepted the grace of God's bounty with
the pride of later times, which "gan exceed/ The measure of
her meane, and naturall first need." And at Sclaunder's house
(IV.viii.30ff.) the innocence of the "antique age" when "loyall
loue had royall regiment" is invoked to justify what in the
present age would be a certain temptation to lust. The fact that
one of these passages apparently identifies this Golden Age with
the setting of the poem, while the other does not, is of relatively
minor importance, save as an example of the poem's shifting
moods. It is less a question of Spenser's consistency than of his
use of the Golden Age as an image of man's self-control and
obedient reliance on Grace. The Christian knows that historically this state existed prior to the Fall; but he also knows that
it can be regained metaphorically by the individual at any time.
For a detailed analysis of the Golden Age as it relates to Fairyland and the present, one must look to the proem to Book V,
the longest of the six proems, which shares with the proem to
Book II the necessity of defending its peculiarly "classical"
virtue through an appeal to historical reality.

Spenser begins by developing the familiar Renaissance theme
of the decline of the present world from the divine order established in antiquity.[4] The precession of the equinoxes has displaced the zodiacal signs; the sun has declined since Ptolemy's
time, and has even shifted its position on occasion; Mars and
Saturn have followed highly eccentric orbits. In view of these
heavenly displacements, it is scarcely surprising that sublunary
standards have gone awry:

> Right now is wrong, and wrong that was is right,
> As all things else in time are chaunged quight.
> Ne wonder; for the heauens reuolution

4. Paul H. Kocher, *Science and Religion in Elizabethan England* (San
Marino, Huntington Library, 1953), pp. 84–86; Don Cameron Allen, "The
Degeneration of Man and Renaissance Pessimism," *Studies in Philology, 35*
(1938), 202–27; George Williamson, "Mutability, Decay, and Seventeenth

> Is wandred farre from, where it first was pight,
> And so doe make contrarie constitution
> Of all this lower world, toward his dissolution.
>
> (V.Proem.4)

Significantly, however, this pessimistic theme is developed with something less than total melancholy. There is an ironic lightness to Spenser's characterizations of the zodiacal signs in terms of an almost Ovidian naturalism:

> . . . in these few thousand yeares
> They all are wandred much; that plaine appeares.
> For that same golden fleecy Ram, which bore
> *Phrixus* and *Helle* from their stepdames feares,
> Hath now forgot, where he was plast of yore,
> And shouldred hath the Bull, which fayre *Europa*
> bore.
>
> And eke the Bull hath with his bow-bent horne
> So hardly butted those two twinnes of *Ioue,*
> That they have crusht the Crab, and quite him
> borne
> Into the great *Nemoean* lions groue.
> So now all range, and doe at randon roue
> Out of their proper places farre away,
> And all this world with them amisse doe moue,
> And all his creatures from their course astray,
> Till they arriue at their last ruinous decay.
>
> (V.Proem.5–6)

As constellations, the Ram and Bull are behaving eccentrically, but their movements are in keeping with their activities prior to being translated to the heavens; thus Spenser minimizes any

---

Century Melancholy," *ELH, 2* (1935), 121–51. The theme appears in Seneca, *Thyestes* IV.2, is developed in a bizarre fashion by the mad Titus in *Titus Andronicus* IV.iii, and forms the subject of Donne's *First Anniversary*.

sense of their having "proper places" in the skies. There are overtones of slapstick in the random motions of Jupiter's menagerie. The parallelism of the mythological allusions (emphasized by the repetition of the word "bore") reinforces the implication that the zodiacal signs are behaving in accordance with their nature as animals, though they may seem to have betrayed our higher estimate of them. Spenser is careful not to continue his enumeration of examples to include the sixth sign, Virgo, for which by contrast he will predicate "an euerlasting place" (V.i.11).

A similar sense of calculated anticlimax informs the description of the sun's decline:

> For since the terme of fourteene hundred yeres,
> That learned *Ptolomæe* his hight did take,
> He is declyned from that marke of theirs,
> Nigh thirtie minutes to the Southerne lake;
> That makes me feare in time he will vs quite forsake.
> (V.Proem.7)

It is difficult to avoid a sense of contrast between the "fourteene hundred yeres" and the "Nigh thirtie minutes," although the two terms are not logically commensurate. But in any case a decline of less than half a degree is scarcely an adequate image of a pervasive corruption of antique order. Nor is the assertion of "Ægyptian wisards"—itself advanced with some skepticism —that the Sun has behaved strangely on four occasions, worthy of seven lines of exposition if the sole purpose of this passage is to document the degeneration of natural order. Spenser seems to be running out of evidence.

The irony of this passage can easily be overemphasized; but it is helpful at least to recognize the tone with which Spenser tempers his contrast between the Golden Age and the world of the present. For to take this passage as one of unalloyed high seriousness is to risk a biographical extension that is one of the great commonplaces of Spenser criticism. The remarks of Legouis are typical:

> It is impossible, then, to call this a poetical fiction used for mere ornament. It is a deep-seated creed, the foundation upon which his poetry was built. His imagination conspired with his private resentments when conjuring up that beautiful image of times long ago. In the great controversy between Ancients and Moderns which was already beginning and was to grow all through the next century, Spenser, without a moment's hesitation, took sides with the Ancients.[5]

The picture of Spenser as a disillusioned courtier, driven by his frustrations to a nostalgic dreamworld, may have some degree of biographical truth; it may even find a reflection among the emotions presented in the poem. But to advance this as the principal motive behind the treatment of the Golden Age in *The Faerie Queene* is to risk a serious misunderstanding of Book V. And more generally, to see Spenser as a poet of vague yearnings and sensuous daydreams is to ignore the tight fabric of allusion and meaning which is one of the most striking characteristics of the style of *The Faerie Queene,* in Book V no less than in the other books. By treating this highly conventional theme of the decline of the world in such a fashion, Spenser directs attention away from the scientific question of an objectively considered phenomenon, toward a consideration of the imaginary and imaginative nature of the cosmic order which is presumed to be violated.

In the present case, too, it should be noted that this presentation of the world's decline in terms of animal imagery anticipates the picture of the present world as a forest in which Artegall is trained "to make experience/ Vpon wyld beasts . . . With wrongfull powre oppressing others of their kind" (V.i.7). Imposing his laws by force, in the tradition of Hercules or

5. Emile Legouis, *Spenser* (London and Toronto, J. M. Dent & Sons, 1926), pp. 36–37; quoted in *Variorum 5,* 154–55.

Bacchus, Artegall is dealing with men who have so far forgotten their nobler part as to deserve classification among the beasts. In terms of this earlier description of the Golden Age, human flesh and blood are now no more sensitive than the stones from which this cruder race is derived:

> For from the golden age, that first was named,
> It's now at earst become a stonie one;
> And men themselues, the which at first were framed
> Of earthly mould, and form'd of flesh and bone,
> Are now transformed into hardest stone:
> Such as behind their backs (so backward bred)
> Were throwne by *Pyrrha* and *Deucalione:*
> And if then those may any worse be red,
> They into that ere long will be degendered.
>
> (V.Proem.2)

This allusion to the Flood may have been suggested by Ovid, whose description of the Golden Age (*Metamorphoses* 1.89ff.) Spenser follows. There, as in other texts, the degeneration of man from his original high estate is punctuated by a universal destruction from which a single just man is saved. The analogy with the story of Genesis is inevitable; if Spenser, like Conti for example, saw Deucalion as a representative of Justice (*Æquitas*) and Piety in the manner of Noah,[6] this allusion appears more directly relevant to Artegall's task. Though in the immediate context of the stanza quoted above the myth of Deucalion relates to man's debased condition, even here it implies that men are yet capable of being "re-formed" under the operation of Justice. The earlier age is irrevocably behind them; their divine descent seems more remote now, for the Flood intervenes between them and their former condition.

6. *Mythologiæ* VIII.xvii; Kircher similarly associates Noah with Deucalion: cf. Don Cameron Allen, *The Legend of Noah: Renaissance Rationalism in Art, Science, and Letters* (Urbana, University of Illinois Press, 1963; first ed. as vol. 33 of *Ill. Studies in Lang. and Lit.*), p. 188.

Only the figure of Deucalion links them to the realm of Saturn, when Justice was universally revered and war was unknown.

The virgin Astraea is a fitting symbol of the innocence and purity of the earlier age, when justice could be administered without the need of armed force. Her withdrawal from the increasingly lawless and violent world is followed by a different kind of justice, with attributes which are better suited to dealing with this harsher situation: the "furious might" of Bacchus and the club of Hercules (V.i.2). If the earlier age submitted willingly to the decrees of Justice without constraint, this new age is that of the lawmakers, and of organized society and royal might: "The club of Iustice dread, with kingly powre endewed." It is to "a caue from companie exilde" (V.i.6) that Artegall is led by Astraea for his education in the new tradition of enforced justice. He is a hero on the order of Bacchus and Hercules, able to repress tyranny and establish a rule of law. The presence of willful evil in the human world has rendered Astraea's rule impossible; when confronted by a corrupt actuality, the Ideal, in this case that of Justice, must retire from the field. In her place she leaves a surrogate, Artegall, whom she has trained to imitate her, but whose involvement in the world makes him better equipped to deal with actuality on its own terms. She provides Artegall with an attribute which was never hers: Chrysaor, the golden sword with which Jupiter put down the Titans. Talus, on the other hand, is described as having been her groom; but although some sort of executive force may be presumed to have existed even under Astraea, Talus' role as a police agent is destined to become far more conspicuous under his new master. Both Talus and Chrysaor become symbols of an enforced order, and as such are foreign to the image of Astraea.

By contrast, Astraea's balance or scales ascend to the heavens with her: she has taught Artegall

> . . . to weigh both right and wrong
> In equall ballance with due recompence,

And equitie to measure out along,
According to the line of conscience.

(V.i.7)

But with her assumption into the Zodiac the scales disappear as
an attribute of earthly justice. It is significant that throughout
Book V Artegall is at no point associated with this image. On the
contrary, in his debate with the giant in the second canto he
demonstrates the absurdity of any human attempt to evaluate
or adjust the divinely established order. The limitations of
human understanding militate against any radical approach to
the apparent inequities of nature or of the human situation.
Appropriately, it is a giant who attempts to weigh the universe:
for his radical egalitarianism is an act of insurrection similar
to that of the Titans against Jupiter. And like Mutabilitie's bid
for supremacy, the struggle is at heart illusory; both she and
the giant are participants in the very order which they pretend
to control. When the giant angrily turns against the scales,
Artegall quickly emphasizes that they are only as good as the
intelligence which employs them. It is in the mind that the
weighing must take place; and to confuse this image of the
scales with the idea it represents is to misunderstand the character of Justice.

Spenser is careful not to blur this point: it is remarkable that
in so lengthy a presentation of Justice in Book V, the words
"balance," "measure," "scale," "weigh," and "weight" occur
exclusively in the description of Astraea's education of Artegall
and in the incident with the giant. In fact, the use of "measure"
in the irrelevant context of a conventional formula—"they
measur'd mickle weary way" (V.ii.29)—is no exception; it
occurs solely at the beginning of the latter incident. This is so
even though Artegall's speech to the giant in no way debases
the image of the scales as a fitting symbol of the operation of
justice in the abstract—or in the human mind. Rather, it seems
that the image is too ambitious to be suited to the practical
sphere of human justice. Man's awareness of the limits to his

understanding, and even more perhaps his awareness of his own ultimate involvement in a divine judgment, militate against any aspiration to a complete or absolute justice.

In this connection Shakespeare's treatment of the problems of justice in *The Merchant of Venice* provides a basis for comparison. There too the image of the scales is consistently rejected as a standard for judgment:

> Therefore, Jew,
> Though justice be thy plea, consider this—
> That, in the course of justice, none of us
> Should see salvation.

(IV.i)

By relying on the scales for his accounting, Shylock works his own downfall. He discovers, as Spenser's giant had discovered, that human life is compounded of too many interrelated elements to permit a simple weighing of one or the other. One cannot cut flesh without shedding blood as well. Portia's legal quibble is a comment on Shylock's refusal to temper his adherence to the letter of the law. Shylock's justice is a legalistic one, and is bounded by the limits of constraint:

> *Portia.* Then must the Jew be merciful.
> *Shylock.* On what compulsion must I? Tell me that.
> *Portia.* The quality of mercy is not strain'd . . .

Shylock has already stopped listening. If such a man is to be the consequence of the codification of laws, then it is with reason that Astraea may be said to have left the earth.

In *The Merchant of Venice* the contrast is obviously between an Old Testament emphasis on Law and a New Testament emphasis on Love. Shylock, the Jew, is forced to retreat from his former insistence on nothing less than justice, and to beg for the mercy he had refused to yield. Once the logic of his position has been so thoroughly undermined, his conversion to Christianity follows almost as a matter of course. Spenser's presentation of the Christian context of *The Faerie Queene* is for the most part far less overt. His emphasis on the struggle between Protestantism and Catholicism tends further to blur any awareness of a unified Christianity opposed to the non-Christian world—despite the opposition of Christian and Infidel implicit in its chivalric subject matter. Reference to Shakespeare's treatment of Christian justice is especially important, however, for the light it sheds on two related aspects of Book V.

In the first place, Shakespeare's opposition of Hebraic and Christian ideas of justice explains why Spenser does not represent Astraea returning to earth to restore a Golden Age under the patronage of Elizabeth. This is a less trivial question than one might think; for Ovid's picture of Astraea leaving the blood-drenched earth (*Metamorphoses* 1.150) was no more familiar to the Renaissance than Virgil's evocation of her return, as the symbol of Augustan imperial glory, at the beginning of his Fourth Eclogue: "Iam redit et virgo, redeunt Saturnia regna . . . " It was a simple matter to adapt this motif to contemporary political situations. Ariosto, for example, employs it in his praise of Charles V:

> Astrea veggio per lui riposta in seggio,
> anzi di morta ritornata viva;
> e le virtù che cacciò il mondo, quando
> lei cacciò ancora, uscir per lui di bando.
>
> (*O.F.* XV.xxv)

Spenser was almost certainly familiar with these lines, for other parts of this prophecy of Andronica to Astolfo seem echoed in Merlin's prophecy to Britomart (III.iii), with its vision of the glorious age introduced by Elizabeth. But even without Ariosto's example, the motif of Astraea's return was widely current in Elizabethan England, as an almost inevitable form of compliment to the Virgin Queen.[7] An easy syllogism leads one

7. For a detailed discussion of the use of this image with respect to Elizabeth, see Frances A. Yates, "Queen Elizabeth as Astraea," *Journal of the Warburg and Courtauld Institutes, 10* (1947), 27–82. A more general survey is given by E. C. Wilson, *England's Eliza* (Cambridge, Mass., Harvard University Press, 1939).

to find such an identification in Book V. In the proem Artegall
is called Elizabeth's "instrument"; in the first canto he is shown
to be Astraea's instrument; therefore, Spenser identifies Astraea
with Elizabeth. But in the shifting sands of Spenser's allegory
syllogisms are often treacherous: one is constantly finding that
the various images directed at a single idea tend to correct one
another and consequently are not interchangeable. In the present instance, Astraea and Elizabeth have certain characteristics
in common; but it is more significant that Spenser shows considerable restraint in avoiding too extensive a comparison.

This restraint becomes meaningful in terms of the theological
division of human history into the periods *ante legem, sub lege,*
and *sub gratia.* Seen in this light, the Golden Age and the rule of
Astraea are characteristic of the prelapsarian period *ante legem;*
the education of Artegall as a heroic representative of legality
in the tradition of Bacchus and Hercules constitutes mankind's
development *sub lege;* and with the emergence of such tempering influences as Britomart and Mercilla, the emphasis passes
to a vision of the era *sub gratia,* that of a Christian justice. Thus
in setting the myth of Astraea in the context of the Christian
view of history, Spenser avoids a conventional humanist suggestion of a return to the Golden Age, and moves toward a more
searching examination of the problems peculiar to Christian
justice. Artegall, like Elizabeth herself, is operating not in an
idealized past, but in a degenerate world that affords no simple
solutions. In one sense it is true that the Redemption implies a
return to man's happier state. But the newly raised Eden must
cope with the problem of evil, and must learn to live with man's
fallen nature. The result is necessarily a greater emphasis on an
interior balance, an act of understanding that bridges the gap
between ideal and actual. It is in this sense, finally, that Astraea
is blazoned in the heavens, removed from this world but shedding light upon it.

If this Christian view of history helps to explain the role
played by the motif of the Golden Age as a symbol of man's
lost perfection, it also illuminates the larger question of the

pattern of development of Book V. Artegall's entry into the action, armed with his sword and accompanied by Talus, is as a representative of Old Testament justice. It is no coincidence that in his first action, the arbitration of the dispute between the Squire and Sanglier, he imitates the judgment of Solomon. Similarly, the following episodes display his competence in maintaining order. He strikes down tyrants, both those of the far right (Pollente) and those of the left (the egalitarian giant); pity does not keep him from stamping out the practice of bribery (Munera). Among his peers at Florimell's wedding feast he is, as Guyon calls him, "our iudge of equity" (V.iii.36). And in the dispute between Amidas and Bracidas he ventures into civil law where he offers a similar insistence on man's submission to the turns of fortune. The justice which Artegall represents in these preliminary incidents is above all else conservative in its scope: the simpler cases of oppression and misappropriation are redressed, but there is no meddling with the divine order as it is expressed by the operation of fortune.

From the beginning, it is clear that Artegall's virtue is closely akin to that of Temperance, and his meeting with Guyon in the third canto reinforces this sense of relationship. Significantly, each knight is shown restraining the other's anger at Braggadochio. A more serious test of Artegall's sense of balance is seen in his battle with Radigund, where his Aristotelian self-control is insufficient to restrain him from falling prey to his emotions. That Radigund is as much a representative of abandon as Acrasia seems apparent from her name, "reckless woman."[8]

> The cause, they say, of this her cruell hate,
> Is for the sake of *Bellodant* the bold,

8. Draper, "Classical Coinage," p. 103. J. H. Walker, *"The Faerie Queene: Alterations and Structure," Modern Language Review, 36* (1941), 51, sees an allusion to the legend of St. Radigund's refusal to consummate her marriage. This would at least be consistent with the picture of Spenser's Radigund as a representative of extremism. The allusion to Hippolytus in connection with the death of the Souldan (V.viii.43) and elsewhere suggests that an excessive commitment to chastity can be a fatal instance of uncontrol.

> To whom she bore most feruent loue of late,
> And wooed him by all the waies she could:
> But when she saw at last, that he ne would
> For ought or nought be wonne vnto her will,
> She turn'd her loue to hatred manifold,
> And for his sake vow'd to doe all the ill
> Which she could doe to Knights, which now she doth
>   fulfill.
>
> (V.iv.30)

Radigund's intemperance follows the pattern of frustrated love by which the concupiscent impulse is translated into the irascible: the same pattern is echoed ironically in the perverse frustration of her overtures to Artegall (V.v.29–57). When Artegall first permits himself to accept her terms of battle—themselves a violation of the natural relation of one sex to the other—and then to be blinded by her beauty, his defeat seems owing to the limitations of the classical justice he represents. He has been described as following in the tradition of the lawmakers Bacchus and Hercules, and now his defeat is likened to a similar humiliation of Hercules:[9]

> Who had him seene, imagine mote thereby,
>   That whylome hath of *Hercules* bene told,
>   How for *Iolas* sake he did apply
>   His mightie hands, the distaffe vile to hold,
>   For his huge club, which had subdew'd of old
>   So many monsters, which the world annoyed;
>   His Lyons skin chaungd to a pall of gold,
>   In which forgetting warres, he onely ioyed
> In combats of sweet loue, and with his mistresse
>   toyed.
>
> (V.v.24)

9. C. W. Lemmi, "Symbolism of the Classical Episodes in *The Faerie Queene*," *Philological Quarterly*, 8 (1929), 283–84, links this passage to Conti, *Mythologiæ* VII.i.

The classical hero differs from the Christian in being wholly dependent on the resources of his own nature. The virtuous pagans in Dante's Limbo are excluded from both the punishments and the rewards afforded by a participation in God's larger design. Their sole offense, as Virgil remarks, was that they spent their lives in a longing devoid of hope.[10] This characteristic of an insufficient motivation is seen in the story of Mars and Venus, to which the concluding lines of the stanza quoted above seem to allude. The classical deities are treated as embodiments of appetites. The stories of their rivalries portray conflicts of interest which are basically uninformed by any sense of subordination to an inclusive purpose. When Mars submits to Venus, or Hercules to Iole, the bellicose instinct is temporarily forgotten in favor of the erotic: one cannot adhere forever to a single, narrow line of conduct. The victory of one god over another is never permanent; Mars will eventually put on his armor again and go back to fighting.

Similarly, Artegall appeared in the earlier cantos as the embodiment of a single appetite, "inspired with heroicke heat" (V.i.1) like Hercules and Bacchus, a single-minded champion of justice. As such, he has dominated every situation; in accordance with his remark that one's judgment of right must depend on one's inner sense of balance, he has acted as the spokesman for justice, handing down one decision after another. With his defeat at the hands of Radigund, it becomes apparent that his self-contained balance has not been sufficient, and that he needs outside help. At this point the image of justice is modified. Formerly Artegall had functioned alone, and his temperance had been seen less as a balance of opposing sentiments, each with its own claim, than as a simple matter of discipline, of repressing any temptation to stay the course of rigor. Henceforth, in contrast, Artegall has company. Britomart is called upon to rescue him, to play Isis to his Osiris: "That part of Iustice, which is Equity" (V.vii.3). With Britomart's departure

10. *Inferno* IV.41–42.

following the defeat of Radigund, Arthur in turn arrives to
collaborate with Artegall in the succeeding episodes. Following
somewhat the pattern established by Guyon in Book II, Artegall
at least partially shares his later exploits with Arthur. Furthermore, he no longer functions as the sole spokesman: as the
problems of justice become broader and more complex, his
role becomes increasingly one of an agent and even, at Mercilla's court, of a simple onlooker.

Certainly it is not sufficient to say that the "natural" virtue
of Justice—or of Temperance—has now reached its limits,
and that Grace, through the agency of Arthur, must appear on
the scene.[11] The action of Book V remains within the order of
Nature: its purview remains the world of political activity. But
Spenser's presentation of Justice has progressed far beyond the
period of Artegall's education in the forests, where he had
practiced on the wild beasts "With wrongfull powre oppressing
others of their kind" (V.i.7). The eighth canto concludes with
a scene which fittingly reverses the pattern of Artegall's departure from the forest into the world of men: that of Adicia,
driven by her passion into the "wyld wood," to the point of
metamorphosis into a tigress. The opening of the following
canto comments significantly on this change:

> What Tygre, or what other saluage wight
>   Is so exceeding furious and fell,
>   As wrong, when it hath arm'd it selfe with might?
> Not fit mongst men, that doe with reason mell,
> But mongst wyld beasts and saluage woods to
>   dwell;
>   Where still the stronger doth the weake deuoure,
>   And they that most in boldnesse doe excell,
>   Are dreadded most, and feared for their powre:
> Fit for *Adicia,* there to build her wicked bowre.
>
> (V.ix.1)

---

11. Woodhouse, "Nature and Grace in the *Faerie Queene,*" pp. 194–228.

This image of the forest, taken with the similar metamorphoses of Malengin in the episode which immediately follows, provides an appropriate frame for Artegall's history to this point. Man's baser nature is constantly in danger of assuming dominance: when the controlling power of reason is lacking, man becomes a wild beast and society becomes a jungle. Temperance and Justice are directed against these risks to the individual and to the social order, respectively. Their role in the moral scheme is to maintain the degree of development currently attained by man, individually and collectively. Seen in this context, Artegall's early practice on wild beasts is revealed as a precise image of his function. And whereas the forest had originally borne overtones of a refuge against the wickedness of mankind, it now stands revealed as a negation of man's highest attempts at community.

At this point in the action of Book V, Artegall's role has focused on defending the social order against the unrestrained passions of individuals. It has become increasingly evident that the restraining powers of justice must be directed toward a higher goal than is afforded by the natural order alone; that self-control for its own sake is powerless to keep up this defense indefinitely. The allegorical core of Book V, the trial of Duessa at Mercilla's court, is concerned with defining this larger view of Justice. As an allusion to Elizabeth's treatment of Mary, Queen of Scots, this scene is also an example of the prominent role played by historical allusions in the later cantos of Book V. This fact has prevented many readers from seeing it as anything beyond an unconvincing attempt to provide a justification for Elizabeth's duplicity. But if one approaches these historical allusions from the other direction, and sees them as attempts on Spenser's part to justify his own view of Justice by testing it against contemporary issues,[12] it is possible to arrive at a more charitable evaluation.

---

12. That the moral problems attached to royal policy were considered appropriate and interesting subjects for public discussion may be seen from the fact that during Elizabeth's visit to Oxford in 1592 debates were held on

The most notable fact about the picture of Mercilla is that her action as judge is an incomplete expression of her attitude toward the situation. She recognizes that the only action possible in view of the gravity of the situation and the danger to society is to condemn Duessa. But her chief characteristic, as her name suggests, is that of the merciful sovereign. In the present instance her mercy finds no expression beyond her refusal to do more than acquiesce in Duessa's execution, and her shedding a few tears—gestures that offer scant consolation either to Duessa or to most readers of the poem. But the earlier picture of her court gives greater significance to what would be otherwise an unsatisfactory view of regal justice. Her chief attribute is the royal sceptre which she holds in her hand, "The sacred pledge of peace and clemencie" (V.ix.30); by contrast, the sword with which she enforces this peace lies rusted at her feet. Her retinue similarly reinforces this sense of a peaceful stasis:

> And round about, before her feet there sate
> A beuie of faire Virgins clad in white,
> That goodly seem'd t'adorne her royall state,
> All louely daughters of high *Ioue,* that hight
> *Litæ,* by him begot in loues delight,
> Vpon the righteous *Themis:* those they say
> Vpon *Ioues* iudgement seat wayt day and night,
> And when in wrath he threats the worlds decay,
> They doe his anger calme, and cruell vengeance stay.
>   (V.ix.31)

One recalls the picture of Astraea during the Golden Age, sitting "high ador'd with solemne feasts" (V.Proem.9). But if Mercilla represents a new Astraea, the peace which she has

---

such subjects as "An Judex debet judicare secundum allegata & probata, contra Conscientiam?" and even more significantly, "An licet in Christiana Republica dissimulare in Causa Religionis?" (Nichols, *The Progresses and Public Processions of Queen Elizabeth, 3,* 158–59).

introduced depends on a precarious balance of action and inaction. It is not for her to expect the unconstrained obedience to her judgment which Astraea had enjoyed in her time. Rather, if she is to minimize the violence and turmoil which she has inherited as a condition of life, it is by means of a subtle mingling of strict justice with the restraining powers of prudence and mercy.

For Artegall self-control has meant a single-minded devotion to the performance of his role. Mercilla's temperance is of a different order, for it balances justice against the opposing ideal of mercy, and recognizes the demands of each: it tempers justice with mercy. The peace which her rule has made possible entails a broader understanding than that enjoyed by Artegall as an agent of Justice; it is in the light of this broader understanding that the concluding incidents of Book V must be viewed. Artegall himself continues to act as the champion of an untempered justice: decisive action is still necessary, and there is nothing culpable about his continued pursuit of evildoers. But it is now clear that he is an agent of a larger policy. This is emphasized by the name of Irena, the maiden on whose behalf he has undertaken his quest against Grantorto. In a limited sense her name may be an anagram of Ierne, or Ireland, the scene of Lord Grey's rigorous policies. But she may also be viewed as a representative of the Peace[13] which was the most surprising aspect of Elizabeth's reign. As a servant of that peace, Artegall can enjoy only a limited victory, putting down the major sources of injustice and then moving on to other tasks in other places. Though blameless—Detraction and Envy cannot hurt him—he is only part of a larger pattern.[14]

The presentation of the motif of the Golden Age in Book V

13. The existence of an Eirene in this sense at Mercilla's court (V.ix.32) does not seem to me to exclude such a secondary meaning to Irena's name.
14. In this connection, Samuel C. Chew, *The Virtues Reconciled: An Iconographic Study* (Toronto, University of Toronto Press, 1947), offers a summary of the traditional conflict between Justice and Mercy, frequently expanded to include Truth as an ally of Justice and Peace as an ally of Mercy.

goes far beyond the simple nostalgia which many readers have emphasized. Far from representing a momentary intrusion of personal sentiment, it may be seen as a carefully developed contrast that points to the central movement of the poem's action. Man's original state of innocent communion with his environment is symbolic of what in a fallen world can only be realized as a spiritual state. The view of human history and of human capability which this fact implies helps in turn to explain certain aspects of Spenser's treatment of the chivalric milieu of *The Faerie Queene*.

The insufficiency of Artegall's viewpoint is expressed through a series of comparisons with other figures which are developed —or hinted—with a bewildering simultaneity. Indeed, it may be that the imaginative failure of Book V derives from its very complexity of imagery, unguided by any single, dominant strain. There is the expected comparison with Arthur, as in other Books of the poem, but with the added qualification that Artegall (as his name may suggest[15]) is perhaps Arthur's "equal" in his dynastic role as well as in his task of adjudicating conflicting claims among the characters from other Books (as at the marriage of Marinell and Florimell). And there is the more complex comparison with Britomart, involving not only the modified view of Justice described above, but more obscurely hinted sexual parallelism which echoes motifs from earlier Books.

The vision accorded Britomart at Isis Church prior to her encounter with Radigund is in itself a dream allegory which educates her to a clearer sense of her personal destiny. This vision also sheds light on her perilous closeness to the condition of her opponent, who has similarly vanquished Artegall (cf. Britomart's victory in IV.iv) without gaining him as lover. The opening stanzas of canto vii spell out with unusual literalness the "meaning" of Isis and Osiris. Most real, Spenser begins, is the divinity of "this same vertue, that doth right define";

15. Nelson, *The Poetry of Edmund Spenser*, p. 257.

Justice is the means by which Jove "containes his heauenly Common-weale":

> Well therefore did the antique world inuent,
>   That Iustice was a God of soueraine grace,
>   And altars vnto him, and temples lent,
>   And heauenly honours in the highest place;
>   Calling him great *Osyris*, of the race
>   Of th'old Ægyptian Kings, that whylome were;
>   With fayned colours shading a true case:
>   For that *Osyris*, whilest he liued here,
> The iustest man aliue, and truest did appeare.

> His wife was *Isis*, whom they likewise made
>   A Goddesse of great powre and souerainty,
>   And in her person cunningly did shade
>   That part of Iustice, which is Equity,
>   Whereof I haue to treat here presently.
>
> (V.vii.2–3)

The human Osiris gives his name to the virtue considered anthropomorphically as a deity. The pairing of husband and wife, Justice and Equity, is further associated with that of Sun and Moon, "For that they both like race in equall iustice runne."

The euhemerism of Spenser's account of the Egyptian myth[16] at the midpoint of Book V has some relevance to the Proem's treatment of the world's apparent decline. It will be recalled that the astronomical evidence was drawn partly from the authority of "those Ægyptian wisards old" (V.Proem.8), and some doubt seemed directed against the bases of their judgment. Here, in contrast, Jove's heavens are simply said to be contained, "rul'd by righteous lore." If the contradiction is conscious, Spenser must be answering his own challenge of mutability in the heavens. In any case, the carefully reasoned tone of the present

---

16. Spenser may be relying on Plutarch's account in *De Iside et Osiride*. Cf. Jean Seznec, *The Survival of the Pagan Gods* (New York, Pantheon Books, 1953).

passage suggests that Spenser is now concerned with demonstrating the means by which a purely pragmatic, repressive
view of Justice can be transcended. His answer, Britomart's
dream, is like that adopted by the antique world in forming a
cult of Osiris and Isis: to create an imaginative fusion of several
loosely related pairs, held together by the analogy with a sexual
synthesis of opposites.

The dream receives its orthodox, "allegorical" interpretation at the hands of the priest the following morning. The
obvious aptness of this interpretation to the theme of Book V as
well as to the traditional iconography of the Isis and Osiris
myths suffices to allay the sense of dismay and foreboding with
which Britomart first responds. Yet Britomart, for all her heroic
valor in other confrontations, and the unqualified indignation
with which she repudiates Malacasta's incautious advances
(III.i.62) and confronts Busyrane's images of lust (III.xii.29),
shows a conspicuous tendency to be upset by the thought of her
future husband. The vision of bearing a lion by one's crocodile
suitor might be enough to give any chaste virgin pause; but for
Britomart this is only the most bizarre of a series of reports
concerning Artegall. Her original vision of him, in Merlin's
mirror (III.ii.25ff.), has led her to compare herself to Narcissus,
in love with a self-generated shadow: the imagery of Book III
has in fact explored the problem of love as a threat to personal
integrity in just these terms of the confusion of sexual distinctions, and the resistance to love on the part of those who see
in it (as for Marinell) only the risk to the self.

In the present instance, the sexual connotations of Britomart's
dream are implied largely as a result of the location of the
episode. In the preceding canto Britomart has shown herself
to be weak and irrational in her response to Talus' news, and
on leaving Isis Church she proceeds to a confrontation with
Radigund in which the two Amazons are evenly paired, "As
when a Tygre and a Lyonesse/ Are met at spoyling of some
hungry pray."[17] By techniques similar to those employed in

17. Hamilton, *Structure of Allegory*, p. 172.

describing the battle of Redcross and Sans Joy (I.v.1ff.), Spenser suggests the extent to which Britomart may be fighting a battle against forces within herself: to restore her beloved to his proper masculine role, she must destroy the misdirected lust represented by the Amazon. In battle the two women are seen as equally reckless in their disregard for femininity:

> But through great fury both their skill forgot,
> And practicke vse in armes: ne spared not
> Their dainty parts, which nature had created
> So faire and tender, without staine or spot,
> For other vses, then they them translated;
> Which they now hackt and hewd, as if such vse they
> hated.
>
> (V.vii.29)

Britomart's victory resists translation into rational abstract terms: hers is the paradoxical task of using her reign over Radigund's victims to repeal the usurped liberty of women and restore them to male subjection. In this one might read no more than a rather unimaginative allusion to the necessity of distinguishing between the exceptional, legitimate Virgin and/or Queen, like Elizabeth, and the general rule against such inversions of the normal order of nature. What seems to make Britomart rather more interesting in her own right is her tendency here, as in Book III, to respond with feminine and even girlish uncertainty to such revelations of her destiny. She does not take her allegorical role for granted—like Mercilla, for instance—and hence what happens to her has a sentimental value as well. The effect is a double perspective that enriches the texture of Book V, especially as regards the protagonists' relationship to their symbolic roles. The value of the Isis Church vision, for example, is not exhausted by the priest's explanation. We have already been reminded that Osiris and Isis were man and wife before they were made emblems of Justice. Britomart herself subjects her dream to a variety of interpretations, "With thousand thoughts feeding her fantasie"; and the reader likewise is reminded of various images elsewhere in the poem—

Duessa with her Apocalyptic beast controlling Redcross, or
Venus containing the Boar while cherishing Adonis. Such reminders do not direct our understanding of Britomart's role
in a positive sense, so much as they suggest the dangers of too
simple a translation of an abstract, celestial virtue into anthropomorphic terms. Or again, if we people the skies with mythical
creatures, we must expect them to show a certain sublunary
degree of error, as the Proem has lamented.

The battles at the end of Book V are filled with half-suggested
parallels of this sort. The battle with the Souldan in canto viii
entails Artegall's disguise as a Pagan knight; Arthur and the
Souldan confront each other "With like fierce minds, but meanings different," in terms which recall again the ambiguous
opposition of Sans Joy and Redcross.[18] As a figure of unbridled
obsession, the Souldan in his fall before Arthur's exposed shield
is compared to Phaethon and more conspicuously to Hippolytus,
similarly the victim of his own ungovernable steeds: "So was
this Souldan rapt and all to rent,/ That of his shape appear'd
no litle moniment" (V.viii.43; cf. I.v.38).

To these two mythological parallels, which appear throughout the poem as images of ambitious self-indulgence, a third
—that of the Thracian Diomedes—is added in the case of the
Souldan:

> Like to the *Thracian* Tyrant, who they say
>   Vnto his horses gaue his guests for meat,
>   Till he himselfe was made their greedie pray,
>   And torne in peeces by *Alcides* great.
>   So thought the Souldan in his follies threat,
>   Either the Prince in peeces to haue torne
>   With his sharpe wheeles, in his first rages heat,
>   Or vnder his fierce horses feet haue borne
> And trampled downe in dust his thoughts disdained
>   scorne.
>   (V.viii.31)

18. *Ibid.,* p. 177. The ironic parallelism is further stressed in stanza 35,
when Arthur is said to be roaring like a mad lion.

A likely source for this allusion is found in *Metamorphoses* 9.194ff., where the dying Hercules recalls his acts as a champion of Justice. These deeds include not only the destruction of Diomedes, but other episodes which figure prominently as metaphors in *The Faerie Queene:* those with Antaeus, Busiris, Cerberus, and Geryon. Though neither Artegall nor Arthur is the object of any consistent or exclusive parallel with Hercules, it should be noted that Herculean imagery is important to the poem, especially in relation to the classical pole of motivation, the virtues of restraint or control. As a figure in the tradition of Bacchus and Hercules (V.i.2), Artegall is particularly close to the antique heroes: he wears (or will wear) the armor of Achilles,[19] according to Britomart's vision of him (III.ii.25); he resembles Mars and Achilles and Hercules in his effeminate submission to Radigund (and Britomart); and his savage rusticity leads him more frequently than other of Spenser's protagonists to recall Hercules, the most rugged and least wily of heroes, bearing as his chief attributes the lion skin and "club of Iustice dread."

References to Hercules in *The Faerie Queene* are persistent but intermittent, often dimly felt rather than explicitly stated. The twelve Labors may be suggested in the poem's twelve-part structure; references to them sometimes appear in the specific quests of individual Books. But Arthur, though he appears throughout the poem in his search for Gloriana, does not earn her through any precise imitation of Hercules. His role as an aid in synthesizing the various concerns of the poem makes him larger than Hercules in his implications. In general, though, Hercules may be felt to provide a useful reference point for classical virtue in its most polarized form:[20] his relative lack of sophistication and reliance on native strength make him a

19. Kathleen Williams, "Venus and Diana: Some Uses of Myth in *The Faerie Queene*," *ELH, 28* (1961), 101–20.

20. Cf. Erwin Panofsky, *Hercules am Scheidewege und andere antike Bildstoffe in der neueren Kunst* (Leipzig, Teubner, 1930).

particularly "pure" and consistent figure of a virtue considered to derive from force (*vis*) and virility.

Though it is doubtless futile to speculate on the possible nature of the subsequent Books of *The Faerie Queene*—Spenser's mastery of technique leaves him especially free to choose his subject matter as he goes along—it is at least conceivable that the promised union of Arthur and Gloriana, with its implied synthesis of the two realms of Faery and Briton, might have made further use of Hercules in his role as the liberator of Prometheus. In any case, Hercules' life seems to guide the Faeries much as that of Christ informs the Britons. Thus the poem provides a view of moral involvement which compares imitations of Hercules with imitations of Christ, virtues of control with virtues of love.

To some extent, too, the contrast between Hercules and Christ, like that between Belphoebe and Amoret, is between the two faces of primitivism, between the Wild Man, denizen of the forests and teacher of the stern lessons of self-reliance to overcivilized man, and the Shepherd whose apparent removal from the pressures of courtly society gives him the *otium* in which to pursue the restorative and integrating arts of love. In his figurative representations, Hercules' club and lion skin occasionally led to his confusion with the medieval wild man.[21] And in this same context, Hercules' choice of an active life contrasts with Christ's more passive, if no less heroic, virtue.

In a number of ways, then, Book V may be seen as a preparation for Book VI, which it requires for an imaginatively satisfying resolution of the issues which it has so obscurely raised. The Herculean Artegall is surrounded by images suggesting a more inclusive virtue than he at present possesses. Though we know from Merlin's account to Britomart (III.iii.26) that he is no Faery but, like Redcross, a changeling, his role in Book V does not require his knowledge of this fact. Within his present limitations of knowledge and action he can enjoy security from

21. Bernheimer, *Wild Men in the Middle Ages,* pp. 101 ff.

the libellous Blatant Beast (V.xii.42); he is rather like Guyon in his smugness. But he is also bound to the unpredictable demands of Gloriana, and he cannot yet see his destiny. Though his world touches on issues of religious allegiance (Burbon, whom he rescues and restores to a life of virtue as Guyon does Verdant, is restored to a specifically Protestant virtue, for he owns his armor from Redcross), he tends to resolve these issues in secular terms of fidelity to one's received identity. And his victory over Grantorto, though it is absolute, is so briefly and even casually described as to be anticlimactic: "He lightly reft his head, to ease him of his paine" (V.xii.23). The image of Justice as a sexual union of opposite forces has been fostered by the marriage themes in Book V; but Artegall is still far from his own marriage when the Book concludes. At this point it appears that Justice must be seen in terms of the bonds that knit society; and the opening cantos of Book VI provide through their repetition of situations from Book V a new perspective on the world which Artegall had evaluated from his own severely limited viewpoint.

5. *Wild Man and Shepherd*

The introductory episodes of Book VI, prior to Calidore's abrupt disappearance in the middle of the third canto, trace the operation of Courtesy within a specifically chivalric milieu. A virtue that draws its name from the court and is rightly called the "roote of ciuill conuersation" (in a broader sense than is at first apparent), Courtesy is first examined in terms of the rules of polite behavior. The antagonists presented in these early cantos pretend to be adhering to the forms of chivalry even when—like Crudor and Briana—they are grossly violating its principles. Calidore, the titular patron of Courtesy, variously employs both tact and force to correct the mistaken appeals to rank and the unwarranted assumptions of personal dignity and freedom which have offended the dignity and freedom of others. He is asked to discriminate between conflicting imputations of shame; his judgments constantly emphasize that courtesy is better expressed by generous and positive actions than by niggling adherence to superficial and largely negative formalities. He rebukes Priscilla for her squeamish reluctance to carry Aladine to shelter; he acquits Tristram of his failure to observe due respect for rank as against the more important consideration of avenging injustice; he turns aside the charges of murder and "treason" which Briana has directed against him:

> Bloud is no blemish; for it is no blame
> To punish those, that doe deserue the same;
> But they that breake bands of ciuilitie,
> And wicked customes make, those doe defame
> Both noble armes and gentle curtesie.
> No greater shame to man then inhumanitie.
>
> (VI.i.26)

Subsequent episodes of Book VI portray Courtesy as the principal motive in man's collective efforts toward civilization, the expression on the social plane of man's awareness of his own "humanity" and of the dignity and responsibility which that awareness entails. First, however, Spenser presents Courtesy in its more conventional aspects. Calidore is here shown as a Renaissance Courtier, adept not only in the manners of his court but in the principles which inform them. It is not surprising that students of Spenser's indebtedness to the ideal courtiers described by Castiglione, Della Casa, or Guazzo, should rely heavily for their evidence on the incidents of these early cantos, in which the conventions of chivalric behavior form the subject of a running debate between Calidore and his opponents.[1] In the later episodes of Book VI this debt is of minor importance, for Spenser is less concerned with the excellences of an ideal court—Gloriana's court is never presented directly, here or in any other book of the poem—than with the radical threats posed to man's precarious estate. Only after carefully distinguishing between virtuous and vicious manners or usages, and showing that courtly manners, rightly understood, may be an expression of Courtesy in its deeper sense of a generous, "gracious" motive, does the poem indicate the more

1. Cf. *Variorum 6*, Appendix I, 317–48.

serious threats directed against the virtue; first by its defect and
excess (seen respectively in the churlish Turpine and the syco-
phantic Blandina) and then by the more radically "inhuman"
qualities represented by the savages, the pirates, and the Blatant
Beast itself.

Significantly, Calidore is described from the outset as combining "gentlenesse of spright" with a physical presence that
enables him "To please the best, and th'euill to embase" (VI.i.3).
Whether this emphasis on his martial vigor is an indication of
his descent from the standard continental descriptions of the
Courtier, or a reminder of the heroic Sidney, or a simple and
obvious necessity in view of the chivalric action, he is clearly
a fitting successor to Artegall with regard to knightly valor.
More importantly, his training and personal disposition give
him qualities which had been lacking in his predecessor. In
his fallen world, Artegall cannot hope for an unqualified success: his is at most a corrective role, which is necessarily interrupted before the "ragged common-weale" can be thoroughly
reformed. It is thus that Artegall appears in the opening scene
of Book VI, "yet halfe sad/ From his late conquest, which he
gotten had" (VI.i.4). And it is with an awareness of the problems
and limitations of their respective quests that Calidore responds
to the story of his predecessor's accomplishments:

> Now happy man (sayd then Sir *Calidore*)
> Which haue so goodly, as ye can deuize,
> Atchieu'd so hard a quest, as few before;
> That shall you most renowned make for euermore.
>
> But where ye ended haue, now I begin
> To tread an endlesse trace, withouten guyde,
> Or good direction, how to enter in . . .
>
> (VI.i.5–6)

In themselves, these lines may simply show Calidore's characteristic tact and courtesy in contrasting Artegall's good fortune with his own uncertainty and difficulties. Yet it is probably

more than politeness that causes Calidore to lament, a few lines
later, that he must look forward to

> . . . labours long and wide,
> In which although good Fortune me befall,
> Yet shall it not by none be testifyde.

(VI.i.6)

Artegall's slaughter of Grantorto, though it has not sufficed
to restore perfect Justice, has at least been an unqualified success in its own right. The individual tyrant can be killed, injustice can be pursued with the sword, and on this level of action
permanent victories can be achieved. But the Blatant Beast
appears to be immortal. Calidore speaks not of killing him, but
simply of pursuing him, of hoping to "ouertake, or else subdew"
him. At the end of his quest the most he can do is restrain the
Beast temporarily. However much modesty and tact we may
assign Calidore in his conversation with Artegall, it seems
reasonable to assume that this same conversation is intended to
illuminate the relationship between the two heroes. This assumption is supported by the prominence given to the transitional episodes at the end of Book V and at the beginning of
Book VI.

Earlier in the poem, at the Tournament of the Girdle, Artegall appeared as a savage knight, bearing as his motto *Sal-
uagesse sans finesse* (IV.iv.39); the description of his education
suggests the appropriateness of this disguise. In the wilderness
he is trained by Astraea in "all the discipline of iustice"; and in
the absence of human subjects he is led by her

> . . . to make experience
> Vpon wyld beasts, which she in woods did find,
> With wrongfull powre oppressing others of their kind.

(V.i.7)

Feared alike by men and wild beasts, Artegall appropriately
achieves his quest on "the saluage Island," as he calls Irena's
home in speaking to Calidore (VI.i.9). His education has not

encouraged him to speculate too closely on the differences separating mankind from the lower creatures: the principles of Justice are not concerned with such distinctions. His misadventure with Radigund further suggests that his lack of analytical "finesse" seriously limits his capacity to temper his pursuit of a rigorous justice. Given the logic of his viewpoint, a rigid consistency, however ruthless, seems the only possible course for him to follow.

Artegall's isolation from the concerns of civilized society explains his indifference to Detraction, Envy, and the Blatant Beast:

> And still among most bitter wordes they spake,
> Most shamefull, most vnrighteous, most vntrew,
> That they the mildest man aliue would make
> Forget his patience, and yeeld vengeaunce dew
> To her, that so false sclaunders at him threw.
> And more to make them pierce and wound more
> deepe,
> She with the sting, which in her vile tongue grew,
> Did sharpen them, and in fresh poyson steepe:
> Yet he past on, and seem'd of them to take no keepe.
> (V.xii.42)

If the threat posed by Calidore's ultimate adversary is to be evaluated solely on the basis of his effect on Artegall, then the pursuit of the Blatant Beast is of trivial importance. But the events of Book V have already indicated the ultimate need of tempering "pure" justice with mercy, and have suggested that Artegall's role, though essential to a healthy society, deprives him of any balanced view of the social context within which he operates. The ending of Book V, rather like that of Book II, shows the hero in a hurry to return home, unwilling to concern himself with a problem which is not properly his. The implications of these two concluding incidents differ widely, and Gryll's obstinate bestiality does not anticipate the theme of the following book, as do the slanders cast against Artegall.

But the incidents resemble one another in their emphasis on
the need of returning from island to mainland "whilest wether
serues and wind," of employing the same self-control and single-
mindedness which have accomplished the quest, to resist any
temptation to extend the victory. And like Guyon, Artegall
tends to be self-righteously aware of his own invulnerability,
to the point of complacency; as he tells Calidore, "I that knew
myself from perill free,/ Did nought regard his malice nor his
powre . . ." (VI.i.9).

Calidore would be unlikely to express a sentiment of this
order. Obviously he possesses the "finesse" that Artegall so
conspicuously lacks. This finesse is apparent not so much in
his practical skill (for the incident with Sanglier has clearly
attributed to Artegall the judiciousness of a Solomon), as in the
authority with which he evaluates an individual or a situation.
He is a product of Gloriana's court, and embodies its refine-
ment as a consequence less of his education (about which nothing is said), than of his innate gifts:

> In whom it seemes, that gentlenesse of spright
> And manners mylde were planted naturall;
> To which he adding comely guize withall,
> And gracious speach, did steale mens hearts away.
>
> (VI.i.2)

His experience has been acquired not among wild beasts, but
among men, and his talent is to recognize the true conditions of
men and to accord fitting treatment to all:

> Ne was there Knight, ne was there Lady found
>   In Faery court, but him did deare embrace,
>   For his faire vsage and conditions sound,
>   The which in all mens liking gayned place,
>   And with the greatest purchast greatest grace:
>   Which he could wisely vse, and well apply,
>   To please the best, and th'euill to embase.

> For he loathd leasing, and base flattery,
> And loued simple truth and stedfast honesty.
>
> (VI.i.3)

The episodes of the first three cantos illuminate this description of Calidore, and justify the inclusion of Courtesy among the twelve moral virtues. In presenting Courtesy as a virtue of sufficient magnitude to warrant comparison with the five already treated in his poem, Spenser assumes a double burden: first, of giving that virtue a significance beyond its conventional implications regarding courtly behavior, and secondly, of relating these conventional implications to that larger significance. In combination, these two responsibilities explain why Calidore is not shown in his role at court, or more precisely, why his training there is not discussed at length. Spenser's broader definition of Courtesy pertains to mankind's attempts to rise above its animal aspects toward the divine. Civilization appears as man's collective striving upward in this sense, and the question of rank or degree is related to the cultural or spiritual attainment of the given individual. The courteous man is skilled in evaluating the worth of others and in according to each an appropriate respect. But Gloriana's court, by its definition, already offers an unexceptionable recognition of human merit: social rank and intrinsic worth are indistinguishable there. Consequently, Calidore's behavior at court would be a test not of his capacity to interpret appearances, but simply of his skill at budgeting his graces according to a recognized scale of values.

The relationship between conventional courtesy and its broader implications is therefore to be explored not at Gloriana's court but in the outer world of chivalric activity, with its deceptions and confusions which demand interpretation and correction. Consequently, after the briefest introduction of terms which will subsequently have a broader range of connotations —"ciuill conuersation," "gentlenesse of spright," "gracious" and "grace," "faire vsage"—Calidore takes up a quest which, unlike Artegall's, leads to no fixed place. Indeed this quest offers no probability of an unqualified victory, since its object is identified with no single outrage. The Blatant Beast, whose indiscriminate annoyance not merely of knights and ladies but of all orders of society betokens the universality of Calidore's problem, is not approached by a predictable route. The meeting between Calidore and Artegall underscores the uncertainty with which the new quest is undertaken. This uncertainty is not merely the product of Calidore's modesty, but more importantly the result of his awareness of the slender bonds which Courtesy must preserve and strengthen.

As a figure of human bestiality, the Blatant Beast is at once the most and the least formidable of the poem's major antagonists. His infernal origins and infrahuman form suggest a comparison with the Dragon of Book I; but his different scope indicates how profoundly the poem's frame of reference has changed. Strong in the Faith and nourished by Providence, Redcross can achieve a transcendent, definitive victory over the challenge of a fallen Nature. He has learned from his first experience in the Wood of Error that man is surrounded by highly ambiguous emblems, and he has found within himself a similarly infected physical nature. But he has been further educated in the workings of a beneficent Providence, and has been given a vision of a New Jerusalem lying beyond the realm of Death. Accordingly, he triumphs over an opponent who represents the totality of hostile elements in man's environment. Where the catalogue of trees in I.i had naïvely seen Nature as orderly and friendly, the Dragon now sums up the opposing view of Nature as wholly brutish and bent on man's destruction: he is "like a great hill" (I.xi.4); his scales reflect heaven's light and turn it back on itself; he cheerfully addresses himself to battle like a "chauffed Bore" (I.xi.15). Redcross overcomes this force by seeing that it is an incomplete view of Nature, as much so as had been his earlier, wholly naturalist faith, and by drawing assistance from the Well and Tree of Life. Seen in terms of the Christian scheme of salvation, Death loses its sting; it is killed by the act of understanding which denies its power.

But if the Dragon represents mutability's threat to the self, Calidore's opponent challenges something less durable, the fragile texture of human community. The transcendent victory is possible with regard to the purely personal challenge. One must be a Puritan in defending one's private integrity, even to the point of recognizing (like Spenser through Guyon, or like Milton's Christ in *Paradise Regained*) the stage at which the poetic vision itself must be repudiated. But the successive Books of *The Faerie Queene* have moved toward an increasing concern for the values of human achievement, however precarious. The view of Ate at the beginning of Book IV stresses the destruction of both cities and private relationships: tokens of betrayal deck her walls, "Their girlonds rent, their bowres despoyled all" (IV.i.24). Where it had previously been a means to personal integrity, Puritanism seems now to be a force destructive of the bonds of friendship or "ciuilitie"; though the Blatant Beast surely includes more than an indictment of Elizabeth's Puritans, his indiscriminate railing does suggest an iconoclasm so radical as to ravage both Church and State (VI.xii.25–28).

In stature the Beast seems closer to the minor antagonists of preceding Books, to the gnatlike perturbations of the flesh to which man is inextricably subject, which can sometimes be temporarily defeated by various means but more often must be borne in silence and avoided wherever possible. Such he is to Artegall. In confronting him, Calidore champions those who find the Beast a menace—individuals who like Timias or Serena lack Artegall's self-confidence and in surrendering themselves to amorous commitments leave themselves vulnerable to festering wounds of reproach. Calidore's sense of the value of human intercourse gives meaning and substance to the Blatant Beast. Repeatedly in Book VI he sees the interruption of idyllic moments; sometimes he himself inadvertently plays the Beast's role of rending the bonds, as when he intrudes on Calepine and Serena or on Colin's vision. It seems that the Blatant Beast includes among his thousand tongues, "Of sundry kindes, and sundry quality" (VI.xii.27), many which are less consciously malevolent than self-righteously reproachful without regard for the consequence. To control such a beast requires a high degree of personal forbearance, even within the "antique" context of Fairyland; in the actual world it is clearly impossible.

In Book VI diplomacy is less a technique than a symbol, and Spenser does not show Calidore's exquisite tact simply in order to make him more convincing as a Renaissance courtier. More significantly, he suggests that the cohesiveness of society depends on its willingness to look beyond superficial differences of rank or circumstance, to the basic relationships underlying these differences. A strict regard for the privileges of rank, or even for factual detail, is less important than an awareness of the considerations of mutual self-respect which are essential bases for any human communion. Spenser anatomizes these considerations in the introductory episodes of Book VI by showing how ill-considered are the tendencies of certain individuals to assume freedoms which by their nature deprive others of more important rights.

The introductory episodes of any given Book suggest the outlines of the virtue under consideration. All tend to draw heavily on traditional exempla, maxims, and commonplace chivalric situations; they all tend, for obvious reasons of decorum, to be of secondary dramatic importance with respect to the main purpose of the quest, and to provide the hero with opportunities to demonstrate his virtuosity, usually with little danger of failure. But the incidents of the first cantos of Book VI warrant more detailed comparison with the corresponding incidents of Book V, with regard to the intrinsic nature of the challenges facing the heroes of these two Books. Allowing for transposition of detail and for obvious differences in the implications of these challenges as they are interpreted by the heroes, the reader may still note the appearance of roughly similar characters in both Books: a squire whose relative weakness in arms renders him powerless to defend his lady against an oppressor (V.i.13ff.; VI.i.11ff.); a proud, discourteous knight who kills or mistreats his own lady after he has come on another couple "in ioyous iolliment/ Of their franke loues," and seeks to avail himself of the other lady (V.i.16ff.; VI.ii.16ff.); and an oppressor who plunders travellers for the sake of a lady (V.ii.4ff.; VI.i.15ff.).[2] Calidore and Artegall seem to address themselves to problems which differ more in degree than in kind, and which offer grounds for comparing their different approaches to generally similar conditions.

Most importantly, Calidore tries to reform offenders whenever possible, while Artegall moves decisively and forcefully against injustice with little concern for the feelings of his victims. Thus Sanglier in Book V is made to bear the shameful burden of his lady's severed head with obvious ill humour, and is treated by Talus like a "rated Spaniell." The animal imagery is appropriate in this case: Artegall continually shows the effects of his education. In Artegall's world wild beasts oppress others of their kind, and his answer to this situation is expressed in his attributes of golden sword and iron servant. Calidore indirectly derives his approach to human wrongdoing from the view of tempered justice suggested by Mercilla:

> For if that Vertue be of so great might,
>   Which from iust verdict will for nothing start,
>   But to preserue inuiolated right,
>   Oft spilles the principall, to saue the part;
>   So much more then is that of powre and art,
>   That seekes to saue the subiect of her skill,
>   Yet neuer doth from doome of right depart:
>   As it is greater prayse to saue, then spill,
> And better to reforme, then to cut off the ill.

>   (V.x.2)

Where the first canto of Book V concludes with the spectacle of the once proud Sanglier ignominiously bearing the badge

2. This last parallel may seem more remote, since Maleffort and Pollente have little in common. But such verbal details as the mention of hair in both cases, together with the emphasis on Munera's pride and her refusal to marry any of her suitors, combine to suggest a general similarity between the two scenes, though scarcely one that will reward closer analysis.

of his shame, the first canto of Book VI ends with the reformation of Briana and Crudor.

It is significant of Calidore's approach to the disorders of civilization that the "shamefull vse" of Briana is traced to an interruption in the free interflow of courtesy which throughout the Book is taken as the image of civilization:

> She long time hath deare lou'd a doughty Knight,
> And sought to win his loue by all the meanes she
>   might.

> His name is *Crudor,* who through high disdaine
> And proud despight of his self pleasing mynd,
> Refused hath to yeeld her loue againe,
> Vntill a Mantle she for him doe fynd,
> With beards of Knights and locks of Ladies lynd.
>   (VI.i.14–15)

Crudor's churlish obstinacy recalls similar motives in Book V— Bellodant's indifference to Radigund, or Munera's proud disdain for her suitors—but here the refusal to return the gift of love is expressed in terms that anticipate the vision of the Graces. The emphasis throughout Book VI is on the positive responsibilities of mankind: men are blamed not so much for what they do as for what they refuse to do. In this respect there is an obvious contrast with Artegall's more negative virtue, which represses wrongdoing and in this sense is limited to separating the tyrant from his victim. Thus Artegall's sword finds its counterpart in these "bands of ciuilitie" which constitute Calidore's chief concern.

Calidore's approach to the unhappy Squire here indicates the peculiar importance which he attaches to fortune as a result of these more positive diplomatic concerns. Once he has freed the Squire from his bonds he interrogates him as follows:

> Vnhappy Squire, what hard mishap thee brought
> Into this bay of perill and disgrace?

> What cruell hand thy wretched thraldome wrought,
> And thee captyued in this shamefull place?
> To whom he answerd thus; My haplesse case
> Is not occasiond through my misdesert,
> But through misfortune, which did me abase
> Vnto this shame, and my young hope subuert,
> Ere that I in her guilefull traines was well expert.
>
> (VI.i.12)

This emphasis on fortune as the determining factor in human situations, rather than on considerations of human desert or blame, is repeated at the close of this incident, when Calidore lectures Crudor on the need for mercy:

> All flesh is frayle, and full of ficklenesse,
> Subiect to fortunes chance, still chaunging new;
> What haps to day to me, to morrow may to you.
>
> (VI.i.41)

In both instances, it is clear that this line of discussion furthers Calidore's more positive goals, by distracting the victim from a sense of the shamefulness of his position and hence from any desire for revenge, and by emphasizing man's common vulnerability to the caprices of Fortune and his consequent need for solidarity in confronting this challenge. It is precisely as a result of the role played by fortune in human affairs that the chivalric ethic demands that the strong and/or lucky knight avoid pride and cruelty by tempering his demands with a merciful restraint. This need for mercy is in fact the major point of Calidore's speech to Crudor:

> Who will not mercie vnto others shew,
> How can he mercy euer hope to haue?
> To pay each with his owne is right and dew.
> Yet since ye mercie now doe need to craue,
> I will it graunt, your hopelesse life to saue.
>
> (VI.i.42)

By means of this appeal to the common cause of mankind in the face of chance, or mutability, Calidore seeks to repair the broken bonds of courtesy, and to build a world in which love and lesser "gifts" are freely offered, received, and rendered anew.

Yet any simple contrast of Artegall and Calidore is obviously impossible. There is as much bloodshed in Calidore's world as in Artegall's. The "counterpart" of Sanglier suggested earlier is not Crudor, who can be reformed, but the "proud discourteous knight" who has been killed by Tristram and has therefore received a rather more decisive punishment than that meted out to Sanglier by Artegall. In this connection, it should be stressed that the virtue which forms the subject of Book VI is not Mercy. Consequently Calidore does not complement Artegall in the sense that Mercy complements or tempers Justice in the Christian ethic. Rather, the contrast between these two heroes suggests that the one does in fact pick up where the other has left off, in that Calidore is operating in a world which resembles Artegall's with regard to the varieties of social disturbance requiring attention. He accepts the validity of his predecessor's approach: "A shamefull vse as euer I did heare,/ Sayd *Calidore* [about Crudor's demands], and to be ouerthrowne" (VI.i.14). And he is careful to admonish Briana, reminding her that blood shed in the pursuit of justice "is no blemish." But he is engaged in a quest that is beyond Artegall's capacity. Just as Artegall's self-confidence has given him an impenetrable defense against the Blatant Beast, so his exclusive concern with suppressing injustice and asserting the rule of law has deprived him of any positive ability to assist man in his task of self-education beyond his natural state of freedom, toward the achievement of community.

This contrast between positive and negative approaches implicit in the natures of Calidore and Artegall, and in the virtues with which they are associated, suggests a similar contrast between Redcross and Guyon, this time on the level of the individual rather than on that of society. In this connection Wood-

house's familiar contrast of Nature and Grace in Books I and
II may be relevant beyond the superficial appropriateness of
these terms to Artegall's connections with the wilderness, and to
Calidore's complementary talents. Obviously, it is unwise to
attempt any simple identification of the "grace" emphasized in
Book VI (the social grace of the courteous man, the classical
Graces who appear to Calidore) with the theological Grace
central to the Christian dispensation. Courtesy, unlike Holiness, can be portrayed adequately within the classical mythology available to Fairyland; it may be for this reason that
Calidore himself remains an Elf throughout the Book. But there
is an important area of correspondence between these two concepts of grace: both are gifts which invite reciprocation and
hence lead to the establishment of bonds of communion. Divine
Grace reunites man with God: the victory of Redcross over the
Dragon suggests the harrowing of Hell and the consequent defeat of Death as a permanent separation of man from God. In
the area of personal relationships considered in Books III and
IV, the motives of Friendship and Chaste Affection similarly
provide a positive basis for the union of individuals. In the more
generalized area of societal relationships, the free interchange
of gifts symbolizes the establishment and maintenance of bonds
of civility. Once again in Book VI, then, Love is clearly relevant to the virtue under consideration. Crudor's refusal to
reciprocate Briana's love, and still more conspicuously Mirabella's proud insistence on her own "libertie," provide clear instances of offenses against the spirit of a courteous abandonment of personal freedom in the interest of an exchange of the
gifts bestowed by a gracious Nature.

Calidore's encounter with Crudor and Briana thus introduces
a theme repeated throughout Book VI, as successive incidents
give increasing significance to man's responsibility to respect
the bonds linking him with others. Crudor's reformation, with
his marriage to Briana and his promise to adhere to the spirit
of chivalry by showing mercy to others in recognition of his
own dependence on the graciousness of fortune, represents a

restoration of normality to the chivalric world. Shameful cus-
toms are overthrown and goodly manners replace them. With
Tristram's appearance at the beginning of canto ii, the relevance
of this theme to the development of the individual personality
begins to emerge. In a number of respects Tristram suggests the
character of the incidents that follow. He is a representative of
the Arthurian world, and is the first Briton to appear in Book VI
thus far. He is disguised as a woodsman, but his nobility is
clear from his stature and features, from his clothing, and above
all from the pregnant wit with which he answers Calidore's
questions. Finally, he is a youth trained in "gentle thewes" in
the wilderness and dubbed squire by Calidore. Each of these
three aspects of Tristram's character relates significantly to the
pattern of escape, disguise, and continuing chivalric responsibility developed in the action of Book VI.

As a mortal and an intruder into Fairyland, Tristram is, at
least by implication, a representative of the larger view of
human responsibility embodied in the Christian "magnificence"
of the ubiquitous Arthur, who arrives on the scene in the fifth
canto. Like Arthur, Tristram displays an easy competence,
addressing himself directly and forcefully to the proud knight
whom he sees abusing his lady. But unlike Arthur, he is an
untutored youth, manifestly gifted with the unconcealable traits
of nobility, but limited in his education to the training that he
and his noble feres have acquired in the wilderness. Consequently, his direct approach to discourtesy, though justifiable
and even laudable, lacks the subtlety and diplomacy which
Calidore has demonstrated; it also lacks the equally devious
though far less conciliatory "policy" which Arthur shows toward Turpine. Tristram may in fact be considered an intermediate figure, suggestive of an intentional blurring of distinctions which Spenser has polarized sharply elsewhere. It appears
that the order of chivalry links Faery and Briton: Calidore can
make Tristram his squire, and the relationship symbolized by
this action explains the absence of a specifically Christian imagery in Book VI (even the Hermit in cantos v and vi invokes

classical rather than Biblical authority). It also explains the presence in Calidore of a Grace that resembles divine Grace even though it is obviously operative on the level of human society, and hence has no direct contact with the Christian context. In Book VI there is as yet no formal union of the two worlds, no marriage of Arthur and Gloriana; but there seems to be an *entente cordiale*.

Similarly, the extent to which elements in the incident with Tristram anticipate the full range of succeeding incidents suggests that all the figures in Book VI are involved in a common range of concerns. Tristram's disguise anticipates the figure of the Salvage Man who, though more radically uneducated than Tristram, similarly displays his noble birth and the emotional justness of his actions; this same disguise looks even further ahead to the pastoral disguise that Calidore adopts later. Book VI is studded with disguises of this nature: the Hermit is a former knight who has adopted his role voluntarily as a form of retirement; Pastorella, like the Salvage Man, has a noble background of which she is unaware; the infant whom Calepine saves from the bear and presents to Matilda seems destined to a similar fate; and to reverse the metaphor, even Meliboe has had experience in the Prince's garden and has chosen to return to his simpler life. All these individuals share a mixed identity. None is fully a member of his natural environment, and each bears the responsibility of maintaining a harmony among the diverse parts of his personality.

Within Book VI parallel incidents and rhetoric further extend this sense of a common involvement. Tristram, going on foot while his lady rides her dead knight's horse (VI.ii.39), anticipates Calepine's painful passage with Serena (VI.iii.28). The picture of Arthur asleep with his armor cast aside (VI.vii.19) picks up the repeated emphasis on Calepine's tendency to cast off his own armor (VI.iii.20 and passim). Arthur's fight with Disdain (VI.vii.8ff.) echoes the strategy of Calidore's fight with Crudor (VI.i.33ff.). Arthur, like Tristram and Calidore, rescues a lady whom he sees being mistreated. The individual reader will sense some of these parallels and feel that others are simply coincidental, the result perhaps of the predictability of chivalric subject matter. But the net result seems to be one of a common involvement in circumstances that resemble one another at least as often as they differ. It would be futile to analyze this network of repetitions (some of which are certainly tenuous) as suggestive of a carefully organized anatomizing of the moral allegory. We are probably not meant to ask too closely in what ways Arthur's courtesy resembles or differs from Calepine's, or Calidore's, or Tristram's. Rather, these half-suggested parallels, and more generally the quality described as the structural looseness or the relaxed tone of Book VI as a whole,[3] seem designed to contribute the groundtone of a common chivalric milieu against which the specific concerns of Courtesy may be seen more clearly.

It is Calidore who provides the commentary on the action of these first cantos. As suggested above, his remarks are consistently directed toward the reconciliation of ill-considered antagonisms and the elimination of interference with the free exchange of courtesy on every level. At the opening of the second canto, the narrator defines the courtesy demonstrated by Calidore as the capacity of men

> . . . to beare themselues aright
> To all of each degree, as doth behoue . . .
> For whether they be placed high aboue,
> Or low beneath, yet ought they well to know
> Their good, that none them rightly may reproue
> Of rudenesse, for not yeelding what they owe:
> Great skill it is such duties timely to bestow.
>
> (VI.ii.1)

In Calidore's case this knowledge appears as his ability to see beyond the claims of individuals to the more positive bases of

3. Cf. Bennett, *The Evolution of the "Faerie Queene,"* p. 207: "Book VI has a more reflective tone than is apparent in the other books." Lewis, *The Allegory of Love,* p. 350: "From this stony plateau—for the fifth book would

courtesy on which concerns of etiquette and rank are founded. Surely Calidore is Spenser's most self-effacing hero: the patient diplomacy with which he placates the conceived displeasures of others attends him throughout the Book, and is as conspicuous in his speech to Calepine (VI.iii.22) as in his treatment of Coridon or Colin Clout during his pastoral sojourn. This self-effacement differs from the self-control of such figures as Guyon or Artegall in that it is less an end, or even particularly admirable in itself, then a means to a goal that lies outside the individual and his personal concerns. In the preliminary episodes Calidore has been presented as a skilled courtier restoring harmony in a world where a hero like Artegall has directed his efforts instead to the simple enforcement of order. These episodes tend to suggest the proportions of a virtue

> Which though it on a lowly stalke doe bowre,
> Yet brancheth forth in braue nobilitie,
> And spreds it selfe through all ciuilitie.
>
> (VI.Proem.4)

Furthermore, the structure of Book VI, with Calidore's seemingly unaccountable absence from the central section, becomes significant only in light of the conception of courtesy as a virtue which subordinates personal heroism to the achievement of human community. Calidore—the extraordinarily gifted man who combines graciousness with the physical prowess necessary to impose his standards of behavior on others— is an appropriate arbiter in a society which at least pays lip service to those standards; he is a fitting champion of courtesy against its ultimate opponents. But in order to dramatize more fully the difficulties attached to the painful evolution and main-

---

have been severe even if it had been successful—the sixth leads us down into the gracious valley of Humiliation." Hallett Smith, *Elizabethan Poetry* (Cambridge, Mass., Harvard University Press, 1952), p. 338: "But in Spenser's view Chastity is a more heroic virtue than Courtesy; it is more positive and more capable of representation in a heroic manner."

tenance of a civilized society united by a common acceptance of the principle of courtesy, Spenser temporarily replaces Calidore with a more typical representative of mankind: an individual whose efforts do not inevitably prevail, and whose understanding is limited. Calepine, Calidore's less gifted surrogate, is himself an illustration of one of the dangers inherent in civilization. Tending to rely on the courtesy of others, he is typically shown in a disarmed condition, powerless to combat discourtesy. Dependent on aid from the undomesticated Salvage Man, he prepares the reader for the pastoral episodes which constitute the Book's climax, for he provides graphic evidence that man must never permit his civilization to render him incapable of defending himself against the enemies of that civilization. He and Serena are relatively tame products of a civilized world; their survival is contingent on the tameness of those with whom they come in contract. The central cantos of Book VI emphasize that man must maintain contact with the natural world, with its rigors and its unadorned simplicities, if he is to defend his civilization against the forces for chaos that take nourishment from this same natural world.

Earlier protagonists—Redcross, Guyon, Artegall—experienced a period of inaction during which the exploits of other characters were presented as a means of elaborating the central quest of each Book. But Calidore's disappearance in canto iii is not seen as a personal setback, as had been the case to varying degrees with these others. He is actually in hot pursuit of his quarry during the intervening period until his reappearance in canto ix. His own lapse from duty coincides with his period of education, his pastoral truancy in the later cantos. In its gross organization about a central protagonist and his quest—in the terms postulated by the Letter to Ralegh—Book VI resembles Books I, II, and V; it is further related to these Books through its repetitions of theme and situation to suggest innumerable elements of symmetry shaping the poem's present six-Book structure. But in its looser episodic technique and its reliance on parallel exempla of the virtue rather than a single pattern of quest, frustration, restoration, and fulfillment, it resembles the central Books. Though he performs his expected role, Arthur does not establish contact with Calidore directly. The central cantos of Book VI may be seen as implicitly breaking down the figure of Calidore into the complementary figures of Courtier and Savage, as a means of describing those "bonds of Ciuilitie" which constitute the delicate fabric of society.

CALEPINE AND THE SALVAGE MAN

In the third canto of Book VI Calidore discovers Calepine and Serena under circumstances that clearly recall the earlier scene in which Aladine and Priscilla had been surprised by the proud discourteous knight. The descriptions of these two incidents are extremely close verbally. Only the note of condescension in the mention of Priscilla's beauty betrays the different point of view (that of the proud knight's lady) from which the earlier incident is being narrated:[4]

> This day, as he and I together roade
> Vpon our way, to which we weren bent,
> We chaunst to come foreby a couert glade
> Within a wood, whereas a Ladie gent
> Sate with a knight in ioyous iolliment
> Of their franke loues, free from all gealous spyes:
> Faire was the Ladie sure, that mote content
> An hart, not carried with too curious eyes,
> And vnto him did shew all louely courtesyes.
>
> (VI.ii.16)

---

4. J. W. Mackail, *The Springs of Helicon* (New York, Longmans, Green, and Co., 1909), pp. 125–26 (quoted in *Variorum 6*, 194), stresses the feebleness of VI.ii.16–23: "all as bad as bad can be." It may be noted that in the analogous scene in V.i.13 ff., an even greater weakness can be seen in the inexplicable silence of the Squire's lady, who seems ready to accept decapitation without identifying herself. Spenser seems to have continued to experience trouble in assimilating all the points of view inherent in this minor but essentially unwieldy incident.

> So as he was pursuing of his quest
> He chaunst to come whereas a iolly Knight,
> In couert shade him selfe did safely rest,
> To solace with his Lady in delight:
> His warlike armes he had from him vndight:
> For that him selfe he thought from daunger free,
> And far from enuious eyes that mote him spight.
> And eke the Lady was full faire to see,
> And courteous withall, becomming her degree.
>
> (VI.iii.20)

The insistence on the relaxed, "jolly" mood of both scenes, in which the knights are defenseless (Aladine too is unarmed, as Priscilla mentions later, VI.ii.43) and ill-prepared for any interruption, underscores the risks attached to such an incautious interchange of courtesies. Both couples assume they are safe in their covert glade or shade, and fail to realize that they have no right to expect their retreats to remain inviolate.

Clearly the primary function of this recapitulation of an earlier scene is to enable Calidore to meet the test of courtesy raised by such an interruption. The active discourtesy shown Aladine and Priscilla constituted a form of tyranny and, as mentioned earlier, fully justified Tristram's action. There it had been a question of voluntary action, of "misdesert" rather than "misfortune" (in the terms introduced by the hapless squire in VI.i.12), for the proud knight willfully sought to avail himself of the other's lady. But in this new version of the incident, Calidore feels obliged to offer apologies to Calepine and Serena for the involuntary discourtesy shown them by his interruption of "their quiet loues delight":

> Yet since it was his fortune, not his fault,
> Him selfe thereof he labour'd to acquite,
> And pardon crau'd for his so rash default,
> That he gainst courtesie so fowly did default.
>
> (VI.iii.21)

Here the rhyme-words emphasize the contrast between *fault,* an active misdeed, and *default,* in this case an unfortunate blunder, which may interfere with the flow of courtesy. Calidore's apology might seem no more than an instance of his willingness to go to any extreme of diplomatic self-abnegation to allay the displeasure of others,[5] were it not that this motif of an interrupted courtesy is repeated throughout the Book. It appears in the earlier case of Aladine and Priscilla, and more significantly in the case of Calidore's intrusion on the private vision of Colin Clout (VI.x.18), where his arrival again interrupts the courteous exchange and calls for a new demonstration of Calidore's skill at graceful apologies. The knight's offense against Aladine and Priscilla was an active discourtesy not unlike the examples of injustice confronted by Artegall in Book V. But with this restatement of the situation, Artegall's world of guilt and retribution, the world of Chrysaor and Talus, has been left behind. Here chance alone, unaccompanied by any question of individual guilt, has been responsible for breaking the bonds of courtesy.

In rescuing Aladine and Priscilla and restoring them to their respective parents, Calidore has already begun to demonstrate the special skills required of him. The case of Priscilla, who starts to worry about her injured reputation as soon as Aladine's physical injuries have responded to treatment, clearly calls for a graceful tempering of truth. Calidore's courtesy is seen here in his willingness to narrate a somewhat edited version of her rescue (VI.iii.18), producing the severed head of her oppressor as the focal point of his narration. This movement away from the poem's earlier treatment of discourtesy to a more searching examination of the positive skills of Calidore's diplomacy is continued, now, by the encounter with Calepine and Serena.

5. H. C. Chang, *Allegory and Courtesy in Spenser: A Chinese View,* (Edinburgh, Edinburgh University Press, 1955), p. 186, takes Calidore's apology as an example of his tendencies toward courtliness which must be overcome before he can capture the Blatant Beast.

At this point the center of attention begins to move away from Calidore. Though the apology to Calepine is appropriate to the situation it is not very effective dramatically, and in fact transfers the emphasis to Calepine and Serena. Although Calidore can defend mankind against open assaults on the fabric of society, he has effectively broken this courteous exchange and can offer in its place only the prospect of polite shop talk between himself and Calepine.

Given the nature of the intercourse which Calidore has interrupted, it is to be expected that the scene should be light and even comic in tone. The suggestion of comedy makes the shift of thematic emphasis more graceful. It reminds the reader that the progression to a more profound treatment of courtesy is also leading to what might normally be considered one of the more trivial problems of etiquette. Hence it is an ironic justification of an insistence on the *forms* of courteous behavior as reflections of the more serious aspects of that virtue, that Calidore's blunder should "breake bands of ciuilitie" as surely as did the willful outrages of the actively discourteous knight. Courtesy is important not simply as an adjunct of Justice, involving a due respect for rank and for the rights and property of others, but in its own right as well, requiring subtle, diplomatic manipulation which lies essentially outside any consideration of individual merit or guilt. At the same time, the comic elements implicit in this situation keep it within bounds dramatically, so that decorum is not violated by too emphatic a presentation of the Book's theme at this point. One of Calidore's chief diplomatic assets is his skill in directing conversation away from awkward subjects and along relatively safe lines. He equips himself with the severed head of Priscilla's oppressor as a means of ensuring that her father's interest will not wander from the story of her assault and rescue. And now he is careful to lead Calepine away from the subject of his interrupted dalliance to the discussion of chivalric adventures. But Serena's boredom with his masculine subject matter provides an indirect commentary on the dangers and limitations of this diplomacy, for her exclusion from the knights' conversation leads her to expose herself to the Blatant Beast.

When Calidore departs in pursuit of the Beast, the focus of the action shifts wholly to Calepine and Serena; it is appropriate that Calepine's name is announced only after Calidore has left. The naming of characters in *The Faerie Queene* is seldom fortuitous. Spenser tends to redeem his characters from anonymity at the point when their individual characteristics have first emerged to such an extent that their names become pertinent to their roles. A relatively uncomplicated instance of this tendency is seen in Serena, who is introduced by name when she leaves Calidore and Calepine to wander into the fields:

> Of which whilest they discoursed both together,
> The faire *Serena* (so his Lady hight)
> Allur'd with myldnesse of the gentle wether,
> And pleasaunce of the place, the which was dight
> With diuers flowres distinct with rare delight,
> Wandred about the fields, as liking led
> Her wauering lust after her wandring sight,
> To make a garland to adorne her hed,
> Without suspect of ill or daungers hidden dred.
>
>   (VI.iii.23)

Her name emphasizes her serene trust in her surroundings, which is promptly shown to be unfounded. More specifically, the fact that a reference to the "myldnesse of the gentle wether" is immediately juxtaposed to this first mention of her name stresses her reliance on an apparently friendly natural environment, to the extent that she is beguiled by that aspect of nature which is most subject to instantaneous change. Allusions to the weather in *The Faerie Queene* treat it as a prime object of mutability. A sudden shower drives Redcross and Una to the Wood of Error and introduces the reader to the poem's world (I.i.6); Guyon hurries away from his victory over Acrasia "whilest wether serues and wind" (II.xii.87); the same awareness of man's reliance on chance informs the persistent nautical imagery with which the narrator typically welcomes his safe arrival in port at the end of a canto or Book. More immediately pertinent in Serena's case is the fact that the discourteous knight who had lusted after Priscilla bore as his device "A Ladie on rough waues, row'd in a sommer barge" (VI.ii.44). Both ladies are defenseless against any unseasonable disruption of the clement weather which characterizes their pastoral seclusion from the cares of society. Serena, like Milton's Proserpina in her gathering of flowers, is ignorant of the dangers lurking beneath the placid surface of the natural setting. The repeated motif of the pastoral garland here as in Book I suggests the contrary implications of such floral tribute. In her ill-advised attempt to gather her own garland, Serena invites comparison with Pastorella (VI.ix.8) and Colin's lady (VI.x.12), who are so celebrated by others. Apparently she has wandered into danger by seeking for herself what can properly come only as a gift or "grace" from without.

The origins of Calepine's name are far less clear. Yet the number of apparently unrelated interpretations which this name has received is a tribute less to the incautious ingenuity of commentators in search of garlands for their own heads, than to a multiplicity of allusion characteristic of Spenser and basic to his technique. At heart this is the same multiplicity seen in the variety of allegorical levels so frustratingly apparent to the systematic reader of the poem. One of the premises of Spenser's allegorical method seems to be that all realms of human experience—religion and classical myth and contemporary event—converge on the poem so as to provide a confirmation of its universality and a commentary on the actions of its characters. On the level of the individual word as on that of the incident, an attempt is frequently made to suggest a number of distinct allusions, linked only by their common relevance to the situation in the poem. Hence one cannot say that a single etymology is pertinent to the name of a given character, or that the relevance of one interpretation excludes all others. It seems more probable that Spenser welcomed such a multiplication of meaning as an index of the consummate aptness of the name. Behind this multiplicity of allusion for its own sake, moreover, there lies also the criterion of "conspicuous irrelevance." Just as the allegorist maintains a careful distinction between image and object, as a guide to an ironic awareness of the imperfect capacity of the real world to reflect the ideal, similarly in the details of Spenser's choice of names for his characters one finds a richness and variety of allusions which ensure that no single allegorical framework can become dominant.

Calepine's name might be taken as an emblem of his various roles in Book VI, as a figure who mediates between the extremes of courtesy and its opposite, providing a dramatic illustration of the difficulties and perils confronting man in his social role. A survey of the possible implications and origins of his name is of interest not merely as an insight into Spenser's use of his sources, but as a guide to the structural principles operating in the central cantos of Book VI.

Spenser was presumably familiar with the name Calepine or Calepin[6] as the anglicized surname of Ambrogio Calepino (1435–1511), whose Latin–Italian dictionary (1502) was expanded in subsequent editions into a polyglot lexicon which Spenser may have known and used through a copy in the library of the Merchant Taylors' School.[7] Calepino can have furnished Spenser with little more than the external form of Calepine's name: it is hard to see any respect in which the man or his work can be reflected in the character of his Spenserian namesake. A more significantly inappropriate name, however, is that of Ariosto's Pinabello, a churlish figure on whom Spenser may have modelled his own Turpine, as Dodge suggests.[8] The

6. The name Callipine appears in Marlowe's *Tamburlaine, Part II,* and in *The Jew of Malta.*

7. DeWitt T. Starnes and E. W. Talbert, *Classical Myth and Legend in Renaissance Dictionaries,* (Chapel Hill, University of North Carolina Press, 1955), pp. 17, 77–80 ("Spenser and Calepine").

8. Dodge, "Spenser's Imitations from Ariosto," p. 203.

name Pinabello, or Pinabel, is found in the chivalric tradition prior to Ariosto, and in all probability is derived innocently enough from a place name. Possibly its use in the *Orlando Furioso* bears a suggestion of its ironic inappropriateness, as an element of Ariosto's own commentary on the chivalric idealizations of his predecessors. It seems probable, though, that if Spenser was thinking of Pinabello when he created the figure of Turpine, he chose the latter name—itself a name of good standing in the romance tradition (witness the Terpine of Book V)[9]—as providing a closer approximation to the true nature of its bearer. Given the natural association of Latin *bellus* with Greek *kalós,* it is possible that Pinabello's name may be echoed ironically in that of Calepine, who is paired off against Turpine in the action of these cantos. And even if Spenser intended no direct allusion to Ariosto, Draper's suggestion that the *-pine* suffix is a means of linking the two adversaries seems certainly valid.[10]

Similarly, Calepine and Calidore are unquestionably paired with one another by their common first syllables. This is made abundantly evident by the fact that Calepine becomes the central figure (and is first named) when Calidore leaves in pursuit of the Blatant Beast. If Calepine is taken as a surrogate Calidore, the difference between them may be seen further in their different names. Through his actions in the early cantos of Book VI, Calldore has begun to give evidence of what his vision of the Graces will bring into clear focus as the central principle of Courtesy: the view of giving as a mutual process, involving a responsibility on the part of the recipient to give in return, continuing the interchange of gifts which lies at the heart of courteous behavior and the establishment of human society. In this context it seems certain that the final syllable

9. V.iv.26. Even here, though, note that Artegall asks, "Sir *Terpine,* haplesse man, what make you here?" and offers three possible explanations for his unhappy fate. Thus Spenser seems clearly to be playing on Terpine's name as implying "thrice wretched." This may provide further justification for a similar reading of the *-pine* endings of Turpine's and Calepine's names.

10. Draper, "Classical Coinage," p. 100.

of Calidore's name (*dōron,* gift) is meant to anticipate the moral of the Graces' dance: "That good should from vs goe, then come in greater store" (VI.x.24).[11] Calidore's chief qualification as a patron of Courtesy is his capacity to use the graces lavished on him by nature as a means both of giving pleasure to others and of convincing others to overcome their unwillingness to give of themselves. The mixture of active and passive, "gentle" (in both the sense of mild-tempered, yielding, and that of well-born, belonging to an honorable rank) and fierce, in his character accounts for his ability to be both a representative of the level of civilization already attained and a defender of that civilization against its enemies.

Clearly Calepine fails to meet these standards. His fault is not one of a proud unwillingness to abandon his own freedom by returning the love of another, as is the case with Crudor or Mirabella; nor is he in any other respect opposed to the exchange of courtesy. Rather, his difficulties arise from his inability to elicit courteous responses from others, notably his major opponent, Turpine, and from his consequent helplessness in the presence of a discourteous refusal to abide by the accepted standards of chivalric behavior. In view of Calepine's unhappy history, it seems probable that his name is further intended to convey the sense of the English verb *pine.* In fact Serena plays on the two words in her speech to Arthur in canto v:

> I was erewhile, the loue of *Calepine,*
> Who whether he aliue be to be found,
> Or by some deadly chaunce be done to pine,
> Since I him lately lost, vneath is to define.
>
> In saluage forrest I him lost of late . . .
>   (VI.v.28–29)

---

11. Mrs. Bennett's suggestion (*The Evolution of the "Faerie Queene,"* p. 215) that Calidore's name may be derived from Latin *calidus* (Calidore as the "living spirit" of courtesy) seems less illuminating than the more generally accepted derivation from the Greek.

The covert shade in which Serena and Calepine had first been revealed has become by now a savage forest; the refuge from an envious society has been seen to contain unsuspected dangers. It remains to ask how Calepine's inability to defend himself against Turpine demonstrates his failure to appreciate the full responsibilities of the courtesy which he attempts to practice.

Any discussion of Turpine must take into account the presence of plot elements which are introduced without explanation and seem to show a considerable degree of revision in the course of the composition of Book VI. Thus Turpine's porter describes him as

> . . . one of mickle might,
> And manhood rare, but terrible and stearne
> In all assaies to euery errant Knight,
> Because of one, that wrought him fowle despight.
>
> (VI.iii.40)

And again Turpine's "homely groome" seems to be alluding to this earlier insult when he repulses Arthur, who is posing as a wounded knight: "for why his Lord of old/ Did hate all errant Knights . . ." (VI.vi.21). Yet Turpine is chiefly notable for his craven disregard for his own reputation, his lack of courage in battle, and his persistent use of treachery as a means of avenging his defeat. The action of Book VI provides no illustration of his "terrible and stern" qualities, and offers no further comment on the origins of his hatred for errant knights. Moreover, Arthur speaks of a "wicked custome" inaugurated by Turpine which is mentioned nowhere else in the poem:

> Yet further hast thou heaped shame to shame,
> And crime to crime, by this thy cowheard feare.
> For first it was to thee reprochfull blame,
> To erect this wicked custome, which I heare,
> Gainst errant Knights and Ladies thou dost reare;
> Whom when thou mayst, thou dost of arms despoile,

> Or of their vpper garment, which they weare:
> Yet doest thou not with manhood, but with guile
> Maintaine this euill vse, thy foes thereby to foile.
>
> (VI.vi.34)

All these details attributed to Turpine's history are precisely those which Spenser drew from Ariosto's presentation of Pinabello. There Ruggiero is told of a "costume . . . iniquo e fiero" (*O.F.*, XXII.xlvii), by which Pinabello, "il peggior uomo che viva," avenges an earlier, similar insult against his lady by stopping all who pass by his castle and divesting the knights of their armor and the ladies of their clothing. Pinabello, like Turpine, is weak and cowardly, but has managed by guile to bind four bold knights to fight his battles for him.

Possibly Spenser was unwilling to give Turpine the prominence in the action of Book VI that a full imitation of Pinabello would entail. In any case, this wicked custom has been anticipated by the practice instigated by Crudor, who unlike Turpine proves to be courageous in his maintenance of wrong and honorable in his acceptance of defeat at Calidore's hands. Whatever may have been the role originally planned for Turpine/Pinabello in Book VI,[12] his actions as they now appear are clearly designed to stress the cowardice of his "knightlesse part," far more shameful than any wicked custom, as Arthur says:

> And lastly in approuance of thy wrong,
>   To shew such faintnesse and foule cowardize,
>   Is greatest shame: for oft it falles, that strong
>   And valiant knights doe rashly enterprize,
>   Either for fame, or else for exercize,
>   A wrongfull quarrell to maintaine by fight;

12. Conceivably, Turpine was originally imagined as a major adversary of Calidore; but the long-standing misprint at VI.vi.17.7 (first emended by Hughes in 1715, but retained even in Smith's Oxford text—though the latter concedes the rightness of the emendation), whereby Turpine is said to have offended Calidore rather than Calepine, seems a flimsy basis for such an inference, especially since the rest of the stanza refers clearly enough to the scene with Calepine and Serena.

> Yet haue, through prowesse and their braue
>   emprize,
> Gotten great worship in this worldes sight.
> For greater force there needs to maintaine wrong,
>   then right.
>
> (VI.vi.35)

Turpine thus provides a striking contrast with figures like Tristram or the Salvage Man, whose innate nobility is apparent despite their humble or even brutish disguises; he is unable to hide his baseness despite his pretensions to the dignity of knighthood (VI.vii.1). Such a man can menace only those who put their faith in the appearances of rank, and who permit their own courtesy to leave them unprepared for the ignoble discourtesy of others.

One index to the specific defenses required against the challenge to Courtesy is seen in the motif of abandoned armor which recurs throughout the Book. Calepine in particular seems inclined to remove his armor for purposes of rest or amorous dalliance. On his first appearance he is compromisingly discovered by Calidore in this condition (VI.iii.20); and when he runs to aid the wounded Serena he again shows his impatience by casting aside his weapons (VI.iii.27).[13] The oppressive burden of his armor is stressed again during his painful progress on foot (VI.iii.29); it appears that Calepine welcomes any opportunity of avoiding it, since he is unarmed again in the forest after his rescue by the Salvage Man (VI.iv.17ff.). Although his disarmed state is clearly associated with his mistaken assumption that he is free from danger, there are several factors that make it impossible to see this armor as man's defense against the discourtesy of others: it is not simply his lack of armor which distinguishes Calepine from Calidore.

---

13. It should be stressed, however, that Spenser makes no attempt to trace the career of Calepine's armor with any consistency. Its absence or presence at a given moment is relevant only to its appropriateness at that moment, not to its position a few stanzas earlier.

In the first place, it must be noted that Calidore's chief advantage in pursuing the Blatant Beast and forcing him to abandon Serena is that he is "more light of foote and swift in chace" (VI.iii.25), a description echoed later when Calepine rescues the infant from the bear:

> Well then him chaunst his heauy armes to want,
>   Whose burden mote empeach his needfull speed,
>   And hinder him from libertie to pant:
>   For hauing long time, as his daily weed,
>   Them wont to weare, and wend on foot for need,
>   Now wanting them he felt himselfe so light,
>   That like an Hauke, which feeling her selfe freed
> From bels and iesses, which did let her flight,
> Him seem'd his feet did fly, and in their speed delight.
>   (VI.iv.19)

In this scene Calepine has regained his strength during his stay in the forest and is able to act with decision and forcefulness. Since he is now accustomed to bearing arms, he is positively aided on this occasion by their absence. Furthermore, his earlier weakness culminated in his humiliating retreat before Turpine's assault (VI.iii.47), where he was reduced to taking shelter behind Serena's back while she sought in vain to placate his assailant;[14] in that scene he was explicitly described as being armed. This insistence on armor implies the need for a flexible adaptability to the various challenges to courtesy, and along with it the requirement of good fortune. Calidore's earlier em-

---

14. Serena's attempts to protect Calepine anticipate the scene in which Turpine takes shelter in Blandina's chamber and seeks her aid in appeasing Arthur (VI.vi.30ff.). The two scenes, and the earlier one in which Crudor appeals for mercy, provide three instances of a reversal of fortunes and a plea for mercy. Turpine, Arthur, and Calidore illustrate three distinct ways of treating such a situation: with treacherous disregard for the rules of chivalry, with a grudging and contemptuous acceptance of those rules (since they are invoked in so cowardly a fashion), and with a gracious and diplomatic welcoming of the opportunity to spare rather than spill.

phasis on the role played by chance in human events applies throughout Book VI. One of the main differences between Calidore and Calepine is in their respective fortunes: Calepine lacks the gifts which have been so abundantly showered on Calidore, both in the graces with which he was born and in his capacity to adapt himself to the varying demands of circumstance.

Calepine also lacks Calidore's habitual alertness. This deficiency is particularly apparent during the incidents in which Turpine insults him with impunity. His rescue by the Salvage Man introduces the contrast between a simple, even Spartan natural environment which, though lacking in the positive values of civilized society, is capable of fostering in its inhabitants the strength needed to defend that society, and the all too comfortable civilization which along with its positive values entails an enfeebling temptation to rely on the good will of others. Thus Calepine's unwillingness to wear his uncomfortable armor may indicate his submission to this latter temptation. But the Salvage Man is invulnerable by his nature, and in this respect he recalls the earlier scene in which Artegall, similarly "savage" by training and inclination, was able to ignore the threats of the Blatant Beast. Far more clearly than Artegall, however, he represents an unnurtured nature. Though we are later told that he is of gentle birth (VI.v.2), his ignorance even of human speech emphasizes the extent to which he has been isolated from human society and forced to draw his knowledge from the savage forest. Though his birth, or at least his status as a human being, provokes him to sympathetic action in behalf of Calepine, it is his upbringing in the forest that enables him to cure the wounds inflicted by Turpine. Presumably Calepine learns from his example to bear his armor patiently without exhaustion, as he is shown after his visit to the forest, returning to rescue Serena from the cannibals (VI.viii.47).

The Salvage Man's kindness to Serena and Calepine necessitates a qualification of the simplified view which derives courtesy exclusively from court society. As Serena remarks to Arthur in defending the Salvage Man:

> In such a saluage wight, of brutish kynd,
> Amongst wilde beastes in desert forrests bred,
> It is most straunge and wonderfull to fynd
> So milde humanity, and perfect gentle mynd.

(VI.v.29)

Although Serena is mistaken in her belief that he is of brutish kind,[15] her comment nevertheless points to the necessity of a fuller understanding of the "mild" and "gentle" aspects of courteous behavior. If they are fully incompatible with savage wildness, then they can scarcely be taken as absolute values for a civilized society, since they would condemn that society to certain extinction at the hands of its wilder elements. The Salvage Man therefore provides another, larger significance to the emphasis on diplomacy seen throughout Book VI: his presence suggests that in order to create and maintain a flourishing society, man must make use not merely of his higher powers but of his lower powers as well. He must unite his brutish and gentle

15. For a survey of Spenser's treatment of Wild Men in various forms, see Herbert Foltinek, "Die Wilden Männer in Edmund Spenser's *Faerie Queene,*" *Die neueren Sprachen,* 1961, 493–512. Although the Salvage Man certainly owes much to his predecessors among the "wild men" of art and legend (cf. Bernheimer, *Wild Men in the Middle Ages;* H. Janson, *Apes and Ape Lore,* London, Warburg Institute, University of London, 1952), in Spenser's version his savagery is a disguise, albeit an unconscious one which he never abandons during his appearance in Book VI. Basically it seems that the emphasis on disguise running throughout this Book must be taken as a consequence of the peculiar nature of Courtesy, which as suggested earlier does not demand a distinction among dispensations, as had virtues treated in the preceding Books. On the contrary, Courtesy requires a recognition of the fundamental kindred of all ranks of humans, as a basis on which a civilization may be founded; it also requires a concentration on the qualities held in common by individuals, rather than on those which serve to separate them. It may appear paradoxical that the same insistence on the "gentle birth" of all the courteous characters of Book VI, which has drawn criticism from some readers on the grounds of its presumed aristocratic bias, seems to derive from what might almost be called egalitarianism, in its desire to eliminate the aspect of social distinctions which interferes with the free flow of courtesy.

natures to achieve a cultured mildness of manner which is constantly being invigorated, strengthened, and defended by contact with the rigors of nature.

Appropriately, then, the Salvage Man is of service not merely to Calepine and Serena, but also ultimately to Arthur, whom he accompanies in the role of page after Timias has been incapacitated by his wounds from the Blatant Beast. And appropriately, too, Arthur is exposed to Turpine in a position of unwary ease clearly reminiscent of Calepine's first appearance:

> Wearie of trauell in his former fight,
> He there in shade himselfe had layd to rest,
> Hauing his armes and warlike things vndight,
> Fearelesse of foes that mote his peace molest;
> The whyles his saluage page, that wont be prest,
> Was wandred in the wood another way,
> To doe some thing, that seemed to him best,
> The whyles his Lord in siluer slomber lay,
> Like to the Euening starre adorn'd with deawy ray.
>
> (VI.vii.19)

Arthur's sleep provides Turpine with an opportunity to show the full extent of his treachery and cowardice. More significantly it provides the Salvage Man with an opportunity to show his ability to rescue his master, even though in this case Enias' incorruptibility makes the danger only theoretical. Yet there is no suggestion that Arthur is merely feigning sleep, as he had earlier feigned exhaustion and helplessness in his appeal to Turpine for hospitality (VI.vi.20): this time he apparently is genuinely defenseless and dependent on fortune and the courtesy of others. It seems clear that the incident (whatever its weaknesses on the score of dramatic implausibility) is designed to emphasize the universal vulnerability of civilized man. The Salvage Man illustrates the practical argument against a courtesy which refines itself to the point of ignoring the lower levels both of human society and of the individual personality.

The parallels between Arthur and Calepine suggest that the

two knights differ not so much in kind as in degree. After his visit with the Salvage Man Calepine is stronger and more alert, and hence is better able to combat savage discourtesy wherever he may encounter it. But his approach to discourtesy has been from the beginning, and remains, that of the affronted knight. Despite his weakness there is no trace of conciliatory diplomacy in his nature; his humiliating retreat before Turpine is far removed from Calidore's gracefully apologetic persuasion. Similarly, Arthur's treatment of Turpine is motivated throughout by the desire for a just revenge; he is

> . . . in mynd to bene ywroken
> Of all the vile demeane, and vsage bad,
> With which he had those two so ill bestad.
>
> (VI.vi.18)

A comparison of the therapeutic diplomacy that Calidore showed in accepting the pleas of the defeated Crudor (VI.i.40ff.) with the righteous scorn shown by Arthur to Turpine in a similar situation (VI.vi.33ff.) suggests a further significance to Arthur's subsequent period of vulnerability. For however justified his reproach of Turpine may be, it is clearly useless as an attempt to reform the latter: it merely provides another affront to be avenged. Perhaps reformation is impossible in the case of Turpine; perhaps his stubborn baseness will remain unresponsive to all appeals to a better nature. In any case, Arthur's treatment of him offers no permanent solution, and there is no indication that he repents after being hung by the heels. Vigor and sternness, though Calepine's misfortunes show them to be vitally needed, are not an answer in themselves.

Calepine's education in the forest is therefore neither more nor less helpful than Artegall's had been earlier. He has made experience on the animals (in this case the bear), and has thereby reached the point where he can defend Serena against the cannibals. But when last seen he is attempting to overcome Serena's shame at her own nakedness: "But she for nought that he could say or doe,/ One word durst speake, or answere him a whit thereto" (VI.viii.50). The courteous exchange between the two remains broken.

Similarly, although the Salvage Man is able to cure the wounds inflicted on Calepine by Turpine, the wounds inflicted on Serena and Timias by the Blatant Beast admit of no such natural cure. The natural environment seen in the Hermit's home shares with that of the Salvage Man an absence of luxury and civilized softness; but it offers no directly efficacious balm for its visitor's inner wounds: "For in your selfe your onely helpe doth lie . . ." (VI.vi.7). Further, positive action is needed beyond that which man can be taught by exposure to a "hard" primitivism based on isolation from civilized society. Such action is ultimately derived from man's knowledge of his own identity, which the individual brings with himself into the wilderness. At most the wilderness can free him of the distracting concerns blinding him to this knowledge.

Thus the Salvage Man's role is necessarily limited. He can make an important contribution to Calepine, who so disastrously lacks the hardness which the forest can teach him. But in accompanying Arthur, who has no such weakness, the Salvage Man serves rather to underscore an element already present in his new master's personality. It is probably no coincidence that his indiscriminate slaughter of the inhabitants of Turpine's castle should be reminiscent of Talus' similar behavior in support of Artegall. Both knights are committed to the sword as a means of avenging injustice; their servants provide an important reminder of the need for a controlling intellect if force is not going to lead, through excess, to a new injustice. Arthur is no more superfluous to the action of Book VI than he has been in the preceding Books. But although chivalric magnificence is essential to the operation of Courtesy it is inevitably defensive in its function. Only Calidore's deliberately unheroic diplomacy can lead to positive achievement. It is to underscore the necessity for such an escape from personal heroics that the action now leads Calidore into a pastoral setting which will test not his hardness —as the wilderness tests and strengthens Calepine's—but his humility, as seen in his abandonment of the last traces of his courtly style. Among the shepherds Calidore will gain a new insight into his origins. The opening lines of Book VI had tentatively accepted the apparent derivation of Courtesy ("Of Court it seemes, men Courtesie doe call"), while recognizing that it is a fair flower growing "on a lowly stalke" (VI.Proem.4), to be "planted naturall" and enhanced by more superficial graces (VI.i.2). In a more natural state Calidore can test his various skills and gauge his efficacy more accurately;[16] his adoption of shepherd's weeds will be seen simultaneously as a disguise and an unmasking.

16. Kathleen Williams, "Courtesy and Pastoral in *The Faerie Queene, Book VI,*" *Review of English Studies, n.s.13* (1962), 337–46, stresses the elegiac role of the pastoral episodes as a means of confronting the problem of change.

6. The Pastoral Vision and the Disrupted Banquet

Calidore's reappearance in Book VI at the beginning of the ninth canto is announced in the terms of a rustic image ("I lately left a furrow, one or twayne/ Vnplough'd") suggesting that the pastoral episodes being introduced are to be viewed as an interruption, however "fayre and frutefull," both of Calidore's quest and of the Book's development. The reader is told that Calidore has diligently pursued the Blatant Beast since his disappearance in the third canto, yet the hero's return to the poem takes place in the one setting where the Beast is unknown. This same emphasis on Calidore's truancy is found again at the beginning of the tenth canto:

> Who now does follow the foule *Blatant Beast,*
>   Whilest *Calidore* does follow that faire Mayd,
>   Vnmyndfull of his vow and high beheast,
>   Which by the Faery Queene was on him layd,
>   That he should neuer leaue, nor be delayd
>   From chacing him, till he had it attchieued?
> . . .
>
> Another quest, another game in vew
>   He hath, the guerdon of his loue to gaine:

With whom he myndes for euer to remaine,
And set his rest amongst the rusticke sort,
Rather then hunt still after shadowes vaine
Of courtly fauour, fed with light report
Of euery blaste, and sayling alwaies on the port.
                                              (VI.x.1–2)

The tone of these lines, in which Calidore's present concerns
are alternatively opposed both to the "high beheast" of Gloriana
and to the "shadowes vaine" of a courtier's rewards, may be
variously interpreted. In W. W. Greg's view of English pastoral,[1] Spenser's awareness of the distance between heroic action and pastoral escape prefigures the end of a convention's
usefulness. Such a reading attaches greater importance to the
first stanza, in which the poet speaks directly to the reader; the
second stanza, with its implicit criticism of Gloriana's world,
might then be taken either as a dramatic presentation of Calidore's own justification of his attraction to Pastorella, or more
generally as an expression of the nostalgic reluctance with which
the poet faces the recognition that his pastoral holiday cannot
last forever.

Aside from the fact that Greg's description of the death of
pastoral seems to have been premature—other critics have
found it rising in its most interesting form from this confrontation with the demands of the civilized world[2]—any interpretation of Book VI which sees these episodes as a simple postpone-
ment of Calidore's main quest depends ultimately on the familiar conflict between poet and moralist. For it seems undeniable
that the Book's interest centers on Calidore's pastoral escape
from the world of courtly motivation. In this respect the opposite of Greg's tendency involves much the same risk of distor-
tion. If the obvious excellence of these cantos leads the reader

1. W. W. Greg, *Pastoral Poetry and Pastoral Drama* (London, A. H.
Bullen, 1906), p. 101.
2. For example, cf. the introductory comments and range of selections
by Frank Kermode, ed., *English Pastoral Poetry from the Beginnings to
Marvell* (London, Harrap & Co., 1952).

to discount Spenser's depreciation of the pastoral world with respect to the heroic, as a conventional gesture deriving perhaps from the traditional emphasis on the shepherd's lowly estate, he is again in danger of blurring the central point of the lines quoted above.[3] An equal emphasis must be placed on both of these opening stanzas.

Preceding chapters of this study have attempted to suggest some of the reasons for the episodic structure of Book VI as a whole: reasons which derive ultimately from the nature of Courtesy as Spenser defines it and contrasts it with Artegall's Justice. It remains to discuss the respects in which Calidore's visit among the shepherds constitutes an education in the operation of courtesy—in a manner similar to that found in similar "allegorical cores" of the other Books—and, at the same time, by its very substitution of pastoral for epic anticipates the limited and anticlimactic nature of the victory possible in the area of courtesy. Book VI concludes with an explicit insistence on Calidore's failure to achieve any lasting victory over the Blatant Beast. Yet more than any other Book, the sixth seems to offer a fitting conclusion for Spenser's presentation of his moral scheme. This sense of completeness which it affords is in large measure the product of the pastoral episodes. Thus it seems natural to discuss first the role adopted by Calidore in these episodes, and secondly the nature of the vision granted to Calidore in this role, whereby his potential as a champion of courtesy is seen in the context of mankind's precarious and impermanent attainments of human rapport.[4]

3. T. P. Harrison (quoted in *Variorum 6*, 242): "Spenser obviously censures Sir Calidore's pastoral aberration; yet he, like Sidney, is inclined to paint the rural picture sympathetically. The digression in Spenser's heroic poem affords him opportunity to describe the delightful life and scenes of this fairy Arcadia . . ."

4. Harry Berger, Jr., discusses some of these aspects of Book VI in two articles, "The Prospect of Imagination: Spenser and the Limits of Poetry," *Studies in English Literature, 1* (1961), 93–120, and "A Secret Discipline: *The Faerie Queene*, Book VI," in Nelson, ed., *Form and Convention*, pp. 35–75. Cf. J. C. Maxwell, "The Truancy of Calidore," in Mueller and Allen, eds., *That Soueraine Light*, pp. 63–69.

PHRYGIAN PARIS: THE PASTORAL DISGUISE

Calidore is first attracted to the pastoral world by the one element in it which seems to him more appropriate to his own courtly society: the beauty of Pastorella. Though as usual he has been "nothing nice" in accepting the shepherds' offer of hospitality, it is not until he has seen her that he is tempted to linger:

> Her whyles Sir *Calidore* there vewed well,
>   And markt her rare demeanure, which him seemed
> So farre the meane of shepheards to excell,
> As that he in his mind her worthy deemed,
> To be a Princes Paragone esteemed,
> He was vnwares surprisd in subtile bands
> Of the blynd boy, ne thence could be redeemed
> By any skill out of his cruell hands,
>   Caught like the bird, which gazing still on others
>   stands.
>
> (VI.ix.11)

Caught off guard by love, Calidore is thus given a motive for his dalliance in this pastoral setting, one which is carefully distinguished from any direct concern for the simple life of the shepherds. In this first presentation Pastorella appears in a position suggestive of her extraordinary qualities: she is placed on a natural elevation, surrounded by the admiring throngs of country lasses and swains, who see her as a "miracle of heauenly hew" (VI.ix.8). The parallels between this description and that of the Graces in the succeeding canto indicate the full significance of her excellence. But for the moment the poet is content to remark that although she thinks herself the daughter of Meliboe, and has received an education limiting her experience to pastoral concerns, she is in fact a foundling child and a member of the society of shepherds only by adoption. It is clear from the beginning, therefore, that the love between Calidore and

Pastorella is presented against a pastoral setting to which both protagonists are essentially outsiders. At the same time, it is suggested that Calidore's diplomatic participation in this world is at least partially disingenuous, being intended as a means of furthering his courtship. In the stanza immediately following the one quoted above, Calidore is presented as

> . . . discoursing diuersly
> Of sundry things, as fell, to worke delay;
> And euermore his speach he did apply
> To th'heards, but meant them to the damzels fantazy.
>
> (VI.ix.12)

Meliboe's invitation is received with a similar awareness of self-interest: "The knight full gladly soone agreed thereto,/ Being his harts owne wish, and home with him did go" (VI.ix.16). Calidore's conversation with Meliboe is thus seen within the context of an ulterior intent which, if nothing else, serves to underscore the distance between the two men. Though both are quick to praise the quiet life of pastoral seclusion, each speaks from his own viewpoint. It is abundantly clear that Calidore's viewpoint combines a recognition of the validity of Meliboe's arguments with a desire for Pastorella which somewhat overshadows the attractiveness for him of a life wholly free of aspiration.

In this connection, it is instructive to compare this conversation with the passage in Tasso's *Gerusalemme Liberata* from which it is largely drawn. Spenser has taken the account of Erminia's visit with the shepherds (*G.L.*, VII.6ff.) and adapted it to his own ends by turning a relatively simple dramatic situation—in which the aged shepherd describes the carefree security of his life to a listener burdened with cares and insecurity—into the expression of a single reference point in a more complex drama. For the hapless and helpless Erminia, the shepherd's life offers a peaceful sanctuary against the wars which rage about her. In terms of her situation, the argument that "il folgore non cade in basso pian ma su l'eccelse cime" easily per-

suades her to adopt pastoral garb. Whatever their differences
in rank, or in the finality with which each retreats from the
trials of the outer world, both Erminia and the shepherd are
in agreement as to their reasons for such a retreat.

In Spenser's version, however, Meliboe's expression of these
reasons—in language so close to the original that the passage
might for all practical purposes be taken as an allusion to
Tasso[5]—provokes in Calidore a "double rauishment":[6]

> Both of his speach that wrought him great content,
> And also of the obiect of his vew,
> On which his hungry eye was always bent;
> That twixt his pleasing tongue, and her faire hew,
> He lost himselfe, and like one halfe entraunced grew.
>
> (VI.ix.26)

Throughout his description of this conversation, Spenser carefully emphasizes Calidore's manipulation of Meliboe's remarks
to suit his own desire to remain in a position where he can court
Pastorella. It is Calidore who begins by offering thanks for the
hospitality shown him, and who, "drawing thence his speach
another way" (VI.ix.18), dwells on the advantages of the pastoral life. The different viewpoints of the two men are emphasized by a counterpoint of motive which suggests not so much
a debate as a conversation carried on at cross purposes. Calidore's introductory statement concludes with the sentiment
"That certes I your happinesse enuie,/ And wish my lot were
plast in such felicitie" (VI.ix.19). Meliboe's answer provides an
indirect rebuke to the knight's envy, for he says that his happiness lies in contentment with the little he possesses: "Therefore
I doe not any one enuy,/ Nor am enuyde of any one therefore"

5. At any rate, even if this passage is not felt as a specific allusion to
Tasso, it seems clearly an allusion to a body of recognizable truisms, as conventional as the sentiments expressed in stanzas 29–30; cf. *Variorum 6,* notes
on these stanzas, 240–42.

6. In Tasso's version, Erminia feels no such conflict of emotions, though
her troubles are only partially calmed by the shepherd's words and she decides
to stay temporarily among the shepherds (*Gerusalemme Liberata,* VII.14).

(VI.ix.21). Calidore, undismayed, again replies by wishing "that my fortunes might transposed bee/ From pitch of higher place, vnto this low degree" (VI.ix.28). Meliboe counters with the argument that "It is the mynd, that maketh good or ill,/ That maketh wretch or happie, rich or poore" (VI.ix.30); an argument which Calidore forcibly wrenches into the context of his own intentions:

> Since then in each mans self (said *Calidore*)
> It is, to fashion his owne lyfes estate,
> Giue leaue awhyle, good father, in this shore
> To rest my barcke, which hath bene beaten late
> With stormes of fortune and tempestuous fate,
> In seas of troubles and of toylesome paine,
> That whether quite from them for to retrate
> I shall resolue, or back to turne againe,
> I may here with your selfe some small repose obtaine.
>
> (VI.ix.31)

And as though to underscore once more the distance between the two men and between their respective views of pastoral contentment, Spenser again echoes Tasso by showing Calidore offering payment to Meliboe, "That may perhaps you better much withall,/ And in this quiet make you safer liue" (VI.ix.32). In Tasso's poem, Erminia's similar offer had been left unanswered, since it had been conditional ("Ché se di gemme e d'or . . . tu fossi vago"—*G.L.,* VII.16), and had been intended simply to emphasize the ironic opposition of her state to that of the poor but happy shepherd. In Spenser's version, Calidore's offer is righteously refused by Meliboe, as a temptation "That mote empaire my peace with daungers dread" (VI.ix.33). The reader is left with the impression that shepherd and knight, for all their courteous discourse, have never made themselves fully understood by one another.

It is easy to overstate the differences between Meliboe and Calidore. Any dramatic relationship between the two men is secondary to the theme of their dialogue, and any half-comic

overtones are similarly incidental to this main emphasis. But
comparison with Tasso reveals that Spenser has placed a conventional praise of pastoral seclusion in a context evocative of
Calidore's personal motives in seeking that seclusion, with the
effect of reminding the reader that it is still a questing knight
who is seeking admission here. The situation of a conversation
between courtier and shepherd seems to suggest a debate of the
sort so commonly found in Renaissance literature. Yet here the
speakers appear to be in perfect agreement; neither is seeking
to defend the life of action or the merits of art. Neither is portrayed with the degree of self-awareness which Shakespeare
gives to Perdita and Polixenes in their famous debate in *The
Winter's Tale* (IV.iii). Rather, Spenser's irony differs from
Shakespeare's in that none of the characters in *The Faerie
Queene* acts as the spokesman for that irony: only the reader
can fully appreciate the significance of the situation. In this
sense Spenser's characters must be seen less as actors in a drama
of their own than as exempla, however fully and subtly they may
be developed.[7]

In the present case, therefore, the conversation between
Calidore and Meliboe serves chiefly to indicate that the knight
has not simply abandoned temporarily his "high beheast," but
has at the same time "Another quest, another game in vew,"
and one which demands comparison with the former quest.
Consequently, it is important to examine the nature of the new
role which Calidore adopts at this point. The conversation with
Meliboe has concluded with the shepherd's advice to Calidore:

> But if ye algates couet to assay
> This simple sort of life, that shepheards lead,
> Be it your owne: our rudenesse to your selfe aread.
>
> (VI.ix.33)

And in fact Calidore immediately discovers that Pastorella has
no taste for his courtly forms: "His layes, his loues, his lookes

---

7. The figure of Colin might be considered an exception to this generalization; but it seems questionable whether he is, properly speaking, a character

she did them all despize." The result of this discovery is the final stage in his adoption of the pastoral disguise, described by Spenser in terms which demand closer scrutiny:

> Which *Calidore* perceiuing, thought it best
> To chaunge the manner of his loftie looke;
> And doffing his bright armes, himselfe addrest
> In shepheards weed, and in his hand he tooke,
> In stead of steelehead speare, a shepheards hooke,
> That who had seene him then, would haue
>   bethought
> On *Phrygian Paris* by *Plexippus* brooke,
> When he the loue of fayre *Oenone* sought,
> What time the golden apple was vnto him brought.
>
> (VI.ix.36)

The immediate basis of this comparison with Paris is clear enough: Calidore is of noble birth, and engaged temporarily in a courtship that brings him into a pastoral setting. But other elements in this description provide a more searching commentary on the present situation. Calidore's abandonment of his armor may refer directly to the results of Calepine's similar tendency, observed earlier. But in any case the change from bright armor to shepherd's weeds, from spear to crook, suggests not simply a humbler condition but a more vulnerable one as well. Similarly, the comparison with Paris carries overtones of menace that are strikingly pertinent to the situation being described. Although the allusion to Plexippus remains obscure,[8]

---

in the poem's action. His brief involvement has rather the quality of a *trompe l'oeil* device whereby an element in the poem's border seems momentarily to spill into the composition itself. He is quick to retreat into the figure of the narrator.

8. Cf. *Variorum 6*, 243, for various theories concerning the possibility of a confused allusion to Pegasus. This is particularly tantalizing since the relevant myths seem to hold promise of some allusion to the role of pastoral *otium* in eliciting the poetic vision. If the "brook" is Hippocrene, the fount on Helicon created by Pegasus' hooves, Spenser has apparently conflated Mt. Ida with Helicon as a haunt of the Muses. The name Hippocrene has a long history

the general outlines of the Paris story seem apparent from the three lines devoted to this allusion. Above all, this passage reminds the reader that during his stay on Mount Ida Paris not only courted and won Oenone, but was involved also in the choice which occasioned the Trojan War. If the sight of Calidore reminds one of Paris, it seems reasonable to assume that one will feel the risks of Calidore's present position, as it may expose him to a similarly disastrous judgment.

The manner in which this stanza chooses these two elements from the story of Paris and sees both in the context of Calidore's abandonment of his heroic and courtly trappings strongly suggests points stressed by Renaissance treatments of the Judgment of Paris. As Edgar Wind points out,[9] the three goddesses come to be identified with the three aspects of the Platonic "tripartite life," with Pallas offering the gift of wisdom to the man choosing the contemplative life, Juno offering power and the active life, and Venus offering pleasure and the voluptuous life. For Ficino, the choice of any one of these over the others

---

of poetic paraphrase: cf. Persius' *fonte . . . caballino* or Spenser's own "sacred springs of horsefoot *Helicon*" (*Teares of the Muses* 271). Spenser or some unidentified source could have stretched a point and made Plexippus, "horse-taming" or "horse-striking," convey the sense of "struck *by* a horse."

Or Spenser may have had in mind the Plexippus who with his brother was killed by Meleager when they disputed his award of honors to Atalanta after the killing of the Calydonian Boar. They were avenged by their sister Althaea, the mother of Meleager and the wife of Oeneus. Oenone was a fountain-nymph, the daughter of the river Oeneus; Spenser may have confused these two myths, and/or found an appropriateness in associating Paris with still another internecine struggle.

9. Wind, *Pagan Mysteries in the Renaissance,* pp. 78 ff. In connection with this mention of the different choice of Hercules, it might be noted that the allusion to Paris finds a counterpart in V.v.24, where Artegall's subjection to Radigund is seen in the context of Hercules' subjection to Iole. The verbal similarities between these two passages are striking, and suggest that in both cases the hero's removal of his heroic trappings is symbolic of the temporary abandonment of the life of active virtue. It is perhaps significant of the limitations of Artegall's world that he is in serious trouble as a result of his wavering determination. He can escape only with the aid of Britomart to play Isis to his Osiris. Calidore manages to balance the various roles within himself.

would court disaster: Socrates, Hercules, and Paris were all "punished by the deities they had spurned." And just as Ficino praises Lorenzo de' Medici for having shown due respect to all three, and for having received graces from each in return, the poets and painters of the Elizabethan period are quick to praise Elizabeth's judgment by contrasting it with that of Paris: Hans Eworth's painting (1569) at Hampton Court, in which Elizabeth in the role of Paris gives the apple to herself rather than to one of the three competing goddesses,[10] is echoed by similar motifs in the writings of Lyly, Peele, Sabie, and Barnfield.[11] Against the background of such an interpretation of the Judgment of Paris, it seems apparent that the courtship of Oenone anticipates Paris' definitive choice of Venus and her rewards. The reader who thinks of Paris in relation to Calidore at this point must wonder, then, whether the latter will similarly progress from his courtship of Pastorella to a total abandonment of his quest and of the life of heroic achievement which that quest implies.

Canto ix concludes with a scene that reinforces the earlier emphasis on Calidore's superiority and suggests the means by which the patron of courtesy is able to avoid the error of Paris. The competition between Calidore and Coridon sets the natural courtesy which derives from the court (as the opening lines of Book VI have remarked) against the loutishness and "cowherdise" of the pastoral cowherd who has neither nature nor nurture to redeem him. Significantly, though, Calidore takes care to placate Coridon, and to accommodate him in the pastoral entertainments:

> But *Calidore* of courteous inclination
> Tooke *Coridon,* and set him in his place,

10. The painting bears the inscription: JUNO POTENS SCEPTRIS ET MENTIS ACUMINI PALLAS. ET ROSEO VENERIS FULGIT IN ORE DECUS. ADFUIT ELIZABETH JUNO PERCULSA REFUGIT. OBSTUPUIT PALLAS ERUBUITQUE VENUS. Cf. *De Triomf van het Maniërisme* (Amsterdam, Rijksmuseum, 1955), p. 61; Yates, "Queen Elizabeth as Astraea," p. 60.

11. Yates, pp. 60–61; Wind, *Pagan Mysteries,* p. 60.

That he should lead the daunce, as was his fashion;
For *Coridon* could daunce, and trimly trace.
And when as *Pastorella,* him to grace,
Her flowry garlond tooke from her owne head,
And plast on his, he did it soone displace,
And did it put on *Coridons* in stead:
Then *Coridon* woxe frollicke, that earst seemed dead.
(VI.ix.42)

Here, and less directly in the wrestling match described in the two following stanzas, Calidore reconciles disagreements by means of an exchange of gifts symbolized in terms of that pastoral garland seen earlier in the description of Pastorella. Just as the maidens surrounding and crowning Pastorella anticipate the vision of the Graces in their dance around Colin's own mistress, here the triple movement of the dance similarly illustrates the courteous exchange by which strife and resentment may be calmed and individuals persuaded to live peacefully in harmony. Calidore's skill in the present instance comes as no surprise in view of his behavior in the earlier cantos. Furthermore, the fact that Calidore excels not only in dancing but also in the sterner discipline of wrestling serves as a reminder that from the beginning of Book VI he has been presented as combining grace with martial vigor.

Yet Paris too might be considered a complete individual. Ovid and Apollodorus speak of his combination of beauty, intelligence, and strength; his surname of Alexander derives from a youthful exploit—routing a band of cattle-thieves—which bears some resemblance to Calidore's own pastoral adventure.[12] The reader who has included an awareness of this aspect of the Paris myth[13] in his contemplation of the image of Calidore as shepherd will perhaps be struck by still broader implications of the comparison. Ultimately, Spenser's allusion

12. Apollodorus III.10.9; Ovid, *Heroides* XVI.51–52, 359–60.
13. The relevance of this aspect of Paris is confirmed by the fact that Calidore's own armor is explicitly mentioned in this same stanza. Paris too is seen as a Mars choosing to submit to the temptations of Venus.

to Paris suggests not simply a possible menace for Calidore, or a simple contrast which belittles the onesided judgment of the Trojan while it extols the diplomacy and universality of Calidore; more generally, it comments on the inevitability of strife as an agent in the advancement of mankind. Here this comment is still largely implicit; yet the reader who accepts Spenser's invitation to see Calidore in terms of Paris' pastoral career may recall that although the award to Venus over the other goddesses led to the Trojan War, this same Trojan War led indirectly to the civilization of Britain. It may well seem fanciful to draw out Spenser's comparison to such an extent; but it should be recalled that the parallel histories in Book II emphasize the element of strife in the advancement of the British race. In a context which blends the Christian concept of the *felix culpa* with the Neoplatonic dialectic (the union of Mars, strife, with Venus, love, producing a daughter, Harmony), this allusion to Paris may be taken as an accurate image, predicting the strife through which Calidore must pass before he can lead Pastorella back to her true identity. Taken in combination with the image of the Graces in the tenth canto, the picture of Calidore in the guise of Phrygian Paris anticipates the book's ultimate development. At the time of its introduction, it serves primarily to open up a prospect which is subsequently explored in greater detail.

THESEUS AND THE INTERRUPTED WEDDING-FEAST

The opening scene of the tenth canto carefully echoes and elaborates the opening scene of the ninth. When Calidore first sees Pastorella, she is described in terms which emphasize her excellence in relation to her pastoral environment:

> Vpon a litle hillocke she was placed
> > Higher then all the rest, and round about
> > Enuiron'd with a girland, goodly graced,
> > Of louely lasses, and them all without
> > The lustie shepheard swaynes sate in a rout,
> > The which did pype and sing her prayses dew,

And oft reioyce, and oft for wonder shout,
As if some miracle of heauenly hew
Were downe to them descended in that earthly vew.

And soothly sure she was full fayre of face,
And perfectly well shapt in euery lim,
Which she did more augment with modest grace,
And comely carriage of her count'nance trim,
That all the rest like lesser lamps did dim:
Who her admiring as some heauenly wight,
Did for their soueraine goddesse her esteeme,
And caroling her name both day and night,
The fayrest *Pastorella* her by name did hight.

                                              (VI.ix.8–9)

In this rustic vision, Pastorella is praised in terms which admit
of a considerable degree of qualification. The diminutive of her
name seems to echo the "litle hillocke" on which she stands;
realistic details (by which the lustiness of the swains is conveyed
by the rhyming of "rout" and "shout") and cautious conjunc-
tions ("as if"; "and soothly sure") suggest limits for the enthusiasm with which she is viewed. Relative to the country
lasses who surround her, Pastorella is certainly extraordinary.
Her beauty dims all the lesser lamps: her excellence is described
in these same terms when she is later the only source of illumination in the pirates' den.[14] This much of the ideal she is able to
embody; but at the same time her very actuality, her physical
and social existence, must be included among the "vain shad-
ows" of the phenomenal world. Earlier chapters of this study
have discussed the extent to which Spenser consistently treats
the physical image as a balance of opposing elements, requiring

14. Berger, "A Secret Discipline," pp. 59 ff., compares the rustic celebration
of Pastorella to the cannibals' worship of Serena in the preceding canto. To
mention only one instance of the insistence on light imagery current in the
literature of the 1590s, *Romeo and Juliet* is similarly couched in terms of an
ironic examination of Petrarchan pretensions; and like Marlowe's *Hero and
Leander* (1598), lines 291–93, it deals as well with the relationship of love
and strife.

a constant analysis and reduction if they are to be comprehended. The analysis of the pastoral world and the development
of secondary images in these cantos provide a further illustration of Spenser's principle of development along these lines.

Against this description of Pastorella, Calidore's subsequent
vision dims all but the "heauenly hew" of Gloriana herself.
Mount Acidale[15] is not simply removed from city and court:
it is removed even from the society of shepherds. "Far from all
peoples troad," it is guarded by nymphs and faeries from "all
noysome things." Not only wild beasts, but even the imperfec-
tions of the pastoral landscape—"ragged mosse or filthy mud"
—are absent from this pastoral vision. So purified and exalted,
the vision is yet strikingly similar to Calidore's first vision.
Instead of the "litle hillocke," there is a hill in an open plain,
surrounded by trees "of matchlesse hight"; and instead of the
"girlond, goodly graced,/ Of louely lasses" and the rout of
shepherds there is here a purified harmony and grace expressive
of an ideal order:

> All they without were raunged in a ring,
>   And daunced round; but in the midst of them
>   Three other Ladies did both daunce and sing,
>   The whilest the rest them round about did hemme,
>   And like a girlond did in compasse stemme:
>   And in the middest of those same three, was placed
>   Another Damzell, as a precious gemme,
>   Amidst a ring most richly well enchaced,
> That with her goodly presence all the rest much
>   graced.
>
> (VI.x.12)

It is a picture purged of the actuality of the earlier scene, yet
it is not entirely removed from the world of the shepherds.

---

15. The phrasing of x.8 makes it clear that Spenser is suggesting both
etymologies for the name Acidale: "freedom from care" and "valley view";
cf. *Variorum 6*, 247. Both are appropriate in terms of the contrast with the
earlier vision of Pastorella.

There is one figure present in both worlds: Colin Clout, the jolly shepherd whose piping Pastorella had preferred to Calidore's repertory of court songs. The central figure in this dance is not a divinity or even a symbol, but Colin's mistress, temporarily "aduanst to be another Grace." Spenser seems concerned here to present the poet as mediator between the two worlds of phenomenon and idea. The introduction of Spenser himself, in the pastoral disguise assumed in the *Shepheardes Calender,* states in the strongest terms the contrast between the idealized world of impalpable images summoned by the music, and the humble, grossly actual world into which they are summoned. At the same time, this very linking of opposites leads to a more persuasive revelation than would be possible otherwise. At the beginning of the ninth canto, Pastorella is seen as she really is: Calidore is free to feast his eyes as long as he pleases. This is the tangible world of nature; if its more exalted aspects demand qualification as they are seen realistically, at least the image is firmly rooted in reality. But Colin's vision belongs to the world of art. Although it is itself more exalted and less subject to qualification, it is by the same token less capable of close analysis, less negotiable so to speak. The harmony of this dance is as fragile and as personal as the exchange of amorous courtesies between Calepine and Serena, and Calidore's intrusion interrupts the one as surely as the other. If the magic of Colin's art is able to achieve a triumphant vision of his "countrey lasse," the "poore handmayd" of Gloriana, as the recipient of the triple gift of the Graces, it is nevertheless in the nature of such a vision that it does not permit the scrutiny of outsiders, but must remain personal and momentary.

Yet for the moment the vision is intensely effective. The success of Spenser's use of personal allusion at this point in the poem represents the most conspicuous example of an effect gained more generally by the contemporary allusions which appear throughout *The Faerie Queene,* as a means of giving immediate relevance to the fictional situations being presented. Here the unexpected appearance of the world of the poet at the center of the Book's "allegorical core" constitutes a shift in perspective which anticipates the final stanzas of the Book, when the narrator concludes by viewing the trials of Courtesy and the menace of the Blatant Beast as a continuing, contemporary problem, one which is no longer clothed in the disguise of fiction (VI.xii.40–41). As an extraordinarily rich and concise statement of this double vision of strife and concord, the simile expressed in the thirteenth stanza of canto x deserves examination:

> Looke how the Crowne, which *Ariadne* wore
> Vpon her yuory forehead that same day,
> That *Theseus* her vnto his bridale bore,
> When the bold *Centaures* made that bloudy fray
> With the fierce *Lapithes,* which did them dismay;
> Being now placed in the firmament,
> Through the bright heauen doth her beams display,
> And is vnto the starres an ornament,
> Which round about her moue in order excellent.
>
> (VI.x.13)

Commentators from Jortin to the present day[16] have remarked on the confused mythology of this simile. Though it may well be that Spenser was indebted to an eccentric mythographer or a typographical error as yet unlocated, there is nevertheless a peculiar aptness to the myth as it is here formulated. The simile itself, it should be noted, relates to two different kinds of rings or garlands. First there is the "goodly band" of dancers, the hundred naked maidens surrounding the inner circle of the Graces "like a girlond," with the Graces themselves providing the setting for the "precious gemme" of the innermost lady. Secondly, there is the "rosie girlond" mentioned in the fourteenth stanza, the pastoral crown bestowed on the lady in this dance. The latter is reminiscent of similar garlands which have figured earlier in Book VI: the garland which Serena was at-

16. *Variorum 6,* 251.

tempting to gather for herself when she was attacked by the
Blatant Beast; the garland bestowed on Pastorella by the
shepherds; the garlands which Calidore received and passed on
to Coridon in courteous actions anticipating the symbolic interchange of the Graces, with its implication "That good should
from vs goe, then come in greater store" (VI.x.24).[17]

As the poem has emphasized from the beginning, both kinds
of garland are short-lived—the flowering garland because as a
natural object it must decay, and the garland of dance because
as a product of art its existence in the phenomenal world depends on magic, on the suspension of disbelief which Calidore's
curiosity destroys. Both, however, are treasured as images of
the concord which, like Astraea's Justice, can find its permanent realization only in the heavens, illuminating the darkened
world of man and serving as a point of reference for the "order
excellent" of the heavenly motions.[18] Consequently the allusion
to Ariadne's crown contains elements of contrast while also
insisting on the validity of the comparison as regards the common emphasis on concord and harmonious union.

It will be noted, therefore, that Spenser's apparent conflation
of several myths helps to stress this double function of his
allusion. Traditionally the crown of Thetis (now the *Corona
Borealis* in the heavens) is held to have been the gift of Bacchus
when he married Ariadne after Theseus had abandoned her.[19]
An alternate myth, however, says that Theseus was given the
crown when he swam down to the palace of the Nereids in
pursuit of the ring of Minos.[20] Possibly, then, a suggestion of

17. The vexed question of the reading of VI.x.24.7, "froward" or "forward,"
remains unresolved, though the meaning of the line seems clear enough in any
case. *Variorum 6,* 475; Wind, *Pagan Mysteries,* p. 33 n.; D. T. Starnes, "Spenser and the Graces," *Philological Quarterly, 21* (1942), 268–82.

18. Spenser is prepared to distort accepted views of astronomy to further
the point of his simile.

19. Pausanias, *Description of Greece* I.20.3; Catullus 64.50ff.; Hyginus,
Poetic Astronomy II.5.

20. Pausanias, *Description of Greece* I.17.3; V.19.1; Hyginus, *Poetic Astronomy* II.5.

the sufferings of Ariadne is present here. If so, it together with the earlier allusion to Oenone serves as a reminder that both Paris and Theseus, as favorites of Aphrodite, did not follow a direct path from courtship to marriage feast, any more than had Scudamour in the action of this poem. But more importantly, and more clearly, Spenser has combined this image of the marriage crown originally bestowed by Aphrodite on Thetis, with the image of the battle between the Lapiths and Centaurs, traditionally described as taking place at the wedding of Peirithous and Hippodameia, when Theseus was present as a guest and participant in the "bloudy fray" that followed. Such a conflation dramatizes the impermanence of any human attainment of concord. Just as Calidore, through bad luck or excessive curiosity, has himself disrupted as many instances of harmony as his courtesy has elsewhere succeeded in knitting, similarly the union—dynastic as well as personal—solemnized by the wedding feast is in constant danger of violation, so that what begins as a celebration of harmony ends as a disastrous example of discord. Paradoxically too, it will be recalled that the very drinking of wine which serves as an image of harmony among men leads to the drunkenness of Centaurs, whose less highly developed culture has left them untrained in the virtues of moderation.[21] Man's own mixture of higher and lower natures is emphasized by the double nature of the Centaur, and the triumph of the lower nature occurs when the civilizing influence of wine is abandoned for its maddening influence.[22]

Some support for this reading of Spenser's allusion might be drawn from such Florentine Neoplatonists as Pico and Ficino, who see these same legends of Paris, the Graces, and the battle of Lapiths and Centaurs as archetypal illustrations of the prob-

---

21. The Centaurs failed to mix their wine with water, the traditional gesture of moderation; cf. V.vii.10, where wine is said by the priests of Isis to be "the bloud of Gyants, which were slaine,/ By thundring Ioue in the Phlegrean plaine."

22. Thus Bacchus, together with Hercules, is seen as one of the great civilizing forces, bringing law to the eastern world (V.i.2).

lems confronting man. But any specific links with Spenser must appear highly elusive. Readers have often sensed an affinity between Spenser's poem and certain allegorical paintings, particularly those which grew out of the spheres of influence of Florentine Neoplatonism; but they have not succeeded in proving any direct awareness of these paintings on Spenser's part. Rather, if the description of the Graces is reminiscent of Botticelli's *Primavera*,[23] for instance, the probability is that both painting and poem derived from a similar concern with the myths being illustrated. Recent research has suggested ways in which Botticelli's treatment of myth drew its inspiration from contemporary writings; these and similar studies[24] are generally relevant to such a work as this, in that they provide evidence of the currency of certain interpretations.

A more immediately significant body of evidence, however, is that provided by Spenser himself, in the mythological allusions scattered elsewhere throughout the poem. It is noteworthy, for example, that in the dwelling of Ate described at the beginning of Book IV the mention of the golden apple among her trophies is immediately followed by mention of

> . . . the relicks of the drunken fray,
> The which amongst the *Lapithees* befell,
> And of the bloodie feast, which sent away
> So many *Centaures* drunken soules to hell.

(IV.i.23)

This juxtaposition, together with the conspicuous role played by Ate and her associates throughout the poem (and her af-

---

23. Janet Spens, in a review of Chang, *Allegory and Courtesy*, in *Review of English Studies*, n.s.9 (1958), 66–69, seems to imply that Spenser was actually familiar with the *Primavera;* but she offers no evidence in support of such an assumption.

24. E. H. Gombrich, "Botticelli's Mythologies," *Journal of the Warburg and Courtauld Institutes, 8* (1945), 6–60; Erwin Panofsky, *Studies in Iconology* and "The Iconography of the Galerie François Ier at Fontainebleau," *Gazette des Beaux-Arts* (September 1958), pp. 113–90; Seznec, *The Survival of the Pagan Gods*.

finities to the Blatant Beast, to Duessa, and even to Mutabilitie
may suggest the scope of her role), reinforces the belief that the
allusion to the Lapiths and Centaurs is another example of
Spenser's use of apparently irrelevant elements in his similes to
suggest the limits of human attempts to capture in a single
image the ideal which has fled to the heavens. Although Ate
in Book IV is seen as a menace to relationships between individuals—lovers or friends—her trophies are described in
terms pertinent to the imagery of Book VI:

> Witnesse their broken bandes there to be seene,
> Their girlonds rent, their bowres despoyled all;
> The moniments whereof there byding beene,
> As plaine as at the first, when they were fresh and
> greene.
>
> (IV.i.24)

Yet it is out of discord's ravages that harmony is built again.
Colin remarks to Calidore that it was as Jove was returning
from the wedding of Thetis (marked by such varied gifts as the
Crown of Ariadne given by Aphrodite, and the golden apple
rolled in by the uninvited Discord) that he sired the Graces.[25]
If strife is the general menace to all human civilization, it is
also the means by which the inscrutable harmonies of the universe are maintained. The paradoxical teaching that *Harmonia
est discordia concors* is central to the poem's view of nature,
and it is echoed in the terms of Mutabilitie's defeat in the judgment of Nature.

In the present case, the allusion to Ariadne's Crown anticipates the strife which interrupts the courteous harmony of
Calidore's own pastoral interlude. The vision is followed by
the incident of the Tiger, in which Calidore's courage is contrasted with Coridon's cowardice. Here Calidore is seen as

25. VI.x.22. Note, incidentally, that the Litae, or Prayers, the "beuie of
faire Virgins clad in white" who surround Mercilla's throne (V.ix.31), were
similarly begotten by Jove.

possessing not merely the attributes of the shepherd, but those of the wild man as well: his unhesitating assault on the beast is reminiscent of the youthful Artegall, and of the Salvage Man, whose lack of nurture is accompanied by an invulnerability which makes him fearless. The Brigands, however, constitute a more serious menace which is not to be confronted with the same directness as was the beast. With their arrival the tone of an idyllic pastoral changes definitively. Meliboe's honeyed quietism is no test for this challenge, and his death expresses the extent to which the element of strife has taken over the pastoral world. In this new, melodramatic context the opening stanza of the eleventh canto would seem comically inappropriate in its complacency, were it not that it continues the poem's earlier insistence on the inevitability of strife as a condition of this life:

> The ioyes of loue, if they should euer last,
>   Without affliction or disquietnesse,
>   That worldly chaunces doe amongst them cast,
>   Would be on earth too great a blessednesse,
>   Liker to heauen, then mortall wretchednesse.
>   Therefore the winged God, to let men weet,
>   That here on earth is no sure happinesse,
>   A thousand sowres hath tempred with one sweet,
> To make it seeme more deare and dainty, as is meet.
>   (VI.xi.1)

It is now clearer what Spenser meant by proposing that "Fierce warres and faithfull loues shall moralize my song"; for his ethic derives from linking these two antithetical elements as the basis of the dialectic working throughout the poem. Mars, Venus, and Cupid are appropriately invoked as presiding spirits alongside Elizabeth (I.Proem.3).

In the doubtful light of the Brigands' cave, Pastorella's own value shines the more strongly, "Like the faire Morning clad in misty fog" (VI.xi.3), or with "starrie beames" like those of a diamond (VI.xi.13). Her increased luminosity seems to be accompanied by an increased experience which leads her through suffering to be reborn as the restored daughter of Lord Bellamour and his Claribell. Her imprisonment in the cave is earlier compared to that of a "flowre, that feeles no heate of sunne" (VI.x.44); and it may be that this comparison looks forward to the discovery of her true identity.[26] At any rate, the general problem of identity and disguise becomes more clearly significant. Pastorella is forced to a series of pretenses as a means of controlling the desires of the Brigand captain; in this she may be learning to cope with the realities of a less protected environment. At the same time, Calidore finds himself in a new pastoral disguise which serves to conceal his weapons (VI.xi.36). In both cases, the poem stresses the necessity of tempering courtesy with strength, to achieve a strategy responsive to the crude demands of this world, which requires the skills of both shepherd and wild man if civilization is to advance and at the same time protect itself against assaults from its rearguard.

Calidore may not be able to recapture the vision which Colin had briefly summoned, but he can rescue Pastorella from the darkness to which she has been abducted. Like Theseus, he can defend civilization against the lower orders which are incapable of understanding it, and which pervert its fruits to their bestial ends; against the "lawless people, *Brigants* hight of yore," for whom societal relationships are inconceivable except in terms of depredation and lust. Once he has rescued Pastorella, and once the herds have been restored to Coridon's care, with these last vestiges of the rustic life the confines of the pastoral world fall away. The setting is now the world of actuality and human involvement: the world not only of the poem's action but also of the narrator, for the history of the Blatant Beast is not ended with Calidore's temporary conquest.

26. VI.xii.18, where Pastorella is said to have derived her name from her birthmark of a "litle purple rose." More generally, of course, this image of feminine beauty or the more inclusive treasures of womanhood as a flower is found throughout *The Faerie Queene*.

It is characteristic of the pastoral mode, as employed by Spenser and the poets of the succeeding century, that it sees the pastoral escape as a temporary one, at the end of which the civilized shepherd has watched his simple, "natural" world lose its innocence and become an exact image of his own fallen world, with the same conflicts arising from man's mixed nature, and with the same promise of nothing beyond a limited and temporary victory in this life.

Conclusion
The Titaness Put Down

By their relation to the six completed Books of *The Faerie Queene*, the *Cantos of Mutabilitie* invite consideration as a coda summarizing and restating the meaning of the poem. Though some critics have found logical or numerological significance in their attribution to a central position in some seventh Book,[1] they are so different stylistically from what has gone before that attempts to extrapolate any further development of the poem seem largely futile.[2] What is particularly novel is their adoption of an Ovidian prosopopoeia (in VII.vi.1–35) so extended as to entail a unique degree of dramatic irony; readers have variously assessed the tone in accordance with their predilections for a sentimental or a doctrinal reading of Spenser. It is enlightening to consider this fragment in relation to the motifs treated in earlier chapters of this study, in an attempt to suggest the balance of emphases maintained through Spenser's dialectic.

1. For example, Fowler, "Numerical Composition," pp. 236–37.
2. The point has been made most recently by Frye, "The Structure of Imagery in *The Faerie Queene*," p. 111.

The program of the *Cantos* is enunciated in their opening stanza:

> What man that sees the euer-whirling wheele
> Of *Change,* the which all mortall things doth sway,
> But that therby doth find, and plainly feele,
> How *MVTABILITY* in them doth play
> Her cruell sports, to many mens decay?
> Which that to all may better yet appeare,
> I will rehearse that whylome I heard say,
> How she at first her selfe began to reare,
> Gainst all the Gods, and th'empire sought from them
> to beare.
>
> (VII.vi.1)

The process of personification is deftly illustrated in the transition from abstract to proper noun. The impersonal relative pronoun "which" in the second line may refer to the wheel of Change, but the logic of the metaphor makes it more likely that Change is swaying mortal things. By the middle of the stanza mutability has received a weak personification (as seen in the "Her" of line 5); but since the poet is still appealing to human experience of the phenomenon, the noun is felt to be essentially abstract. In offering his twice-told legend of mutability, however, Spenser gives substance and human shape to the abstraction. The legendary status which he bestows on her— "Her antique race and linage ancient"—is further expressed in terms of this same controlling irony: though all is flux, her genealogy has been preserved "In *Faery* Land mongst records permanent."

Mutabilitie is therefore a product of the allegorical imagination, as much so as Isis and Osiris were in Spenser's description (V.vii.1ff.) of their worship. She derives from the race of Titans, who figure in Spenser's references as the irrational, anarchic generation which preceded the Olympian pantheon. Like her sisters, Hecate and Bellona, she is associated with the dark, destructive, intuitive forces within the personality. Her proud rebellion against divine authority inevitably bears overtones of Satan's and Adam's. At the same time, the power and authority of the Titans, delegated to them by Jove after his mastery of them (VII.vi.3), suggest the limitations of the fallen world:

> O pittious worke of *MVTABILITIE!*
> By which, we all are subiect to that curse,
> And death in stead of life haue sucked from our Nurse.
>
> (VII.vi.6)

The terms of Mutabilitie's initial presentation imply two contrary emphases. On the one hand it is true that she is seen here in her largest dimensions, that Spenser presents her "darkest implications"[3] in describing her ancestry and her assault on the heavens. But the very superhuman and supernatural scope of her ambition subjects her to a consequent loss in imaginative power. The first half of canto vi is in effect a statement of the problem in semantics which Mutabilitie's challenge involves. The Olympians are being challenged in two senses simultaneously. As astronomical figures within the circle of Creation, they are to some extent subject to change, both in terms of their regularly changing positions and shapes in the heavens, and in their more alarmingly erratic behavior, as Spenser lamented earlier (V.Proem). As anthropomorphic deities they are burdened with the frailties of human imagination in this same way.[4] But as images of man's positive impulses to control and order they are as much a part of his universe as his negative, demonic, "lower" impulses. Mutabilitie's principal claim here remains moot, but she does succeed in demonstrating that Jove is "no equall iudge."

The tone of this first third of the *Cantos* is thus one of a

3. Sherman Hawkins, "Mutabilitie and the Cycle of the Months," in Nelson, ed., *Form and Convention*, p. 84.

4. In this Spenser may be indebted to Lucretius or Bruno (*Spaccio de la Bestia Trionfante*), both of whom stressed the "bestial" elements of classical myth.

detached, ironic wit. After the appeal to human experience in the opening lines, there is no further attempt to make her meaningful in human terms. She has, indeed, left the human world and ascended to dizzying heights of abstraction. Conventional formulae, appropriate to the style and subject of this heroic quest, provide ironic commentary on her absurdity. She has climbed to the moon, "Where *Cynthia* raignes in euerlasting glory";[5]

> And by her side, there ran her Page, that hight
> *Vesper,* whom we the Euening-starre intend:
> That with his Torche, still twinkling like twylight,
> Her lightened all the way where she should wend,
> And ioy to weary wandring trauailers did lend:
>
> (VII.vi.9)

The moon and planets continue to exist; the reader has no serious doubt as to any physical change in the constitution of the cosmos. Mutabilitie is arguing that the planets should henceforth be read as symbols not of changeless order, but of Change itself. The amazement with which the Olympians react to her presence seems a result less of her monstrosity than of her resemblance to themselves:

> Whil'st she thus spake, the Gods that gaue good eare
> To her bold words, and marked well her grace,
> Beeing of stature tall as any there
> Of all the Gods, and beautifull of face,
> As any of the Goddesses in place,
> Stood all astonied, like a sort of Steeres;
> Mongst whom, some beast of strange and forraine
>   race,
> Vnwares is chaunc't, far straying from his peeres:
> So did their ghastly gaze bewray their hidden feares.
>
> (VII.vi.28)

---

5. To a contemporary reader, of course, these formulae might bear an added relevance to his queen, Ralegh's Cynthia, whose motto, *Semper eadem,* could represent a further gesture of defiance to Mutabilitie's claims.

It is her beauty which conquers at this first interview: a beauty which inspires Jove to mellowness, but which also suggests the close family relationship between the Olympians and their excluded cousins.

The debate between Mutabilitie and Jove is thus controlled by its conflicting levels of meaning. As a dispute between opposing branches of the descendants of Uranus, it quickly resolves itself into a search for a competent forum. As a challenge to the "heavenly" (or ideal) status of celestial bodies, it questions the inherent dignity of gods so extensively created in the image of man. Jove's posturings are made to seem merely bombastic, the futile efforts of a tyrant and usurper to appeal to conservative values. Mutabilitie's chief advantage over him is her singleness of meaning. Her name expresses her nature fully and directly, whereas the names of the gods are emblems to be unfolded—proper names pretending to abstract values. Ultimately the Olympians and the Titans are equally the creatures of the human imagination; but Mutabilitie's dominance here suggests that the legendary figure loses his claim to a role as symbol of permanence in proportion as he is shaped and defined in human terms, by the proliferation of legend. Mutabilitie is temporarily the stronger for her lack of circumstantial history; what eventually silences her is the contradiction inherent in her claim to omnipotence. Her role may be conceived rather as that of antithesis in an unending dialectical struggle; and it is thus that Nature will finally define her.

The Nature to whom she submits her appeal constitutes a new concept within the world previously adumbrated by the *Cantos*. Jove had seemed supreme, the equivalent even of the Christian God in proportion as Mutabilitie had suggested parallels with Satan and Adam. But now Mutabilitie introduces a broader context:

> But to the highest him, that is behight
> Father of Gods and men by equall might;
> To weet, the God of Nature, I appeale.

> (VII.vi.35)

It would be difficult to find in classical myth any authority for the cosmology which is being presented here. It does not help particularly to cite, as commentators have done,[6] the Homeric Hymn in which Jupiter is described as a supreme god of universal nature, both male and female in his embodiment of active and passive principles; for Mutabilitie's point here is precisely that the Jove of these cantos is not such a god. Rather, the God of Nature to which she refers is superior to men and the Olympians alike; as she confesses later, "even the gods to thee, as men to gods do seeme" (VII.vii.15). When classical writings refer to a single supreme God of Nature, they generally do so without prejudice to the Olympian pantheon. Spenser's Nature, as his reference to Alanus hints (VII.vii.9), brings the reader back to the world of allegorical personification introduced in the opening stanzas of the *Cantos*. Her veiled face, like Una's or that of Venus (with its similar hint of hermaphroditism, IV.x.40–41), suggests the dazzling brillance of the transfigured Christ: her radiance combines the worlds of Pagan and Neoplatonic conventions, to produce a nexus of meaning characteristic of Spenser's syncretism. But her obscure form enables her to approach the paradoxes traditionally assigned to the Christian God:

> Great Nature, euer young yet full of eld,
> Still moouing, yet vnmoued from her sted;
> Vnseene of any, yet of all beheld.
>
> (VII.vii.13)

In the orderly pageants assembled by Mutabilitie as a demonstration of her case, Spenser demonstrates simultaneously the arguments for and against the dominance of Change in man's world. Not only the completeness of her cyclical parades (which anatomize change so fully as to suggest the pattern which informs it) but the individual forms within them—the tropes which hearken back to the traditional human search for order

6. *Variorum 6*, 281–82.

within Nature—lead the reader, as spectator and judge alongside Nature herself, to the conclusion that

> . . . being rightly wayd
> They are not changed from their first estate;
> But by their change their being doe dilate:
> And turning to themselues at length againe,
> Doe worke their owne perfection so by fate:
> Then ouer them Change doth not rule and raigne;
> But they raigne ouer change, and doe their states
> maintaine.
>
> (VII.vii.58)[7]

Yet Spenser has preceded this climactic scene on Arlo Hill
with a definition of the world in which the confrontation is to
take place. The pastoral and comic interlude at the end of
canto vi constitutes a crucial element in the tripartite structure
of the *Cantos*. The lower style contrasts with the heroic terms
of Mutabilitie's quest; the effect is not simply to deflate
Mutabilitie herself by parodying her folly in the voyeurism of
Faunus, but to give a new, humbler reality to her sublunary
existence. The heroic style in the first half of the canto had
shown a continual risk of degenerating into mock-epic, for the
titaness (rather like Milton's Satan) had been manipulating
abstractions too broad and slippery for her control. But in the
Faunus episode Mutabilitie is no longer an active character;
rather, she figures indirectly and thematically, scaled down to
the level of an Ovidian metamorphosis. Here Cynthia appears
in another aspect, as Diana, driven by the sniggering bestiality
of Faunus into a destruction of her terrestrial bower. Like
Astraea, she abandons the stony world of man, leaving behind
a wilderness as the more accurate pattern of man's habitat:

> Them all, and all that she so deare did way,
> Thence-forth she left; and parting from the place,

---

7. This aspect of the *Cantos* has been traced in detail by Hawkins, "Mutabilitie," pp. 76–102.

There-on an heauy haplesse curse did lay,
To weet, that Wolues, where she was wont to space,
Should harbour'd be, and all those Woods deface,
And Thieues should rob and spoile that Coast
around.
Since which, those Woods, and all that goodly
Chase,
Doth to this day with Wolues and Thieues abound:
Which too-too true that lands in-dwellers since haue
found.

(VII.vi.55)

In this tragicomic incident the catastrophes are averted: Faunus'
punishment recalls Actaeon's but stops short of his death;
Molanna's stoning does not keep her from a watery union with
the Fanchin. Spenser is demonstrating here a highly dexterous
control of his subject matter, to the extent that it seems pompous
to speak of a serious meaning to the episode. He has reduced
the scope of man's subjection to change to the level of the
housewife crying over spilt milk in her dairy (VII.vi.48), and
to the uncomfortable but unsurprising reality of a savage wilderness surrounding man's efforts at civilization. The figure of the
poet, lamenting this as "too-too true," provides a graceful frame
for the whole canto, and defines the human relevance of the
pageants which follow in canto vii.

The overall effect of the *Cantos* is that of a stylistic tour
de force, for the triadic narrative pattern (epic, pastoral, didactic
synthesis) is vastly enriched and complicated by a delicately
ironic balance of tone within each of these three sections. At
no point is the reader permitted to forget the mixture of opposing attitudes with which Mutabilitie is being viewed. One pole
of this opposition is the Christian *contemptus mundi,* the feeling
of exhaustion and disdain for this world and intense longing
for the combination of absolute delight and absolute rest to be
found through death in the "Sabaoths sight" hinted by Nature.
At the other pole is the artist's delight in the inexhaustible

variety and movement of his creation: a delight which is apparent from the moment he begins to unfold his legend, in the effortless tracery of his stanza as in the *copia* with which character, incident, and theme are anatomized. It seems supremely appropriate that the poem should begin and end with a celebration of the seasonal and diurnal cycles, in imitation of the larger creation:

> Loe I haue made a Calendar for euery yeare,
> That steele in strength, and time in durance shall
>   outweare.

> (*S.C.* Dec.235–36)

The poet's triumph over a recalcitrant reality lies in his imitation of its complexity, in his celebration of the endless pattern of oppositions by which the worlds of physical nature and of man's moral nature are to be conceived. Critics who tend to dismiss Spenser's allegory as an incomplete or onesided presentation of reality seem radically insensitive to this aspect of the poem. It is the poem's richness, its refusal to reduce its world to any neat conceptual pattern, or to exclude any discordant impulse when it arises, which must in the end constitute its chief claim to imaginative validity.

Index of Episodes

The following index is designed to provide orientation for the reader of this study. Consequently, Books whose episodic structure receives extended discussion are outlined in greater detail than are the others. Furthermore, page references (the more important ones in italics) are limited to passages where an episode is discussed directly; a more exhaustive list of all occasions in which a character is mentioned can be found in the General Index.

BOOK I

At House of Pride Redcross views Lucifera's court and is challenged by Sans Joy (iv), *49 f.*

Redcross wounds Sans Joy, who is treated by Aesculapius in
underworld; the Dwarf shows Redcross Lucifera's dungeons
and they escape (v), *50–54*

Una is rescued from Sans Loy by Satyrs, who worship her;
Satyrane leads her out of the wood and encounters Sans Loy
(vi), *54–57, 61–66*

Redcross is seduced by Duessa, overcome by Orgoglio, and imprisoned; the Dwarf bears the news to Una, who meets
Arthur and enlists his aid (vii), 54, *66–71*

    Description of Arthur's armor, *68–71*

Arthur defeats Orgoglio, exposes Duessa, and liberates Redcross (viii), 71

Arthur tells of his lineage and quest for Gloriana; Redcross
tempted by Despair but restrained by Una (ix), 70 f.

The House of Holiness; Redcross learns his identity and destiny
(x), 21, 51, 67, 70

Redcross kills the Dragon (xi), 45 f., *71–73, 183 f.*

Redcross and Una are betrothed; Archimago is bound (xii), 31,
48 f., *73 f.*

BOOK II

Proem: Fairyland as the frontier of knowledge, *148 f.*

Encounter and reconciliation of Redcross and Guyon (i.1–34)

Amavia and her bloody infant; the chaste nymph's fountain
(i.35–ii.11)

The House of Medina (ii.12–end)

Braggadochio steals Brigadore, joins with Trompart, meets
Belphoebe (iii)

Guyon binds Furor, stops Occasion, rescues Phedon; Pyrochles
announced (iv)

Guyon defeats Pyrochles, delivers Furor and Occasion to him;
Atin visits Bower of Bliss and stirs Cymochles to revenge (v)

Phaedria's Isle: Guyon and Cymochles fight; Pyrochles burns
(vi), 120

Ollyphant; Britomart meets Scudamour and enters House of
Busyrane (xi)
  Decorations of House, 140
Masque of Cupid; Britomart rescues Amoret (xii), *121–25,*
  140, 170

BOOK IV

Amoret learns Britomart's sex; Ate and Duessa sow discord
between Scudamour and Glauce (i), 184, 234 f.
Paridell and Blandamour compete for False Florimell; peace
restored when Squire of Dames tells of Satyrane's tourna-
ment (ii.1–29)
Story of Agape's children (ii.30–end)
The battle for Canacee, settled by Cambina (iii)
Satyrane's tournament: Artegall defeated by Britomart (iv), 65,
168, 179
Ladies compete for Florimell's girdle; Scudamour visits House
of Care (v)
Scudamour and Artegall fight Britomart; Artegall woos her (vi)
Amoret is kidnapped by Lust, hears Aemilia's story, is rescued
by Belphoebe; Timias in disgrace (vii), 103, *108 f.*
Timias and Belphoebe are reconciled; Arthur, Amoret, and
Aemilia lodge with Sclaunder; Arthur overcomes Corflambo
(viii), 151
Paeana reformed; Arthur encounters six knights in conflict (ix)
Scudamour tells of winning Amoret at Temple of Venus (x), 244
Marinell's wound [III.iv] healed by Tryphon; he comes to
Proteus' house for marriage of Thames and Medway (xi)
Marinell hears Florimell's lament and falls in love; she is re-
leased (xii)

BOOK V

Proem: lament at world's decline, *147–55*
Astraea's education of Artegall and designation of him as her
surrogate (i.1–12), *154–61*

BOOK VI

BOOK VII (CANTOS OF MUTABILITIE)

General Index